## ADVANCE PRAISE

'A woman, a mother, a fighter. A heartwarming inspiration for all who want to make a real difference in this world.' **Christiana Figueres, former Executive Secretary, United Nations Framework Convention on Climate Change**

'Christine Milne has always been much more than an activist. She has long been a powerful inspiration to me and countless thousands of other Australians because of her relentless fight against greed, environmental destruction, war, discrimination and political corruption. Christine Milne will never lose her humanity. She is incorruptible.' **Peter Cundall, author and previous presenter of** *Gardening Australia*

'Christine is a force to be reckoned with, a woman to laugh with and a great mentor. Her deep love for nature, concern for the climate and care for people is best expressed in her tenacity, hard work for decades, and little things like pots of homemade apricot jam. Read this book if you want to be inspired to back yourself and work for a better world.' **Larissa Waters, former Australian Greens Deputy Leader**

'Christine Milne is a powerful champion for the planet and a world-renowned pioneer in Green politics. She has shown the way for many of us, and continues to inspire Greens around the world. Her story is compelling.' **Caroline Lucas MP, Co-Leader, Green Party of England and Wales**

'Christine Milne is one of the world's most important environmental voices; to have the story of where she came from and how she has fought her many battles is a great gift, one which will inspire all of us to fight harder and smarter.' **Bill McKibben, founder 350.org**

Christine Milne was leader of the Australian Greens from 2012 to 2015. She grew up on a dairy farm at Wesley Vale, obtained a Bachelor of Arts with Honours from the University of Tasmania, and taught in secondary schools from 1975 to 1984. Christine was arrested in the Franklin Dam Blockade in the early 1980s and led the campaign against the Wesley Vale pulp mill, after which she was elected to the Tasmanian Parliament in 1989 – the first woman to lead a political party in Tasmania. She was part of the evolution of the Tasmanian, Australian and Global Greens and in the 1990s drove significant reform in the areas of gun control, LGBTIQ equality and economic transformation. As Australian Greens leader her focus was on serious legislative action on global warming, advocacy for human rights and the restoration of our democracy. She was one of Australia's Bicentennial Women 88 Award winners, was appointed to the United Nations Global 500 Roll of Honour in 1990 for her forest conservation work, and was elected to the International Union for the Conservation of Nature Global Council in 2000. In 2015, after her decade-long Senate career, Christine was appointed as the ambassador for the Global Greens. She is a mother and grandmother.

# CHRISTINE MILNE

*An Activist Life*

UQP

First published 2017 by University of Queensland Press
PO Box 6042, St Lucia, Queensland 4067 Australia

uqp.com.au
uqp@uqp.uq.edu.au

Cover design by Sandy Cull, gogoGingko
Cover photo by Chris Crerar
Author photo by Karen Brown Photography
Illustrations by Julie Payne
Typeset in 12/15.5 pt Adobe Garamond Pro by Post Pre-press Group, Brisbane
Printed in Australia by McPherson's Printing Group, Melbourne

All photographs provided by the author unless otherwise indicated.

National Library of Australia
Cataloguing-in-Publication data is available at http://catalogue.nla.gov.au

ISBN 978 0 7022 5981 4 (pbk)
ISBN 978 0 7022 6067 4 (pdf)
ISBN 978 0 7022 6068 1 (epub)
ISBN 978 0 7022 6069 8 (kindle)

University of Queensland Press uses papers that are natural, renewable and recyclable products made from wood grown in sustainable forests. The logging and manufacturing processes conform to the environmental regulations of the country of origin.

# Contents

*To those from whom my generation has borrowed the Earth — my sons Thomas and James, my granddaughter Eleanor and their generations;*
*and*
*To those who have stood in the Earth's defence — activists both inside and outside the parliaments of the world.*

# Preface

OBJECT: *Peg Putt's plastic and aluminium picnic chair.*

I AM LIKE A LOT of people. People who find it hard to talk about how they feel, but will happily explain the history of an object they value. Through their stories of how an object came into their keeping and why it means so much to them you can learn a lot about a person. That is why I have chosen to tell the story of one woman's life, my life, through objects that matter to me.

The political turmoil in Tasmania in 1998 that led to the cutting of the numbers in the Tasmanian House of Assembly is well recorded. People were disillusioned with politics and politicians and a forty per cent pay rise had topped it off. The Liberal Party's obsession and solution was smaller government and deregulation: cut the number of politicians in the state and give business its head. For Labor this was the solution to getting rid of the Tasmanian Greens; for the Liberals getting rid of the Greens was a bonus.

What could a plastic and aluminium picnic chair possibly have to add to that?

In 1998 Liberal and Labor together suspended the Standing Orders of the Parliament, pushed the changes to the Constitution through and called an election based on a much increased quota for election to fewer seats. I knew that night as the legislation passed that it was over for the Greens. We would all lose our seats. I knew what it meant for us, for Green politics and what twenty-five members meant for the quality of government in Tasmania.

I went back to my Leader's office in Parliament House in Hobart and cried. I cried from exhaustion, frustration and a deep upwelling of loss. After almost a decade of holding it together, always being calm, professional, strong no matter the mockery, the insults, even the hate directed across the Chamber of the Tasmanian House of Assembly, I couldn't hold it back anymore: the dam broke.

It seemed so unfair, so unjust, that those who had set out to destroy us had been rewarded and that we who had taken a stand and made so many personal sacrifices were all being punished: my whole family – my husband Neville and my precious little boys Thomas and James, my parents, my late sister Gaylene – and my Wesley Vale farmers, my fellow Green MPs and supporters, and those on whose shoulders we stood.

We had tried to bring about a new order of things in a state that likes things just as they are and it seemed we had lost.

But we didn't all lose our seats. Peg Putt held on in Denison as the sole Tasmanian Greens MP. On election night I had to go to the tally room to make a speech and I did what I had always done: dealt with public life behind a shield. I was determined not to be the crushed person and Party that the Liberal and Labor Parties and many in the media wanted to see. Of course I was devastated but I knew I had to get it together for the Greens and for the future. I told my advisors Rod West and Russell Kelly to go down to Wrest Point and tell the Greens who were lined up to welcome me that they should not approach me, embrace me or make eye contact until after my speech: kindness would have been my undoing. They did as I asked and I gave one of the most memorable and powerful speeches of my life, predicting that the Greens would be back.

When the Parliament resumed with Jim Bacon – the man who

had driven the model most detrimental to the Greens – as premier, the House of Assembly chamber had been physically altered with the crossbenches taken out.[1] It was not enough to get rid of the Greens legislatively and electorally, they did it physically as well. By removing the crossbenches there was nowhere for anyone who was not a Liberal or Labor MP to sit. The message was clear: there was no room for the Greens in Tasmania.

So Peg Putt brought her own chair. It was an aluminium, orange plastic fold-up picnic chair and she walked in, calmly set it up where the crossbench used to be and proceeded to take her place. It was such an inspiring gesture of rebuke, resilience, persistence and hope. All was not lost, the vested interests of the old order hadn't won and far from getting rid of us, they had only encouraged us.

She did it for herself, for me and for all of us who were meant to go home, give up or get out of the state. It screamed, 'never, ever give up'.

That gut-wrenching, demoralising time in Tasmanian politics has now faded to simply a historical point of interest and there is no corporate memory in the media and little in academia as to what really motivated the actions of the period. The 'Clean, Green and Clever' vision for Tasmania that we Greens had championed has now become the state's major competitive advantage. The reduction in the numbers of Parliamentarians is now regarded as a major mistake. People can read about what happened in any number of texts but that chair gives an insight into how it felt to live it.

Unlike information, objects are a point of emotional connection. They have a story and a tactile reality that connects people across generations. We in Green politics and the environment movement across the nation need to hold them and their stories dear for the insights they provide. Like all the objects in this book, that chair goes to the heart of how I felt to be a Green in Tasmania in 1998.

Without its story, that chair is nothing but old plastic and aluminium but with its story, it is precious. People looking at it asking, 'What would have driven the sole Tasmanian Green MP to have taken a plastic chair into the Parliament and sit on it rather than the leather benches?' will get a much better understanding of Christine Milne, Peg Putt, and Green and Tasmanian politics in the 1990s than any information in a constitutional history of Tasmania.

But the chair was almost lost. It was donated to a Greens fundraising auction and fortunately a person who understands Tasmania to his core, author Richard Flanagan, bought it. Having lived through tumult in Tasmania, he recognised its significance in my life, in Peg's life, in the Green story and the Tasmanian story and gave it to me for safekeeping.

So much of the blood, sweat and tears of Australian environmental and Green history is being lost. Successful and unsuccessful campaigns roll into the next. The history is rarely recorded by those who were there. Not only do they not have time for it as they move on to the next campaign, but they often don't feel authoritative enough and so keep their mementos and experiences to themselves, leaving it to historians to make sense of it.

The next generation won't know the stories unless we tell them. They won't really know who people were or what they felt or why they did the things they did if we only leave them history books. That's why the chair is under my house and why it will ultimately go to the Tasmanian Museum and Art Gallery.

This book is a collection of stories, like that of the picnic chair, that flow from the odd things I have collected, how I came to have them in the first place and why I have kept them.

The stories of the people, special moments and events that come to mind when I focus on these objects have helped me over decades to tap into and replenish the wellspring of passion for justice – ecological, social and intergenerational – that has driven my activist life.

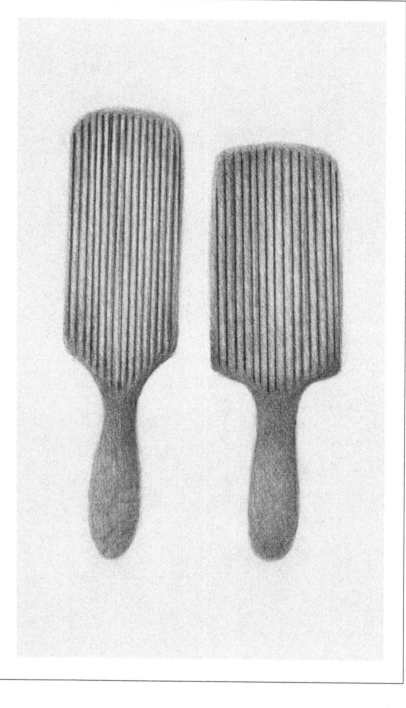

# 1

# My Blood's Country

OBJECT: *Butter pats, traditionally used to shape butter after it has been churned. This pair was handed down to Christine by her mother, June Morris.*

WESLEY VALE IS MY PLACE. It is my blood's country. In north-western Tasmania, it is framed by the Dial Range to the west, Mount Roland and Cradle Mountain to the south, Narawntapu National Park to the east, and Bass Strait and the Australian mainland to the north. I was brought up on a small family dairy farm there in the 1950s and 1960s, where I lived with my parents and sister, Gaylene, almost two years older than me. My mum, June Morris nee Tyler, was a teacher at local schools. My dad, Tom Morris, worked the farm with his brother Barney, and together they milked 110 head of cattle in a six-stall milking machine. It is hard to imagine now that such a farm could be viable, but our experience was typical of many dairying families in the 1950s.

As was the wont of country children then, I roamed around the farm with my father, catching tadpoles and rabbits, and watching the changing seasons and the wild ducks leave and return. I came to know how the light fell across the paddocks on late summer afternoons and the way people helped each other out, and the arguments in milking sheds and saleyards about whether it would rain and the local football team's chances of victory or defeat.

Knowing and loving that country, and standing up for its stories and way of life, formed the wellspring of my political life. I knew that and wanted to express it when, as a new Australian Greens senator for Tasmania, I made my inaugural speech in the federal parliament in 2005. It was the feeling expressed by Judith Wright in her poem 'South of My Days', though she was describing a very different landscape:

> South of my days' circle, part of my blood's country,
> rises that tableland ...
> I know it dark against the stars, the high lean country
> full of old stories that still go walking in my sleep.[1]

The Morris family had come to New Ground, about 190 kilometres north-northwest of Hobart, in the mid-1800s and farmed there. My great-grandfather William Morris left the farm to his daughters, and so his son John bought a property a few kilometres away at Wesley Vale. He and his wife, Alice, had seven children. Their sons Tom and Barney stayed on the farm, and Dad's father helped his other two sons, Harry and Jack, onto another farm in the district.

My mother's family, like my father's, comes from this small area of north-west Tasmania. Both sides of my family were born and farmed the land there, and are almost all buried there, except for my great-uncle John Hancox. He lies in Shell Green Cemetery in Gallipoli on the other side of the world, in a place utterly unknown to my great-grandparents, though not to their sons and daughters. In every country town in Tasmania, no matter how small, there is a war memorial; my grandparents' generation silently remembered the boys of the district who never came home. So great was the pain of their loss, and there were so many, that few spoke of them. Resilience was an article of faith, especially among the women.

Knowing looks and curious questions were answered with vague responses, and conversations were terminated in such a way as to make you understand that some things are not spoken about. Silence is the Tasmanian way of burying, hiding or ignoring that which is too painful, too shameful or too disruptive to bring into the open. I learned very young that the most important things can be read in faces and practical gestures rather than words: the index finger raised from the steering wheel as a friendly hello, casseroles left at the back door, gates or taps fixed in the householder's absence, a farmyard full of neighbours to help bring in the hay, and baskets of hot scones.

What people valued told you a great deal more than what they said. I remember as a child I accidentally dropped one of Mum's Sunday best dessert bowls, which broke into several pieces on the kitchen floor. It was a Carlton Ware green bowl with a sprig of small pink flowers on one side. My mother rarely cried, but she did when she saw what I had done; that bowl was special, having been given to her as a girl. Then I burst into tears because it was so frightening to see her cry. The whole episode had such an impact that for years I scoured antique shops and clearing-out sales looking for a bowl that was the same, but though I have seen hundreds of similar pieces, I have never found an identical replacement. Eventually I came to see that although Mum loved that bowl, she was crying not for its loss per se, but for the loss of the one thing she had that connected her to her youth. An identical bowl could not replace that.

It was a valuable lesson and that's how I came to understand that you can connect with people through the objects they value. By knowing those objects and what they mean, you can come to know a person and their values just as clearly as if they had described them in writing.

That is why the kitchen drawer in my Hobart home contains my mother's wooden butter pats. Technically, butter pats are not the tools that shape butter but the shaped butter itself – but that was never my understanding, nor the source of my memories. When I was little, my mother would lift me up on the kitchen sink to sit on top of the butter churn, my job being to keep the lid on while she turned the crank handle and churned the butter. When the butter was ready, she would divide it into lumps and then shape each one with the wooden pats, making sure each lump had the right shape, weight and appearance. The whole process, from going over to the dairy to get the cream through to the production of the rectangles of butter, took at least an hour.

At that time the farm separated the milk and produced cream for the butter factory owned by a farmers' cooperative, of which my father and his brother Barney were members. Every day the shiny cream cans were loaded onto a horse-drawn dray and taken up to the end of the lane to a shelter, from which they were collected for the factory. The separated milk was let run down an open cement drain to the pigs.

I will never make my own butter, but whenever I open the kitchen drawer to get out the tongs or anything else and I see the butter pats, I am immediately connected to my mother, to a farm kitchen and to a time and a way of life and a place that is part of me. They are not the only objects from the farm that I keep: I have an old pyrex jug I used to carry from the farmhouse across the yard to the dairy for Dad and Barney's afternoon tea, taking care not to spill the hot tea. I also have Mum's cake plates, an oven cloth made out of hessian and decorated with bits of fabric, and bottles of buttons. These things have no monetary value but they are priceless.

Every summer the blowflies would storm the flywire doors as Mum boiled tomato sauce and relish and jam on the stove for later use. Gaylene and I picked and cut up fruit and vegetables, and especially enjoyed cracking open the apricot stones for the kernels, which we would put into the jam for extra flavour. 'Not too many, though; they're poisonous,' said Mum. The Fowlers Vacola outfit was always on the go, with bottle after bottle of fruit preserved and carefully placed on shelves in the storeroom for the winter.

Mum was an excellent cook, and a great knitter and seamstress. She had trained as a home arts teacher and taught at both the Wesley

Vale Area School and Latrobe High School, where she became the senior mistress. She had a reputation for making the best pastry in the district. With her own butter, eggs, milk and cream, she produced the most amazing afternoon teas for special occasions: sausage rolls, egg and bacon pies, cream puffs, cream horns, matchsticks, little apple cakes with orange icing, chocolate, coffee and passionfruit sponges, and pavlovas oozing with cream. A feast for the eyes as well as the stomach.

She taught me to cook but I was a complete failure at knitting and sewing. Mum didn't have the same level of patience with her own daughters that she displayed with her students – and I must admit that patience is not one of my virtues either. After watching the painful progress of my school compulsory knitting, she would grab the needles and do it herself. It was she who turned the heels on the socks knitted on four needles that I had to make to pass my school home economics course.

Like all the families in the district, we had an account at Gardam's store in the hamlet of Wesley Vale, not far from the school where Mum taught. This was the clearing house for the news of the district, conveyed via the windows of trucks and utes. It was a marvellous country store that doubled as a post office and newsagency. It sold everything from gumboots hanging from the ceiling to stock feed, from stationery to groceries, packets of tea and tins of coffee. It also sold lollies. Apart from cobbers and raspberries, my favourite value-for-money lollies were the red or green and yellow all-day suckers on sticks. Every mother in the district loathed them, as they were always shoved into the pockets of school uniforms and shorts, where they set rock hard.

Dad used to take the ute up to Gardam's store every month or so. He bought large sacks of flour and sugar, and those bags were washed and reused. The flour bags became cushions and the sugar bags of hessian were cut up, edged with remnants of pretty material and used as pot-holders. These were thrifty habits that Mum and Dad had developed during the Depression and war years. Everything from rubber bands and buttons to string, brown paper and glass jars was kept in the storeroom because it might come in handy. We raised and killed all our own meat and poultry, cured our own bacon, collected our own eggs, grew our own vegetables, and ate quail and kangaroo. We split the sticks and carted the wood from the woodheap. We lived off the land.

As kids, Gaylene and I fed the fowls and the turkeys. On big killing days before Christmas and Easter our contribution was plucking the poultry once the heads had been cut off and the scalding to loosen the feathers had been done. Unlike most people in political life who bandied the term around the parliaments, I really did know what running around 'like a chook with its head cut off' actually looked like. I knew about raising chickens, was horrified when I found out what battery hen farming did to chickens, and have ever since been a strong supporter of banning it.

Orphan lambs were bottle fed, often from an old long-necked beer bottle with a teat on it. Gaylene and I loved our pet lambs, always known as Billy. They were great pets but inevitably grew too big for the bottle. Then the day came when Billy would disappear while we were at school. Dad always told us that he had been returned to the flock. We would then go down to the sheep and call and call but our pet lambs would never come. It was a mystery to us because they had become so tame, but Dad convinced us that once back with their own they would forget us pretty quickly. Not until years later did we discover that, without exception, our pet lambs had found their way onto the table as the Sunday roast.

The rhythm of life was the same day in, day out. Dad rose every day at 5 am to go down to the bottom paddocks near the beach edging Bass Strait to bring the cattle up for milking, and every afternoon they were milked again. Afterwards Dad would come in for breakfast and report on the weather: 'Cold today, there's snow on Roland'; 'Easterly weather, no good for netting'; or 'Bloody hot out there'.

We were always looking inland to distant Cradle Mountain and Mount Roland or out to sea in Bass Strait for signs in the weather.

We rarely left the farm because of the twice-daily milking, so we found our own things to do. I had two ferrets, an albino and a polecat, and off we'd set with them in a bag and the nets ready to catch rabbits. I remember the pleasure of lying on the grass in the sun, listening to the rumbling in the warren just before the ferrets sent the rabbits running out of the burrows into the nets. My first ever pocket money came from selling rabbit skins. Rabbits were in plague proportions in my grandfather's time. The story goes that he introduced myxomatosis into Tasmania by bringing an infected rabbit in a Gladstone bag back from one of his annual trips to the Royal Easter Show in Sydney. Tasmanian potatoes were grown for the Sydney market, and hot Tasmanian potato chips were a big drawcard at the show. My aunts used to accompany my grandfather, and cooking the chips was a precise affair. Snow Thomas, the local farmer and later Wesley Vale activist who accompanied them one year on his way to agricultural college in New Zealand even remembers the instructions: cook in oil at 320 degrees Fahrenheit for six minutes.

The bottom paddocks of the farm were covered by a freshwater coastal lagoon, and then you crossed the sand dunes and emerged onto Moorlands beach, where we often had picnic teas. We spent hours down there watching the black swans on the lagoon and fossicking around the rock pools on the two reefs that defined the beach. We frightened ourselves with the 'bloodsuckers' (sea anemones), pulled the periwinkles off the rocks and waited for the fairy penguins. They nested right along the foreshore then and would leave their burrows at dusk to head out into Bass Strait to feed.

Often Dad would bring the fishing net down. He would drag it around himself, fully clothed and shoulder deep in the cold water, with one of my uncles or a neighbour or friend tailing it. When it was hauled up on the beach, we loved going through the catch. Dad caught everything from porcupine fish, puffer fish and toadfish to cocky salmon, mullet and flounder plus seaweed and the occasional crab, as well as tiddlies, which we grabbed and threw back on the next wave. Once a pod of pilot whales beached themselves on the shore in front of our place. I couldn't believe it. It was the biggest thing to happen in the whole district, and people came from everywhere to have a look. That was my first experience of whale stranding and decades before any whale rescue was ever thought of.

My sister and I used to lie in a ditch under the flight path at the fence at the end of the runway that bordered the farm. The Fokker Friendships that flew in and out of Devonport Airport would come in low over us, and we would speculate about the people and where they had come from. We knew a bit about Melbourne, just across the Strait. Mum had taken us there when we were in primary school and we saw the zoo and the trams and the shops, but what really dazzled us was a production of *Fiddler on the Roof*. There was a revolving stage and magnificent costumes and wonderful singing. I was hooked on theatre from then on. I was also hooked on travel.

The *Princess of Tasmania* sailed out of Devonport to the mainland, and at nights we could see the lights as she left. We knew there was a wider world, even though we hardly saw it. But my mother was determined that we would know about it and, apart from taking us to Melbourne and Hobart and on occasional shopping trips to Launceston, she bought us a globe and a set of encyclopedias from a door-to-door salesman.

At that time salesmen were welcome visitors to rural properties because they were fairly rare, and a salesman was someone different to talk to. They made a pleasant change from the council inspectors who came to check on dog licences – always too few for the number of dogs on the property. The Rawleigh's man was my particular favourite. Rawleigh's began as an American company and opened a factory in Melbourne in 1928, selling everything from food flavourings and spices to ointment remedies for coughs and sore muscles, and antiseptic creams for cuts and burns. The salesman had big cases that he unlatched on the kitchen table, and everything was beautifully packed in its own little compartment. Mum always bought a large bottle of vanilla essence, sometimes tapioca pudding and with enough nagging could be persuaded to buy a small packet of peppermints for us.

At some stage we got a car: a pink Vanguard ute. I remember being crowded into it as all four of us would head into Devonport for tea on a Sunday to visit my grandparents. We'd stop at a corner store and I would be sent across the road to buy Havelock flake cut tobacco for Dad's pipe. Much later we got a Holden Kingswood, a 'town car', as well as the ute. Sometimes we would go for drives in the countryside and up to Sheffield to see the old house where my mother was brought up. We were given the family history tour of places like Stoodley, where she went to primary school, where she rode her horse or bicycle and where she was terrified of the dogs people owned.

She sometimes told us about Tom, the Italian prisoner of war who had lived on their farm during the Second World War. There were quite a number of POWs on farms around Sheffield. I used to ask questions about Tom, but no one knew what had happened to him when he left and whether he had even returned to Italy safely. This attitude seemed very uncaring, and they were not uncaring people, but it was explained that as they spoke no Italian and he spoke no English, they couldn't be expected to communicate.

Years later I decided to try to find him. I discovered that he was still alive, living in the same town of Forli in Emilia Romagna that he had left when conscripted into the Italian Army. Mum and I visited him and his wife, Lavinia, and their family of two married daughters, Iones and Iris, their husbands both called Sergio and grandchildren Cristian and Chiara in 2000. The visit was just wonderful; they were so pleased to see us. Through an interpreter I learned what it was like to be an Italian prisoner of war on a Sheffield dairy farm during the war. Firstly, his real name was Carlo: they called him 'Tom' because 'Charles' was my grandfather's name, and apparently you couldn't have two people called Charles on the same farm.

He spoke of the loneliness but was philosophical, saying that if you had to spend the war as a prisoner, a farm in Sheffield with the Tylers was as good as it could have been. By law the prisoners were not permitted to sleep in the farmhouse but my grandmother had made clear that he would eat with the family, and he shared whatever they had. Needless to say this did not include pasta or garlic. To Carlo, joining the family for meals was everything, and in return he shared what he had. The Red Cross would call with chocolate and sweet biscuits for the prisoners: Carlo always chose the chocolate to give to my aunt Josephine, who was at primary school at the time. With rationing there were few treats for children, but he went out of his way to be kind to her, and she always spoke warmly of him. The Red Cross also took photos, and it was from Carlo that I got the only photo of my grandparents taken on the farm. My family did not have a camera.

After our trip to Italy Carlo's daughter Iones, along with his son-in-law Sergio and grandson Cristian, visited the Sheffield farm. As is the case in much of rural Tasmania, not much had changed since 1945. They were able to film the shed in which Carlo had lived and the house and vista of Mount Roland. Carlo was very emotional when he saw the photos and video. I visited him in Italy again in 2016, when he was 103.

Probably the most traumatic incident of my childhood concerned our two Clydesdale draughthorses. Wearing their heavy collars, the Clydesdales would be yoked up to a wooden cart or sledge as turnips were pulled, paddocks were ploughed, and hay was cut, raked, baled, brought into the barn and fed out again in the winter time. I loved them. They were huge gentle creatures and we were often lifted up to sit on their backs. When Dad went down the paddocks with a sledge yoked to one of the horses, we went through a certain gate where there was often a huge puddle. The horse would pull us through, but not without a shower of mud. It was one of Gaylene's and my favourite pastimes.

But once the tractor arrived on the farm, the horses had to go.

There was no market for them: everyone was getting rid of horses. One morning Mum told Gaylene and me that we had to stay inside and not come out of our bedroom. This was unusual because we were always roaming around the farm on our own and the doors were never locked. Naturally we climbed out of the window to see what was going on. We sneaked out to the garden gate in time to witness the first draughthorse being shot. Shocked, in tears, we rushed back inside. We railed against Dad and what he had done – but it was the first of many lessons in the heartbreak of farming. You cannot keep animals for sentimental reasons. They have to be fed, and a farm can't support two draughthorses that are no longer needed: they are more useful as dog meat. I have never forgotten it.

A few years later, still in primary school, I saw in a Devonport newsagent a book with the title *They Shoot Horses, Don't They?* and was shocked – why would anyone write a book about that? Not until I was an adult did I discover that it was actually a novel about a dance marathon during the Depression in the USA. When a policeman asks the main character Robert why he shot his dance partner Gloria, he replies with that punchline.

It took Dad no time at all to get used to his tractor. It was the first of many. The metal seats were soon replaced with later model padded ones, and then came cabins. He was always on the tractor heading down to the beach to check on the cattle, ploughing, slashing and feeding out. In later years, when so debilitated by a stroke that he could hardly walk, he could still drag himself up onto it. Mobile again, he could drive around the farm, watching over his cattle with a steady gaze, keeping an eye out for damaged fences or field mushrooms, or throwing a match into gorse. (I don't know how many times I tried to persuade him that he was stimulating gorse growth but he wouldn't have it. What would a city-educated girl know?)

Most weekends during the winter when the cows were dry, Dad would put a wooden frame on the ute, load up the guns and the hunting dogs and set off kangaroo shooting. It is not surprising that he also liked a good western. By 1963 we had a black-and-white television set. At that time almost eighty per cent of television content was sourced from the USA and, apart from the ABC news, *Laramie*, *Bonanza*, *The Lone Ranger*, *Hopalong Cassidy*, *The Cisco Kid*, *Rawhide*, *Whiplash* and *F Troop* were staples. Surprisingly, Dad also took a liking to *Doctor Who*, with Tom Baker being his all-time favourite Doctor.

But the big influence on our house initially was the advertising. We had no idea so many things existed. Dad was fascinated by a new product called Rice-a-Riso and insisted Mum buy it. One day he came into the kitchen and his stomach churned at the revolting smell. 'What the bloody hell is that?' he protested. After that he was never persuaded by advertising and never wanted any 'bought muck', so we stuck with homemade. Growing up, we stayed with friends who had *bought* tomato sauce and *bought* butter. We thought such products were so superior and sophisticated. Fifty years later the complete reverse is true.

I can still see Dad on the tractor, wearing an old worn-out sports coat or a favourite collared woollen jumper with holes in the front, his ever-present old hat on his head, puttering off with his pack of dogs running along behind. Dad loved his dogs and brought home way more than we needed. It was a joke in the saleyards that if you wanted to sell a dog, Tom Morris was your man.

Dad had a great sense of humour. Always at home in his old clothes on the land and around his cattle, he was only awkward when dressed up in town. When Dad died, Nicola, one of my nieces, put into his coffin a photo of him on his tractor, surrounded by turkeys, to help him on his way. It was not quite the ritual followed by the ancient Egyptians or the Chinese with their terracotta warriors, but the sentiment was the same.

I brought one of his early metal tractor seats with me to Hobart and it is cemented in my garden. As the butter pats are my connection to Mum, the tractor seat is my connection to the man himself, to my dad. Together these objects capture hard-working, resilient people, loving and providing for their family, living on the land.

~

I SOMETIMES THINK MY MEMORIES of those days are so acute because I was sent to boarding school at St Mary's College in Hobart in 1964 when I was ten years old. My mother had been sent there and, believing that education makes anything possible, she thought it was critical that her girls got a good St Mary's education. I stayed there for six years. Confined within the school boundaries in the centre of the 'modern' asphalt city, and only allowed home the first weekend of every month, we boarders were isolated. There was no phone, and letters in and out were opened and read by the nuns. Any complaints about the school or the nuns or the food meant that the letters were torn up and had to be rewritten. 'Your parents are not working hard to send you here to have you upset them with this nonsense. Write it again.'

Painfully homesick to begin with, I often went home in my imagination. And when I did go home, I carefully observed every detail and every change – more intensely, I think, than did those who continued to live on the farm every day. I never took it for granted.

People have often asked over the years how I got involved in politics. The answer is the same as that given by the farmers fighting against coalmines and coal seam gas wells. I could not stand by and watch North Broken Hill and Noranda of Canada destroy my blood's country. It is part of who I am and where I have come from, and its stories 'go walking in my sleep'. My grandparents, great-grandparents, and great-great-grandparents are all buried under the prevailing wind that would have dumped pollution from the pulp mill on the land. There was no way I was not going to fight for that country. Mum's butter pats and Dad's tractor seat are a constant reminder that some things are worth fighting for.

# 2

# The Power of Lake Pedder: Awakening

OBJECT: *Pink quartz sand and pebble, known as a Pedder penny, from Lake Pedder. Entrusted to Christine by Margaret Wilkinson.*

I HAVE A XXXX BEER GLASS in the shape of a boot full of pink quartz sand from Lake Pedder, topped with a Pedder penny: a smooth coin-sized pebble from the lake shoreline. It was given to me by Margaret Wilkinson, a great Tasmanian conservationist and life member of the Greens, just before she died in 2009. Together Margaret and I had fought the campaign that stopped the Wesley Vale pulp mill, the campaign to protect the farmlands at Don Heads; we had marched for the forests, and celebrated my election to parliament in 1989 and the official birth of the Tasmanian Greens in 1992. We had even been arrested together trying to protect the Tarkine Wilderness Area from the Road to Nowhere (the link-road carved through the wilderness in 1996).

Margaret collected the Lake Pedder sand and the penny on her last walk into the area in 1972, before it was drowned by the rising waters of the Serpentine Impoundment contained by three dams in the Upper Gordon Scheme and built by Tasmania's Hydro-Electric Commission to generate hydroelectric power. The flooding of Lake

Pedder drowned the glacial lake and its unique pink quartzite beach, formed at the end of the last ice age. It was an assault on the heart of the South West Wilderness of Tasmania.

To her dying day Margaret never gave up the fight to restore the lake. She did not give these things to me as souvenirs; she was passing me the baton in a gesture of faith. She asked me to put them back in their rightful places when this crime against nature had been reversed and Lake Pedder restored. She was confident that if I did not see this happen, the next generation of Greens and conservationists would, sending a powerful signal to the whole world.

Hundreds of people have jars of Pedder sand on their bookshelves. When they look at them, they do not think of a drowned lake, but of hope. They too keep the faith that the lake will be restored and that one day they will take that sand back to the beach.

Lake Pedder is much more than a place in the south-western Tasmanian wilderness, as beautiful and unique as its sand and wide beach may be. It became and has remained a powerful symbol of political expression through action, and its restoration embodies the hope of people and nature reunifying.

~

THE CAMPAIGN TO SAVE LAKE PEDDER solidified at a rowdy meeting in Hobart Town Hall on 23 March 1972. This was when the world's first Greens party, the United Tasmania Group (UTG), was formed, preceding European Greens parties by several years. Its manifesto, written by the chairman of the Lake Pedder Action Committee, Dr Richard Jones, senior lecturer in botany at the University of Tasmania, sets out the four pillars of the Greens political philosophy: ecology, social justice, peace and non-violence, and participatory democracy. These have been incorporated into the Global Greens Charter adopted by every Greens party in more than ninety countries in the world – and the Lake Pedder campaign was where all this began.

Dick Jones drove the establishment of the University of Tasmania's Centre for Environmental Studies in 1974, the year in which he ran for the Senate under the banner of the UTG. His advocacy led to radical changes in people's thinking about conservation; it put the Earth front and centre as our home, with green politics as the political expression of that idea. He argued that the environment is not something to be considered and protected after the imperatives of development, as the Liberal and Labor parties assumed, but is the place from which we human beings derive the fundamentals of our life: water, food, clothing, shelter and, through its beauty and complexity, the sustenance of our spirit. The idea that we are the Earth and whatever we do to her we do to ourselves is central to the lives of all first peoples on this planet, including Australia's Indigenous people. It is an idea that needed to be brought into political discourse.

It was in this political context that in 1971 I enrolled in an Arts degree at the University of Tasmania. I wish I could say that the campus was on fire with environmental ideas, but unfortunately I have a clearer recollection of students burning tyres on the road to secure an underpass to the refectory. However, as time passed my awareness grew, especially when my boyfriend, and later husband, Neville Milne became the treasurer of the north-west coast branch of the UTG. Even so, apart from signing petitions and taking part in marches calling for the lake to be saved, I did not become an active campaigner.

I used to wonder why I was not actively involved in this huge new idea swirling around me. I could have gone to the south-west and absorbed the magnificent beauty of the Lake Pedder beach; I could have been at the meeting when the world's first Greens party was formed. But I didn't. I think this was because I was an eighteen-year-old fifth-generation rural Tasmanian with limited experience not only of life but also of the beauty of my own home. I had no knowledge of the wilderness except for the hydro schemes I had visited on a school trip in 1963 and listening to Dad talking about fishing and hunting 'up the lakes': the Great Lake and the Central Plateau. I had not been anywhere in the south-west, and bushwalking was unknown to me. The south-west was not a place I knew or had any feel for at all – but I had that in common with most Tasmanians.

I think I didn't become involved in environmental activism at university because even being there was a big achievement for me. My mother had been to teachers' college but I was the first person on either side of my family to go to university. Until the 1940s the overwhelming majority of students in rural Tasmania left at the end of primary school. Area schools such as the Wesley Vale one I attended were set up in the late 1940s to provide three years of post-primary education to all children in Tasmania. There were high schools in Hobart and Launceston and some larger towns, but many rural children were sent to private schools that took boarders.

From the time I was very young, I knew that the only way I could afford to continue to study was by winning scholarships. The income from the farm wasn't enough to cover the cost of boarding school, and though Mum was a teacher she was working in an age of unequal pay and societal disapproval of married women working. Bursaries allowed me to complete my secondary school education, and I took a teacher studentship at university, which paid better than the Commonwealth scholarship. It was great: after four years of university with all fees paid, I was only bonded to the Education Department for one year.

It was unusual for any kids – let alone girls – from north-west Tasmania to go on to tertiary education; I was in no doubt about how special it was, and I felt huge pressure to do well. Belonging to a conservative hard-working family, I knew that I was at university to study, to make my parents proud, not to become involved in student politics or any other kind of politics.

The need to succeed was drilled into me, not only by the nuns at boarding school but also by the Dominican nuns who ran Ena Waite Catholic Residential College, where I lived during my undergraduate years. Sister Cyprian, who was in charge, was an extremely intelligent and erudite woman who set up Fellows of Ena Waite, a group of University of Tasmania academics who visited the college for dinner reasonably regularly. It was at one such gathering that I saw James McAuley, the conservative Catholic poet who lectured me in English, playing the piano and singing 'Frankie and Johnny'. I had never suspected he knew such a song, let alone could perform it, which he did well. I doubt that the whole issue of Lake Pedder had ever crossed the radar of most of the academic fellows; its fate was certainly not a subject for discussion. Nor did it feature in my political science course or as a subject for intercollege debating – one of my great interests as an undergraduate.

My awareness of the campaign to save Lake Pedder came through Neville, but I remained an interested onlooker. I was sure that all the work being done by the Save Lake Pedder National Park Committee, the South West Committee and the Lake Pedder Action Committee – the petitions, letter writing, meetings and even supportive TV programs – were all so compelling that MPs would clearly understand the evidence and vote against flooding the lake. And when in 1971 under this growing public pressure Prime Minister Billy McMahon actually offered Tasmania federal funding for an alternative hydro scheme, I thought common sense had prevailed.

I was wrong. The Tasmanian Parliament wasn't going to be told what to do by the federal government or UNESCO or scientists and people from overseas. At the 1972 state election the Hydro-Electric Commission spent vast amounts of public money on its support for the government and the Opposition in their plan to flood Lake Pedder. The UTG ran a people-powered campaign but was defeated by the collusion of political parties and business, and failed to win any seats.

But in May of that year Gough Whitlam, as leader of the federal Opposition, announced his support for a hydro scheme that would save Lake Pedder. When fellow Labor MP Tom Uren followed up by saying, 'Let us be big enough to admit we were wrong, let us rectify our mistake,' the campaign to save the lake was seriously back on the national agenda.

On 8 September 1972 Brenda Hean of the Lake Pedder Action Committee flew from Tasmania to Canberra in a Tiger Moth piloted by Max Price; they planned to skywrite 'Save Lake Pedder' over Parliament House in the lead-up to the federal election. The plane disappeared before they got there. It has never been found. Scraps of recognised clothing were later discovered in a fisherman's nets. As a parliamentarian many years later I accessed the police file under Freedom of Information legislation, but it shed very little light on the investigation, except to confirm how inadequate it had been. We knew that the hangar door had been tampered with and the safety beacon had been hidden, and it was later revealed that Brenda had received a threatening phone call saying, 'How would you like to go for a swim?' The police investigation was disgraceful: none of these facts was even referred to.

The federal election in 1972, when Labor won for the first time in twenty-three years, was a political awakening not just for me but for many, many members of my generation. Even though, not being twenty-one, many of us could not vote, we campaigned for Gough Whitlam – for free university education, to bring the troops home from Vietnam, to save Lake Pedder. Politics, we now knew, had become real; we were personally affected. We had watched friends and family members being devastated as they were conscripted for the war in Vietnam, we had seen our parents' financial struggle to get us to university, and we had watched a lake begin to disappear. In 1972, for the first time in our lives, we understood that the people could change the nation with a change of government, and that knowledge was energising.

In 1973 Gough Whitlam as prime minister established a parliamentary inquiry into the fate of Lake Pedder, when the flooding had already begun. The inquiry said the lake was too important to be destroyed and a moratorium should be placed on the flooding until the feasibility of saving the lake was assessed. The Labor Cabinet rejected the inquiry's findings. However, the full Labor caucus, persuaded by the efforts of Minister for the Environment Moss Cass and a photographic presentation by Olegas Truchanas, overturned the Cabinet decision. The government betrayed the conservation movement. Whitlam never wrote to Tasmanian Premier Eric Reece with an official Government offer for the funding for an alternative hydro scheme or supporting the moratorium; he just informed Reece of the caucus decision. This enabled Eric Reece to proceed unimpeded: as he said at the time, 'As far as Lake Pedder is concerned, the sooner they fill it up the better.' Gough Whitlam was a great Australian, but he bears a grave responsibility for failing to save Lake Pedder.

But others attempted to save it. Trade unionist Jack Mundey from the Builders' Labourers Federation, fresh from his successes with the green bans that had saved Sydney's Rocks and Woolloomooloo, called for a 'blue ban' for workers on the dams, but this was rejected by Tasmania's Trades and Labor Council. Calls for Bob Hawke and the Australian Council of Trade Unions to take on the issue fell on deaf ears: they decided to leave it up to Tasmanian unionists.

In January 1974 the call went global. At its meeting in Buenos Aires the International Union for the Conservation of Nature passed a resolution calling upon the Tasmanian and Australian governments to investigate the feasibility of restoring the original Lake Pedder. But it was too little too late: the lake was flooded. However, its power as a rallying point for the conservation movement was undiminished; it had educated and empowered a whole generation.

Even though I was not directly involved in the intricacies of the campaign, I learned a great deal about how politics works in Tasmania and in Canberra. That experience taught me that argument based on evidence is not necessarily effective. I understood that Tasmania's political parties were embedded in the dream of hydro industrialisation and what they saw as its power for good. I also learned that nothing can be taken for granted, and that eventually a stand must be taken for the things that are important. For me, civil disobedience became an option for the first time.

When the lake shore slipped below the rising waters of the Serpentine Impoundment, many people felt sadness and regret that they had not done enough. I was among those who vowed that I would never allow anything similar to happen again without a fight. And so, a few years later, when the Tasmanian Government of Robin Gray and the Hydro-Electric Commission tried to dam the Franklin River and the call went out for protesters to join the Franklin blockade, people answered in their thousands, and I was one of them.

That was the start of my political activism, and it would see me not only battling to save the Franklin in the early days but also fighting for Pedder as part of the Greens.

Fresh from the Franklin River campaign in 1983, Bob Brown, a member of the UTG, won the seat of Denison in the Tasmanian Parliament following a countback after the resignation of Democrat Norm Sanders. It was Bob Brown's second attempt at being elected on an environmental platform, and his success saw the consolidation of the first Green seat in Australia, which had been won by Sanders in 1980.

Following the 1986 state election Bob was joined by Dr Gerry Bates, who had been a high-profile campaigner against the Electrona smelter in southern Tasmania. Then, in 1989, Di Hollister, Lance Armstrong and I ran with them on 'The Independents' ticket. All of us were elected. The five Independents of 1989 became the Green Independents in 1991, and the Tasmanian Greens in 1992. Later that year the Australian Greens was formed as a federation of state-based Greens parties, and the Global Greens followed in 2001.

In 1990 we Greens pushed for the government to require the Hydro-Electric Commission to conduct a feasibility study on draining Lake Pedder. Of course the Hydro rejected the proposition. In 1992 a study group was formed to research the scientific, economic and ecological issues surrounding the restoration of the lake.[1] A diving expedition made an amazing and inspiring discovery: all major features of the original beach and dune systems were intact, and the accumulation of sediment over the beach was slight, no more than a few millimetres. Not only was the beach intact, but the tyre marks from the last plane to leave the beach were also still clear. Lake Pedder was just waiting to emerge, and people were excited.

A new campaign, Pedder 2000, was launched with the idea of greeting the new century with a decision that would inspire the world: the restoration of Lake Pedder. As Olegas Truchanas had so brilliantly articulated twenty years before, 'If we can revise some of our attitudes towards the land under our feet, if we can accept the role of the steward and depart from the role of the conqueror, if we can accept the view that man and nature are inseparable parts of the unified world – then Tasmania can be a shining beacon to a dull, uniform and largely artificial world.'

Bob Brown and I spoke at the Hobart launch, and for the first time in a long time we began to feel that we could really save the lake. The charge was led by Helen Gee, a brilliant campaigner, organiser and conservationist. Approaches were made to the Keating Labor government, and as a result in 1995 the House of Representatives Standing Committee on Environment, Recreation and the Arts launched an inquiry into the proposal to drain and restore Lake Pedder.

I was leading the Tasmanian Greens in the campaign, and Bob Brown had announced that he would run for the Senate in the upcoming 1996 federal election. Both Tasmania's Liberal government led by Ray Groom and the Labor Opposition led by Michael Field were actively hostile to the proposal, and so were supporters of the Hydro-Electric Commission. Michael Field moved a motion in the Tasmanian Parliament that the investigation into Lake Pedder, a 'tenth-ranking environmental issue', was a waste of public money, especially at a time when unemployment in Tasmania was increasing.

It was a view others shared. Nigel Forteath, professor of aquaculture at the University of Tasmania and well-known trout fisherman, argued against the draining of the lake, though not on the grounds that it had become a mecca for trout fishermen after it was flooded; instead he announced that if Lake Pedder were drained, 2000 platypus would die. It was a sensational statement that captured media and public attention, as it was designed to do. Though his methodology was discredited[2], the publicity furore distracted from the evidence presented to the inquiry. Using an iconic native animal to derail an environmental campaign was a new tactic from the vested interests, and the Hydro, Liberal and Labor parties loved it.

It was a particularly bruising time for Bob Brown and me. T-shirts were produced with a print of a platypus on the front above the writing 'Lake Pedder is My Home, Leave the Lake Alone' and, on the back, 'Ring Dr Bob Brown and Christine Milne'. In the Tasmanian Parliament things became ridiculous and heated as the hearing in Tasmania of the House of Representatives Inquiry into the Restoration of Lake Pedder was set to commence. I went into Question Time one day and the frontbench members of both the Groom Liberal government and Field Labor Opposition took off their coats to reveal the T-shirts. They thought it was hilarious that the image of a platypus was being so successfully used to ridicule the restoration of Lake Pedder and the House of Representatives Inquiry.

The House of Representatives report concluded:

> It is the opinion of the Committee that further research
> or evaluation of the feasibility of draining Lake Pedder
> would be inappropriate at this time. It is unfortunate
> that this beautiful, geologically unique lake was ever

flooded, but with finite resources and many competing
environmental goals it is unlikely that enough of the
other higher-priority tasks will be accomplished in the
near future to make way for the allocation of resources for
the restoration of the original lake … One lesson from
the history of Lake Pedder is that, in future, a greater
weight must be given to the preservation of biological and
geological diversity when considering use of pristine areas.

There was one dissenting voice – that of Labor's Robert Chynoweth,
who wrote:

What price is beauty? What price is a symbol that can
inspire people forever? What price for the wonder of
looking at a scene unspoilt by human intervention?
What price to walk, and listen to the quiet? What price
for restoration of the soul? What price to admire the
Creator's work? These prices were not computed in our
report. Surely they outweigh the other costs.[3]

What price indeed? At the first ever Global Greens Conference, held
in Canberra in 2001, I was talking to a group of young delegates who
had come from Brazil, and asked whether they planned a holiday
after the conference, having come so far. They said they planned
to travel to Tasmania to visit Lake Pedder. They knew that this is
where their hope for a better world had its genesis, but also where it
continues to be grounded.

The summer of 2015–16 was hot and dry. Tasmania's hydro
lakes were at a record low, and not just because of the drought. Lake
Gordon was at only thirteen per cent of its capacity. Talk began about
draining Lake Pedder into its neighbouring lake to shore up energy
generation. Was the dream of restoring Lake Pedder to be realised by
the Hydro itself? What delicious irony!

The Hydro had clearly – once again – mismanaged Tasmania's water storage. The carbon price delivered by the Australian Greens and the Labor government of Julia Gillard had provided Tasmania with a massive annual windfall of more than $70 million, selling renewable energy via Basslink into the national grid. (Basslink is the cable that joins the Tasmanian and national electricity grids by means of a subsea and terrestrial interconnector between Tasmania and Victoria.) However, when Tony Abbott became prime minister in 2013 he announced he would repeal the carbon price, but he needed the new crossbench senators to take their seats in July 2014 before this was possible. The Hydro had a narrow window of opportunity to drive the turbines for all they were worth, to pocket the cash while they could.

Even though the Hydro board knew that an El Niño event was impending and that Tasmania was likely to suffer from a lack of rainfall, they took the risk and ran down the storages, thinking they could access cheap coal-fired power via Basslink to make up any energy shortage. When Basslink was proposed in the first place, one of the key arguments against it had been that it would lock in the profits to the Hydro from maximising hydro energy production, and therefore make it impossible ever to restore Lake Pedder. One of the premier's key advisors told me that I was wrong; Basslink would make it more likely that Lake Pedder could be saved because its place in the Hydro generation system would be compensated by the purchase of electric power from the mainland.

So the Hydro spun the turbines and depleted their reservoirs. In doing so, they ignored the risk of a Basslink outage – and in December 2015 Basslink went down and stayed out of commission for six months. The Tasmanian Government brought in diesel generators. The cost of this debacle was $180 million. The whole episode provoked huge community outrage and a renewed Tasmanian debate about the stupidity or otherwise of giving up our self-reliance and renewable hydro energy source in exchange for cash and extending the life of Victoria's coal-fired power stations.

While this was going on, I decided to break my forty-year vow never to go out to the Serpentine Impoundment until Lake Pedder had re-emerged. I wanted to see exactly how feasible it might be to restore the lake, as some people were suggesting. I stood at the lookout above the relatively full impoundment and tried to imagine Lake Pedder as I had seen it in so many paintings and photographs over the years. I could make out all the surrounding landmarks but could not quite come to terms with the huge mass of water relative to what I knew was a tiny lake beneath. It was shocking to see the state of nearby Lake Gordon, with a broad ring of dead trees poking through the shallow water.

However, before the community conversation could seriously turn to the restoration of Lake Pedder, it rained. The storages filled quickly; the diesel generators were switched off. Another parliamentary inquiry was set up, and the Hydro and Basslink refused to attend. Basslink was up and running again. *Plus ça change*.

The campaign to save Lake Pedder continues. The Lake Pedder Restoration Committee has developed a technical proposal to drain the lake, and they continue to lobby for it. The ravages of time have taken their toll on the dam walls, and soon major decisions will have to be made about whether to maintain or dismantle the masses of cement. New renewable supplies of wind and solar energy are already reducing Tasmanians' former reliance on hydroelectricity. The old bulk power consumers are reaching the end of their days. There is no technical barrier to environmental blue-sky thinking.

The world is seriously pondering what human wellbeing and the sustainability of human life look like in an age of global warming. While I support the active decoupling of fossil fuel energy from economic growth, I believe we need to go further and question the nature of growth itself: there are limits to growth based on exploitation of nature in an increasingly crowded, degraded and warming world. It is clear to me that coming home to our natural world, with the humility to learn from it, to recouple human wellbeing with a healthy planet, is the key to future happiness and prosperity. I have a feeling that Margaret Wilkinson would agree.

Tasmania is still well positioned to be the place to show how it could be done. It could still be the beacon of environmental hope in the twenty-first century that Olegas Truchanas imagined. Restoring Lake Pedder is still as central and critical to that vision as it ever was. It might have slipped below the waters of the Serpentine Impoundment in 1973 but it remains there, intact, preserved, powerful. Not lost, but waiting.

# 3

# Saving the Franklin: Empowerment

OBJECT: *The photo of Christine's arrest during the Franklin blockade in 1983. It was made into a poster thirty years later and includes a personal inscription. The poster is now part of the Museum of Australian Democracy Collection.*

THE CAMPAIGN TO SAVE TASMANIA'S magnificent and wild Franklin River was a coming of age for environmentalists across Australia. In the 1970s and 1980s thousands of people here and around the world came together through marches, rallies, concerts, petitions, parliamentary actions and a celebrated blockade to take a stand for protection of the wilderness against the excesses of industrialisation. During the blockade 1217 people were arrested and 475 jailed in Risdon Prison.

The Franklin River campaign, my arrest and imprisonment were defining moments in my life. I was already an environmentalist, and they turned me into a fully fledged activist. The campaign empowered me. I learned that if you can handle the worst thing that the authorities can do to you for taking a stand for what you believe in, there is nothing to stop you acting and no excuse for not doing so.

The nuns at St Mary's College boarding school had always encouraged us to stand up for what we believed in. Over and over we were told to have the courage of our convictions, to take personal responsibility and not blame others for any predicament. We were never permitted to see ourselves as victims or avoid addressing what was wrong. We were left with no doubt that we had been given the advantage of an education and had a duty to humanity to act. As the prison van was making its way from the court in Queenstown to Risdon Women's Prison, I remember thinking that this way of dealing with such precepts was possibly not what the nuns had in mind.

By 1982 I had been teaching in high schools in north-west Tasmania for eight years. I had had a year overseas travelling in a campervan around Europe and six months' long-service leave backpacking through South East Asia, the Middle East and Africa. The year in Europe was a wake-up call for me. Having had an education that was basically English, with English history and literature the focus of the curriculum, I was keen to see the landscapes, buildings, historic places and wildlife I had come to know through the printed page. I wanted to see Brontë country and couldn't wait to walk to Top Withens on the Yorkshire moors, the inspiration for *Wuthering Heights*, and feel the presence of Heathcliff and Catherine. I went to Thomas Hardy country and was desperate to find the place where the sheep went over the cliff in the 1967 film adaptation of Hardy's *Far from the Madding Crowd*. I had studied the novel at school, and it was one of the very few films we boarders at St Mary's College were allowed to see; it made a big impression on me, and from then onwards Julie Christie was one of my favourite actresses. I went to Sligo in Ireland to see Yeats's Lake Isle of Innisfree and up to Scotland to see the battlefield of Culloden. London was all about red double-decker buses and phone boxes, black taxis, Big Ben, St Paul's Cathedral and Westminster Abbey, Hyde Park and Piccadilly Circus, and walking the streets and squares made famous by Dickens.

It is a pity that I didn't know then that one of my forebears, Sarah Smith, an eighteen-year-old servant of Eleanor and Thomas

McDowell of Kennington Lane, had been convicted at Surrey quarter sessions on 13 January 1818 for stealing a watch, an umbrella and two silver spoons. I would have been fascinated to see the records and visit the places where she lived, worked and was tried. Sentenced to transportation for seven years, she was held at Horsemonger Lane Gaol, transported to Port Jackson on the *Maria 1* and transhipped to Van Diemen's Land on the *Elizabeth Henrietta*, arriving in Port Dalrymple (George Town) on 14 October 1818. Her daughter Mary met John Morris at Westbury, Tasmania, and their son William Morris was my great-grandfather.

Having been brought up on Robin Hood, I couldn't wait to see Sherwood Forest, and I was disappointed that only about 200 hectares remained of the forests that had originally made up about twenty per cent of the whole of Nottinghamshire. In Germany I was on a mission to see the Black Forest, home of Hansel and Gretel and the cuckoo clock that hung in the porch at the farm. But I was horrified to see the forest dying from the effects of acid rain because of pollution from industry and coal-fired power plants. Thousands of hectares of dead and dying trees lined the roads. The great rivers of the Rhône and the Rhine were brown and heavily polluted. The cities were cloaked in pollution, and many of the famous marble and sandstone buildings and statues and gargoyles were blackened or eroded. I realised that clean air, clean water and uncontaminated soil were not to be taken for granted. Nature and the cultural heritage of Europe were disappearing and dying at the hands of humanity.

Because this was the time of the Cold War, Neville and I were not prepared to risk driving behind the Iron Curtain, especially in a very unreliable Commer Highwayman campervan. Years later I found out that probably the only good thing about that artificial division of eastern and western Europe, with its heavily militarised no-man's-land zone, is that an undisturbed wildlife corridor was effectively created for plants and animals, forming the basis of a green belt the length of Europe.

While we were in Europe, the Tasmanian Hydro-Electric Commission announced that a new dam would be constructed on the Gordon River below its intersection with the Franklin. The Hydro was at it again, this time to flood the Franklin River valley. I didn't know about it at the time; news from home was scarce and conveyed from our parents via letters held at American Express's poste restante offices in European cities. Our parents didn't mention the Franklin.

I came back to Tasmania with a strong sense of how special our wild places were, and redoubled my resolve to save them. Momentum for the new dam on Tasmania's west coast was matched by opposition to it. The Tasmanian Wilderness Society, formed in 1976, was actively campaigning to save the wild rivers from any new dams. By 1981 the issue came to a head, with a stand-off between the Tasmanian Labor government's compromise for a dam on the Gordon River upstream of the junction with the Franklin (where it joined the Olga River) and the Legislative Council's backing for the Hydro-Electric Commission's Gordon below Franklin option, which would have inundated thirty-three kilometres of the Franklin River. A referendum was held to resolve the deadlock, and Labor Premier Doug Lowe said that the ballot would include an option of no dams. But the president of the Labor Party wrote to all its Members of the House of Assembly (MHAs) instructing them to withdraw that option.

Doug Lowe was forced into a backdown and was deposed as premier. Harry Holgate, a pro-dams Labor MHA, became premier and the ballot paper did not include a third option of no dams. The Wilderness Society encouraged people to write 'No Dams' on the ballot paper, which they did in their thousands: thirty-five per cent of voters. But 54.72 per cent of Tasmanians voted for the Gordon below Franklin option, and 9.78 per cent for the Gordon above Olga option.

Mayhem followed with the resignation of Doug Lowe and Mary Willey from the Labor Party to sit as independents. Labor lost its majority, and Democrat Norm Sanders moved a no-confidence motion in the government. An election was called for 15 May 1982. Both Labor and Liberal parties campaigned in favour of the Franklin dam in the election, but as a result of the chaos in the Labor Party and the upheaval in Tasmania over the issue, the Liberal Party's 'whispering bulldozer' Robin Gray won the first non-Labor majority in fifty-one years. Bob Brown stood on an anti-dams ticket in the seat of Denison and secured 8.9 per cent of the vote.

Legislation to dam the Gordon below Franklin passed the Tasmanian Parliament, and dam construction began. On 2 September the Tasmanian Parliament revoked large tracts of the Wild Rivers National Park and vested control of the land in the Hydro-Electric Commission to build the dam. Trespass was made an arrestable offence, with a fine of $100 or six months in jail.

With the stalemate of the Fraser government's nomination of south-west Tasmania for World Heritage listing in 1981 and Robin Gray's determination to build the dam, Bob Brown began a national tour calling for the Commonwealth to intervene using its foreign affairs powers (Section 51 of the Australian Constitution grants the Commonwealth power to pass legislation that gives effect within Australia to its obligations under international treaties and conventions).

Rallies were held in mainland capital cities, and planning for a blockade of the Franklin began, with Anka Makovec employed by the Tasmanian Wilderness Society to go to Strahan and start getting organised. In November 1982 Bob Brown announced in front of 14,000 people at the Melbourne rally that a peaceful blockade of the dam site would begin on 14 December.

I watched news of the fifty-three arrests on the first day of the blockade, from the high-profile environmentalists Bob Brown and Professor David Bellamy to well-known business people such as Claudio Alcorso. Their arrests coincided with UNESCO's announcement that it had listed Tasmania's South West Wilderness, including the Gordon and Franklin rivers, as World Heritage sites. The stakes were high. Messages of support for the blockaders flowed in. One of the most memorable came from novelist and environmental activist Xavier Herbert, author of *Poor Fellow My Country*, who wrote:

> The one hope of not only saving Terra Australis from
> eventual ruin but of the terrestrial globe itself, rests with
> you brave hearts now going into battle. My heart and soul
> go with you. They will die like the heart and soul of our
> country if you fail.

The commencement of the blockade and UNESCO's listing of south-west Tasmania as World Heritage was big news, and we talked about it in the staffroom at Devonport High School. A few of us had already decided that we would go to the blockade, including Neville and me. We were joined by longtime friend and neighbour Jon Paice; he had the full support of his partner, Pip Walker, who couldn't come as she was about to give birth to their second child. Another friend, fellow schoolteacher Helen Pryor, joined us.

We left Port Sorell at 5 am on 2 February 1983, having removed our anti-dam stickers from our old Peugeot 404, and travelled via Zeehan to Strahan, where the Wilderness Society Information Centre advised us that because of tensions in the town we should go straight to the blockade base campsite known as Greenie Acres. We drove into the site at ten in the morning, and the first thing we saw was a clean water station with strict instructions about handwashing and cleanliness; gastro was a major risk, because so many people had been thrown together with limited sanitation. We were immediately in a sea of tents of every size and colour, and we shared the mood of hope and anticipation.

There were rules governing the blockade. Training in non-violent direct action was essential before we were allowed to go upriver to the blockade site. Tensions were running high in Tasmania, with anti-dam protesters including Bob Brown being bashed and cars with anti-dam stickers being run off the road. It was critically important that everyone campaigning to stop the dam knew how to deal with threats and intimidating behaviour, as well as with the stress of being arrested and jailed. So we went to register for the blockade and start the training activities.

One of the first characters we met at Greenie Acres was Sydney artist Harold the Kangaroo Thornton, who described himself as 'The Greatest Genius the World Has Known'. He was sixty-seven at the time, one of those larger-than-life characters you immediately want to know better. When we told him we had been in Europe a few years before, he told us he had a studio in Amsterdam and had painted the facade of the city's first cannabis coffee shop, the Bulldog No 90, in 1975. We had never heard of him and knew nothing about the Bulldog coffee shop. Our 1978 Frommer's *Europe on $10 a Day* did not feature it as a 'must see', though it did make reference to 'Alternative Amsterdam', saying, 'For the group variously known as "hippies", "flower people", "freaks", Amsterdam offers special lodgings, special restaurants, special nightspots and markets – even special advice centres for when things go wrong.' Bulldog might well have been among them. After meeting Harold, I wished we had been more adventurous.

We attached ourselves to an affinity group for training. These were described in the *Franklin River Blockade Handbook* as:

> small groups of 6–10 people who know each other well
> and between whom there is a feeling of trust and mutual
> support. In addition group members will have a commonly
> understood commitment to look out for each other and to
> come to each other's assistance in times of need.

The first group we joined was very enthusiastic about games, as recommended in the handbook, to 'enable the blood to circulate and the brain to wake up' and to be used to end meetings because they left everyone feeling 'fresh and positive'. One game, Car Wash, was described as follows:

> Everyone stands in a circle facing the back of the person in front so that everyone is facing in the same direction. With the feet spaced wide apart, one or two people crawl through the tunnel created by everyone else's legs. They rub, scratch, and massage the backs of the 'cars' as they move through the tunnel. When the first two 'cars' have done a lap, two others follow, until everyone has had a turn.

I have always been a practical, organised, self-disciplined person, never overtly emotional or 'touchy-feely', and so I struggled with game playing, not to mention group hugs and affectionate gestures and the recitals and sharing of each person's satisfying daily accomplishments. On the second day we joined another group of people, from Sydney, who became our affinity group because they seemed much less enthusiastic about all this. It was a motley crew: we had a general nurse, a psychiatric nurse, an archaeology student, a clerk, a horticulturalist, a grandmother and four teachers.

Tasmanian Wilderness Society stalwart Cathie Plowman gave us a peacekeeping and tactics briefing, after which we retreated to Strahan's Regatta Point pub, where we heard the momentous news that Prime Minister Fraser had called an early double dissolution election for 5 March and that Bob Hawke had replaced Bill Hayden as Opposition leader. We returned to the campsite in time for a concert by bush band Captain Whiskers.

The next morning, 4 February, we boarded Reg Morrison's boat the *Jay-Lee-M* and headed upriver to the Butler Island base camp. The Gordon River was overwhelmingly beautiful; we felt the majesty and peace of bush and river, as well as nervous anticipation about what we intended to do. But we were also elated; with a federal election imminent and a popular new Labor leader, everything seemed possible.

As we neared the Butler Island base camp, captain Denny Hamill unveiled his plan. We were to go past the Butler Island camp and the Tasmania Police base camp at Sir John Falls, waving enthusiastically to the police before stopping around a bend of the river, where we would wait for half an hour or so. He urged us all to lie down in the boat so that when it returned to the Butler Island base camp apparently empty the police would rush out, assuming that we had all gone bush. Then we were to all jump up and clap. It all went perfectly; the police rushed to their boats and roared onto the river while we all cheered. We were thrilled; they were less than impressed.

The base camp upriver was very well organised, with a large meeting and communications area, excellent cooking facilities and a rudimentary shower and toilet system. It was a beautiful place in the forest, and we pitched our tents under some big trees. On our first night we attended a lengthy planning meeting and then got to know some of the other people already there. David Taylor took his flute in one of the rubber duckies out onto the river. The music, the gentleness of the river and the peacefulness of the wilderness were all glorious.

The next morning news reached us that the *Cape Martin* was towing a barge carrying huge earthmoving equipment up the river, and we were to immediately set up a rubber ducky blockade at Warners Landing and a support protest out on Butler Island. We tried to explain to our German, non-English-speaking affinity group member Emile what the options were, translating 'rubber ducky' (as in rubber inflatable boat) by pointing to gumboots and quacking and flapping furiously. We failed, but that is how our affinity group got its name of the Gumboot Donkeys.

Harold the Kangaroo Thornton and I went out to Butler Island to join the protest while others in our group tried to blockade the *Cape Martin* and its barge. I have never met anyone like Harold. He was nine years older than my parents but there he was, upriver and defiant. I was taken with his mix of individuality and showmanship, his pixie hat, painted enamelled teeth, glasses with handpainted naked women on the side and magic wand with 'Get Fucked' written all over it. I also liked that he didn't care about anyone's opinion of what he did or said.

As an artist he was a keen observer of the detail of the blockade, and he created a painting *Dr Brown and Green Old Time Waltz* that he submitted for the Archibald Prize in 1983. It was later acquired by the National Portrait Gallery. That painting is a great social history of the Franklin River campaign. He captured the experience of being on Butler Island that day when the *Cape Martin* forced its way past. He also captured Reg Morrison's *Denison Star* and Denny Hamill and the *Jay-Lee-M*, which transported so many blockaders up the river. He included the A3-57 RAAF planes doing a reconnaissance mission over the Franklin at the behest of the newly elected Hawke Labor government in April 1983, an episode that resulted in Attorney-General Gareth Evans thereafter being known as Biggles. He even painted recognisable faces of many key players in the tree canopy, and included a cameo of a police officer in uniform having a cup of tea, his hat lying on the ground with a 'No Dams' sticker inside it.

Our experience of the police upriver was a positive one, with a good deal of friendly engagement between the two groups. They had a job to do and so did we, with a mutual understanding that we were protesting not against them but against the government of the day. After the Butler Island protest we returned to the camp and enjoyed the rest of the day. We took a rubber ducky up to the police camp at Sir John Falls and at one stage a policeman called Graeme made life easier for Helen Pryor and me by throwing us a rope and giving us a tow. People went swimming and relaxed. However, increasing pressure was being put on the police to take a tougher stand against us. There had been some ugly incidents regarding protesters.

This was because a new police minister, appointed in late January, had given fresh instructions for the blockade to be undermined. Police actively collaborated with the Hydro-Electric Commission in bringing the first bulldozer to Strahan unimpeded. Telephone and telex wires to the Wilderness Society Information Centre were cut – to this day nobody knows who did that – and police accompanied the bulldozer and blocked protesters from crossing a bridge between the camp and the township. Upriver on one particular day the week before we arrived, more than sixty-five protesters were left in the police compound all day without shelter from the rain, resulting in twenty-one of them suffering from exposure.

Back at the base camp we all discussed the forthcoming federal election and the merits of building up or winding down the blockade during the campaign. Sitting in a remote bush camp in western Tasmania, we found it surreal that decisions being considered by a random group of people upriver had the power to influence the shape of an Australia-wide election campaign. But decisions needed to be made about the capacity of Greenie Acres and the Butler Island camp and its support crew to cope with the logistics of increased numbers and increasingly intense media focus.

While the overwhelming majority of blockaders were there to save the river, it was clear that some people had come because the Franklin blockade was the centre of the most exciting action for young people in the country. One bloke with a stunning mohawk haircut would insert himself into the background of every media event he possibly could. There would be Bob Brown looking so conservative in his suit and short back and sides haircut, and right behind him would be Mohawk Man. The numbers grew to such an extent that the Wilderness Society decided that to save the river, the blockade would be wound down and people would be encouraged to work in their own electorates for a change of government.

The *60 Minutes* crew with Ray Martin arrived to film the activity upriver and so we all gathered on the Butler Island base camp landing under the banner 'Think Globally Act Locally' and sang songs from the *Blockade Songbook* for the TV story. Ray Martin was a well-known media personality and so we all laughed when Harold mistook him for his colleague George Negus and called out, 'George, did you get enough media footage?'

After all the media left, six of us Gumboot Donkeys packed our packs and readied ourselves to row across from the Butler Island camp and help with the blockade of a bulldozer behind Warners Landing, where clearing for a road to the dam site was going on. We knew we would probably be arrested, but we had made that decision before coming upriver. We climbed up a very steep valley to Perched Lake, where we set up a rudimentary camp with tent flies above sleeping bags and settled in. I didn't sleep much, but in a letter from Risdon Prison to my friend and Devonport High School Senior Mistress of English Betty Paterson, I wrote that we 'spent a glorious night under the stars, deep in the rainforest ... We chatted, laughed, listened and really experienced what it is like to be a friend of the Earth.'

The following morning, after a breakfast of muesli bars, Jon Paice, Anne Myers and I walked down to Warners Landing to take a look at the bulldozer with a view to later disrupting work. Its driver, Donny Smith, was a dam supporter, believing that 'you have to develop these areas for progress'. His was the first dozer to plough through the Gordon River rainforest in order to build an access road to the dam site.[1] As we were hiding, crouched behind some fallen trees, another bulldozer driver approached us. Whether he had tipped off the police or not we will never know, but within minutes they arrived.

Constable Ian Radford, disguised as a greenie down to the headband, arrested Jon and Anne, and Constable Hyland in uniform arrested me. I don't know what I had imagined it would feel like to be arrested, but it was pretty straightforward and over in a minute, with a touch on the shoulder and a simple, 'You are under arrest.' Since the whole purpose of the blockade was to stop the dam by disrupting work, having as many arrests as possible, filling up the prisons and keeping pressure on the federal government with maximum publicity, we were on track and I was happy. It was a momentous thing for me to break the law, but I was absolutely convinced that in revoking the national park in favour of the Hydro-Electric Commission land and making trespass an arrestable offence the law was wrong, and so resistance was justified. I will always be grateful to Constable Radford, who carried my bag down to the landing; we were later picked up by a police boat and taken to the police camp.

We arrived at the arrestees' compound at about ten in the morning and spent a long day in the heat, waiting for others to be brought in. The police waited until the evening and then transported us all in a police boat back to Strahan, to the paddy wagons and on to court in Queenstown. I remember as we arrived in Strahan we were buoyed by the support of lots of people from Greenie Acres who had come down to the wharf to cheer us on, as we had done for others before they were taken upriver.

I don't remember much about the trip to Queenstown or the court appearance. The No Dams campaign was strongly supported by the legal profession. Dedicated conservationist and lawyer Lincoln Siliakus had organised a roster of legal professionals for the entire Franklin campaign to represent the blockaders as they were brought to court. Many of those young lawyers were my friends from university days, and I was grateful for their professional and personal support.

We were given the option of accepting bail to appear at a later date on condition that we not 'enter onto, remain on, trespass, lurk, loiter or secrete [ourselves] on any land subject to the control of the Hydro-Electric Commission and commonly known as The Gordon River Power Development Scheme Stage 2' or be remanded in custody. Neville had not come upriver with us, as he had sporting commitments, but he was there to meet us and to drive Jon Paice home to be with Pip, as their baby was due very soon. I decided to refuse bail and go to Risdon Women's Prison. It was a big decision and I was most concerned about what my parents would think. They had worked so hard to provide me with a good education and I had spent so much of my life making them proud. Having a daughter go to prison, I knew, would not impress them, regardless of the circumstances.

Eleven of us – including Gumboot Donkeys Pat Rose, Donna, Steven, John and I – were put in a minibus and left Queenstown at 11 pm bound for Risdon Prison. We had Jon's chocolate for sustenance, and when we changed buses I slept on the floor on Donna's sleeping bag. We arrived at Risdon at 3.30 am. We women were taken from the bus first and herded into a processing area, where we were made to empty our pockets. We were only allowed to keep toothpaste and a brush and comb. No toiletries or tampons were allowed, apparently to prevent women from harming themselves. No writing paper, biros or books were permitted. I was wearing a beanie so I stuffed tampons in the turned-up rim and a few sheets of paper in my shoes and walked away with them. We were allocated bedsheets and a blanket and taken to the cells. The cell door slammed and I was locked in. It was 5.10 am on 9 February.

Being locked in didn't bother me too much. Six years at a boarding school was good training for prison, as it happened. At St Mary's College at night the exterior doors were bolted and the windows facing onto the street or back courtyard were barred. This was all to keep us safe from anyone breaking in, but it certainly kept us from breaking out. As boarders we could not leave after school hours or during the weekend unless it was a designated day or weekend out and we were accompanied by an approved adult. We couldn't even cross the road to buy an ice-cream or a bread roll from the corner shop within metres of the school perimeter. We couldn't post or receive a letter without it being read first and had no access to a telephone except under supervision of a nun, and then only in an emergency.

I measured the cell in terms of the Besser bricks used in its construction; it was thirteen and a half Besser bricks high. It had an iron bed along one wall. In the corner was a sink with cold water and in the other a toilet, and between the two was a window three and three-quarter Besser bricks wide. Along the other wall were a wardrobe and a dressing table. There was a barred window approximately one foot by four feet (30 by 120 centimetres) above the bed, through which guards could look at any time. There was no privacy whatsoever.

At 7 am doors were unlocked. Breakfast was served half an hour later at four laminex tables in the dining area. There were only seven women in prison in Tasmania at the time; our arrival was a welcome distraction, as the women prisoners now had new people to talk to. We were sent for examination by a nurse and a doctor, weighed and given urine and blood-pressure tests. The doctor was very sympathetic. Then we went to the laundry to wash our clothes.

It was in the laundry that I first had an unsupervised talk with a young woman who had been allocated laundry tasks and couldn't wait for her stint there to be over. She had been sentenced to life imprisonment five years earlier, aged sixteen, for stabbing another girl in a women's shelter, and was hoping to be paroled the following April. She was an intelligent person who had begun to set down her thoughts in writing. As access to paper for blockaders was restricted to one letter sheet a day, which was collected at the end of it, I transcribed some of her writing onto the sheets of paper I had smuggled into the prison and brought them out with me.

Work in the prison was repetitive and focused on cleanliness. The floors were constantly swept and washed. Wages were fifty cents a day, rising to seventy-five cents after six months. All toiletries had to be purchased from the canteen with money earned, but half of the wages went into compulsory savings. Uniforms, walls and floors were all variations on blue, grey and white, and the silence was overwhelming. There were two exercise yards, each with a set of garden furniture. While sitting there, I noted that a brown and orange butterfly had landed on a blade of grass. After only a few hours I became conscious of the deprivation of sound and colour.

Whenever I hear the complaint that people in prison have it too easy, I try to explain that it is not what prisoners have that is the issue: the punishment is what they are deprived of. Losing your freedom, having even small decisions made for you, losing control over your own life, having everything censored and becoming separated from the sound and colour of everyday life, let alone the people and places with which you are familiar – that is real punishment.

In a letter Jon Paice wrote to me, he commented, 'The clutter of supermarkets is dispiriting after the peace and calm of the wilderness.' He went on to say that he had told the girls at playgroup in Ulverstone that I was in the 'can' and they had not believed it initially, but then were quite impressed. He concluded with, 'Good Stuff, fellow Gumboot Donkey.' I had one visitor during my stay in Risdon: Alison Grant, a good friend of mine from my university days.

Before I left the prison, I went to see the matron to ask what was permitted as presents for the prisoners, thinking I might buy a colourful pot plant for the young woman I met in the laundry. The matron looked at me with utter contempt and said, 'This is a prison, not a hospital.'

On 11 February I appeared in court with all the others arrested on the same day upriver. I made a speech on behalf of us all, but I have no idea now what I said exactly. In Risdon I had thought I might recite a few lines from Tennyson's poem 'Ulysses', which has always been a favourite – especially the lines 'to strive, to seek, to find, and not to yield' – and so I probably did. I certainly made it clear that we were ready to go back to jail, and when I was presented with the bail document I refused to sign it. The justice of the peace put a cross where my signature was meant to be and wrote, 'The document was read to the defendant who declined to sign same. A copy was then handed to her.' I was being forced to be free, whether I liked it or not.

I returned home to Ulverstone and resumed teaching at Devonport High School. My parents didn't say much; Mum came to Hobart with Neville to pick me up, but Dad never mentioned what had happened again, ever.

Within the first day or two I wrote to the young woman in prison and sent her some books. She replied, telling me that there were few blockaders left, and she had heard that the magistrates were not sending people there after the following Monday. She noted that the election was not far away and said, 'You can only hope – never expect – only hope (at least that is what I do).' In a later letter she told me her studies were going well but that she would never suggest to anyone that they study sociology in prison, saying, 'I do not like to be just another statistic in a file cabinet so I cannot subject these people to be the victims of my study.'

Devonport was the home of many Hydro workers, so I was not surprised when I went into my home classroom to begin a new year to find a notice on the back wall that read:

**Wanted: Protesters for the South West Blockade**
Applicants must be experienced in pot smoking, guitar or tin whistle playing, singing protest songs and must wear trendy clothes. Previous protest experience, although desired, is not necessary (we'll teach you).
    Social dropouts, defeated politicians, and homosexuals especially welcome.
    Dole Money guaranteed to continue.
    We need your help badly.

One day the principal Bob Doran called me to his office to say some parents had made a formal complaint that as I had been in prison I was not a fit and proper person to teach their children. All he said to me was that I should make sure the Franklin stayed out of the classroom. I am forever grateful that Bob Doran stood up for my right to be involved in the Franklin campaign and make the choices I did. Many protesters returned to the mainland as heroes: for those of us who lived in rural Tasmania, it was a different story.

On 11 May I received a letter from the Tasmanian Wilderness Society to say that the police prosecutions section had adjourned all cases of trespass indefinitely and that the police had signed an undertaking that my case would not be listed for hearing again. I had no guilty verdict and no police record. For me, the blockade was over. But not so the campaign to save the river. Bob Hawke won the 1983 federal election and passed the World Heritage Properties Conservation Act, which enabled the Commonwealth to prohibit dam building in the Tasmanian Wilderness World Heritage Area. The Tasmanian Government refused to halt dam construction and challenged the Commonwealth's power under the Constitution to stop the dam. On 1 July 1983 in a 4:3 split decision the High Court upheld the validity of the Commonwealth's use of its external affairs powers. It was a momentous day.

~

I CAME OUT OF RISDON PRISON a different person from the almost thirty-year-old woman who went in. I think I had been quite judgemental about people in prison. Apart from wanting justice to be done, I don't think I had thought about prison very deeply as either punishment or rehabilitation. I almost certainly believed that once people had served their time, they should just get on with their lives. But in prison I came face to face with women who had suffered poverty, sexual abuse, intergenerational disadvantage and lack of education. Reading about it is one thing; knowing it is another. I came to really understand that many people are born and brought up in circumstances from which it is difficult, if not almost impossible, to escape. I heard about mistakes repeatedly made and saw broken lives and spirits. It made me a better person, a better teacher and a far better member of parliament to have sat with people who taught me about the complexity of women's lives from a perspective I had not until then really understood. People who help you to know what you don't are giving you a gift, and I am grateful.

And as far as being an environmental activist was concerned, going to Risdon Prison was empowering. As I've said, thereafter I knew I could do anything, because I could survive the worst that governments could do to me for taking a stand. I wrote at the time in a letter from prison:

> My decision to become so actively involved in this
> campaign is one of the best things I've ever done. I've met
> some fantastic people and I feel as if I'm doing something
> to save the river. Being up there in the wilderness was
> good for the soul and I'm now even more convinced of
> the necessity to save it.

For me, the Franklin River campaign was, as Ian Paulin's blockade song of the same name predicted, 'The face of things to come'. In 2013, on the thirtieth anniversary of my arrest on the blockade, my office staff in Canberra decided to commemorate the occasion by making a poster of the photograph of my arrest upriver. It was displayed in the front window of my office in Parliament House. Along the top I wrote:

> Thirty years ago, I was arrested during the peaceful
> campaign to save the Franklin. The bulldozers had
> already started into the forest. We didn't give up and we
> won. Today the fights to safeguard our environment and
> climate are not over. Together we can be the difference.
> And we will win.

# 4

# Wesley Vale: First Steps in Activism

OBJECT: *Brown briefcase, stickered.*
*Used by Christine since the mid-1970s.*
*It is now part of the Tasmanian Museum and*
*Art Gallery Collection.*

IN 1987 MY BROWN BRIEFCASE, battered from many years of teaching, emblazoned with a 'No Mill at Wesley Vale' sticker, became my constant companion. Always on the back seat of the car, it accompanied me everywhere locally, and to Canberra and back. It carried our hopes and aspirations, and was crammed with the sum total of our research and arguments. It was never out of my sight. Now an oddity, replaced by the laptop and satchel of the hipster, the briefcase – mine and everyone else's – has largely disappeared. But when I look at mine, I think of the airline overhead locker, walking the corridors of power, handing over documents and standing at the photocopier, and I see the safekeeping of facts, figures, photographs and scraps of paper covered in scribble. That briefcase became an important part of my sense of being a woman driving change. It was also the necessary accessory of the professional – essential if you wanted to be taken seriously by the men who also carried briefcases. Over time it has become a physical legacy and a prompter of memory.

Of all the campaigns I have been involved in, saving northern Tasmania's Wesley Vale district from its proposed pulp mill in the late 1980s was the most personal. I went from being a supporter of environmental activism to being a leader and driver of a campaign. Before the Wesley Vale campaign I was a well-respected local mother and teacher. Afterwards I was an independent member of the Tasmanian Parliament, either fair game for every abuse hurled from a passing car or held up as Boadicea of the Bush. Before, politics was something I encountered through campaigns and mostly at arm's length; afterwards politics framed my day-to-day existence and my challenge was to fundamentally change it.

The older generation who lived along the ridgelines and coastal flats of Wesley Vale and populated my childhood have mostly gone. Farms have been passed to the next generation or reluctantly sold, crops have changed and there are even wind turbines powering a poultry farm and a flower farm. Port Sorell, Shearwater and Squeaking Point have boomed, with the predictable and short-sighted loss of native coastal vegetation. But the coastal beaches are as wild as ever. Bass Strait is cleaner now than before, and Tasmania's Clean Green Future envisioned in 1989 has come to pass.

I sometimes look at people enjoying their holidays, building their homes there or establishing their vineyards or ploughing their paddocks and wonder whether they ever stop to think that without a small group of committed people their experience of clean air, a clean marine environment and magnificent rural vistas would not have been possible. The great campaigns to save iconic places of natural and Indigenous cultural heritage – to save the Franklin or the Daintree, or to stop drilling on the Great Barrier Reef or uranium mining in Kakadu – have rightly taken their place in Australia's modern history, but campaigns to save farmlands, rivers and oceans from pollution hardly warrant a mention.

Wesley Vale was the first national environmental campaign to go beyond wilderness protection 'out there' and to address pollution 'at home', by telling the story of ordinary people fighting for their precious place, their clean air, clean water and uncontaminated soils, and their right to be heard. But it was something more. The Wesley Vale campaign was started to save a community from the environmental impacts of a pulp mill (which converts native forests to woodchips and into pulp for making paper), but it rapidly morphed into a campaign to restore democracy and give the people a voice. That was its power.

In 1987 the mining and resources company North Broken Hill announced on the front page of *The Advocate* that it intended to build a billion-dollar kraft chlorine pulp mill at Wesley Vale, using Tasmanian native forests as feedstock. I was horrified and immediately rang Geoff Law, the Tasmanian campaigner for the Australian Conservation Foundation, and asked him what the foundation was going to do about it. I will never forget that conversation. Instead of the empathy and promises of help that I thought would be forthcoming, he bluntly explained that the Australian Conservation Foundation was up to its neck in the Helsham Inquiry established earlier that year into the Lemonthyme and Southern forests and had no capacity to do more. He then asked what I was going to do about Wesley Vale. It was a clear challenge to take personal responsibility. If I didn't want the pulp mill, I had to do something about it. My course was set. If I didn't start doing something, who would?

I had the experience of the Franklin campaign behind me, and as a teacher I had the organisational skills to do something. But what gave me the confidence to take on this fight was my experience in campaigning to save the about-to-be-demolished Waldheim huts in the Cradle Mountain National Park the year before.

I had begun making an annual trip to Cradle Mountain when I was at university, and always stayed in the huts, where I had learned to love wilderness. I was captivated by the vision of Gustav Weindorfer, who had campaigned for the area to become 'a national park for the people for all time'. I wanted people like me, who had not been brought up camping and bushwalking, to learn to love wilderness too. The huts had a long history; it was not as if any new incursion into the wilderness was being proposed. I started to organise, write letters to the paper and put out press releases, and I did my first ever TV interviews on saving the huts. Graham Richardson, the federal Labor minister for the environment, came down to examine the situation. It was at Cradle Mountain that we first met and worked together. He was persuaded to save the huts and stop the pollution by building new shower and toilet blocks. After that I knew I could lead a campaign.

Everyone in the Wesley Vale district had lived with the small 1960s pulp mill on the ridge overlooking Bass Strait, but there was a great deal of nervousness about what a huge new one would bring. People remembered the 'no pollution' promises made and broken when the mill was originally built. The farmers in the district were already suspicious of what spewed out of the chimneys and loathed the dark stain in the sea visible from the beach or from the air. The pipe dumping the effluent only extended to the low tide line, and dead fish were often washed up along the shore. Moore's Point under the water was occasionally coated by the kaolin clay used to coat paper. Batches deemed not up to scratch were sometimes dumped. In heavy seas at Burnie, just along the coast, huge banks of brown froth rolled into the shallows, and the stench from the chimneys was nauseating.

I met with New Zealander Mike Carr, a newcomer to the district who had the lease on the Wesley Vale service station, and local farmer Snow Thomas. We decided to hold a meeting of residents in the hall of the local primary school. The meeting was advertised by word of mouth, and we had a full hall. We knew that several sites for the new mill were under discussion, from Bell Bay to Dulverton, and the community decided to elect a committee to represent it in the anti-mill campaign. In those early days people did not necessarily believe that a pulp mill was a bad thing, but they were convinced that it should not be in their district, destroying first-class agricultural land or polluting Bass Strait.

We formed a committee consisting of farmers with a long family history in the district: Snow Thomas, Tony Loane, Alan Wilson, Shirley Saville, Leanne Hall, Patsy Hoare, the local vet Gilbert Walker, and teachers Di Hollister, Peter Conroy and me. At our inaugural meeting at the home of Patsy and John Hoare we decided to call ourselves Concerned Residents Opposing Pulp Mill Siting (CROPS), and I became the spokesperson. We quickly fell into a routine of regular meetings at the Hoare home, with briefings and updates delivered by word of mouth to and from the Carrs' service station. Our strengths were our local knowledge and our legitimacy as locals, chosen and supported by and speaking for the district. Our voice was authentic. No amount of propaganda could undermine that.

As one of our first moves we decided to hold a public meeting at Port Sorell, as the prevailing winds and sea current would take the stench and effluent into and across the Rubicon Estuary. Snow Thomas presented me with a corsage from his garden before we went up on stage – such a kind, supportive, if old-fashioned gesture. Di Hollister delivered an outstanding performance: not just a great speech but a complete capture of the audience. We were thankful for having a science graduate on our team as Peter Conroy patiently and clearly explained the pulping and bleaching sequences and pollution involved in kraft pulping and elemental chlorine bleaching. The meeting was reported in the local press, and I was interviewed on ABC radio. We were under way.

The campaign was intense. For my family and me, it was a twenty-four-hours-a-day, seven-days-a-week commitment. I had two small children at the time, with Thomas three years old and James just sixteen months. My husband Neville was teaching and we lived at Ulverstone, a twenty-minute drive from Wesley Vale. As I had resigned from the Education Department when my accouchement leave ran out, we were on a single income. We had a second-hand blue Datsun station wagon and our technology consisted of a wall-mounted telephone.

Before the days of home computers or mobile phones, communication meant pen and paper at the kitchen table. Fax machines had just come into vogue; the post office at Ulverstone had one, as did the local solicitor's office, so any extremely important document could be sent quickly, but the cost was high. Mostly I had to rely on the post. The public library in Devonport had a photocopier, and before documents could be sent on to others, critical pages needed to be copied for future reference. It is hard to imagine campaigning with so few tools now, given the ease of email and internet links in conveying reference material. Whenever something had to be moved quickly, we relied on the Redline bus that travelled daily between Hobart and the north-west coast. I would have large documents such as the Environmental Impact Assessment sent to me by post. I would then read and highlight them and put them on the bus to Hobart for Bob Brown to pick up and use in the parliament.

On one occasion I went to Hobart to meet with Graham Richardson in a last-ditch effort to persuade him to reject the mill. He and I were already talking regularly about this, and so I met him for a private meeting unbeknown to the media. Then we held the publicly announced lobbying meeting, followed by a press conference at which a male journalist asked me, 'What makes you think you can deal with Senator Richardson?' I felt I had been slapped in the face. His tone made it a full-on sexist insult and putdown, making it clear he thought a woman, mother and housewife from Ulverstone was no match for Senator Richardson. It was a revelation about what a rural, female teacher was up against in the male chauvinist world of politics, business and media. That man's bias cost him a scoop. But apart from the sexist overtone, what he said was also a comment about the disassociation of politics from ordinary people.

In those pre-Google days we had no way of finding out quickly whether the claims made by North Broken Hill or Noranda about their proposed technology and the performance of their pulp mills in Canada or Scandinavia were true or not, but we started with a high degree of scepticism. We knew from the experience of the Burnie mill that any pulp mill stank and polluted the sea. We knew also from the Greenpeace International campaign against pulp mills that the effluent dumped into lakes or the marine environment was highly toxic.

We needed information from everywhere, and we looked for it. The collaboration among a range of groups all speaking from their area of expertise was one of the great strengths of the campaign. This was not an alliance; it was a coordinated campaign. Perhaps it could be described as like a child's game of Twister: just when the government or company thought they had one objection under control, apparently out of left field another issue of concern to another group would pop up. My job was to keep across every development, inform everyone else and maximise the effectiveness of each objection by making CROPS the echo chamber for them all.

Scientists at the University of Tasmania formed United Scientists for Environmental Responsibility and Protection (USERP), and they became an important force for critiquing the companies' documents. Even though university academics were afraid that speaking out would jeopardise their careers and their research funding by corporations, they formed an organisation with a courageous and highly effective spokesperson in Gustaaf Hallegraeff. We were also fortunate to have input on the sulphur-based pulping process from Charles Turner, who had been an industrial chemist at Associated Pulp and Paper Mills in Burnie and who had developed a superior method of pulping that did not smell. Interestingly, the North Broken Hill executives did not question his expertise but dismissed the idea because the market knew and accepted their kraft pulp, no alternatives.

Dr Juliet Lavers, a GP from Burnie, attended our rally in Launceston and immediately established the Environmental

Health Alliance to raise awareness of the health issues associated with organochlorines and dioxins. Greenpeace International's Australian campaigner Robert Cartmel quickly brought us up to speed on campaigns against pulp mills around the world. Dr Gerry Bates, independent member for Franklin in the Tasmanian Parliament, was an environmental lawyer. He accessed the expertise of University of Oregon environmental law academics John Bonine and Michael Axline, and Mary O'Brian from Oregon's Northwest Environmental Defense Center. These academics visited Australia and made influential media appearances, confirming the dangers of the pollution from pulp mills and the legal issues surrounding their regulatory oversight.

The Tasmanian Abalone Divers' Association, led by Dean Lisson, spoke out about the impact on the fishery in Bass Strait. Local campaigner Annie Willock raised issues concerning dioxins. The Tasmanian Farmers' and Graziers' Association, with Ferdie Foster and George Rance at the helm, took up the concerns about the proposed railway spur to the mill that would bisect many properties. The Tasmanian Wilderness Society and the Australian Conservation Foundation took on the feedstock issue as part of their campaigns to save Tasmania's native forests, and in the context of the Helsham Inquiry.

In the Tasmanian Parliament Dr Bob Brown was a stalwart from the start; Dr Gerry Bates was also soon on board as the flagrant abuse of environmental law became more evident. It was brilliant having them both ready to follow up and pursue ministers on pulp mill and forest matters. Without Bob and Gerry's presence, the Tasmanian Parliament would have unanimously supported the pulp mill without any criticism or scrutiny. That's why it is essential to have Greens in parliaments, asking the questions that all other parties would prefer were buried.

We decided to organise a tractor demonstration from Wesley Vale into Devonport. We had read about French farmers taking their tractors to town in protest and decided to do the same, with a rally to be held on the Devonport High School netball courts once the tractors had arrived. The excitement on the morning of the rally was palpable. We had homemade signs of every kind. Our little son James held a sign 'No Smell on Pa's Farm'. Farmers who had never protested about anything in their lives were taking to the road in a long procession. It was the first ever farmers' rally in Australia. Eighty-seven-year-old Clive Loane drove himself in his ute. Peter Cundall, by then a national gardening guru, described the mill as a giant vacuum cleaner ready to suck up Tasmania's forests and spew out the filth into the sea.

Bob Brown also spoke. It was my first meeting with Bob in person, although I had previously spoken to him by phone. Some of the farmers were uncomfortable about Bob's sexuality and his high-profile anti-logging stand and would have preferred Gerry Bates to be there, but once they had met Bob and heard him speak – including referring to the interjectors as 'poddy calves' – they changed their minds. Joker Piper, a local farmer, summed up their attitude: 'Before Wesley Vale, if Bob Brown was up a tree, I would have cut it down. Now I would take him his lunch.'

The companies began the hard sell of the pulp mill full of confidence.[1] With Robin Gray as Liberal premier of Tasmania and a pro-development Labor Party in Hobart and Canberra, they thought that in a state desperate for jobs it didn't matter what the community thought. They had encouragement and tacit planning and development approval at every level and considered final approval to be a formality. They knew that, regardless of what we said, those in power wanted the mill to proceed and would blindly back them. At a pro-pulp mill rally at Ulverstone the local mayor Terry Stuart, backed by legislative councillor Reg Hope, rallied the crowd in support of North Broken Hill by making the ridiculous declaration: 'More dioxin, not less'. Dioxin was already known as a carcinogen. Thereafter he was known in anti-pulp mill circles as Toxic Terry.

Once CROPS was formed, we called on Premier Robin Gray and the leader of the Labor Opposition Michael Field to meet us in Wesley Vale. Michael Field came and we met in an old farm shed, on the side of which was stamped an advertisement from before the First World War: 'Preservene Soap: No Toil, Only Boil'. The locals were mostly Liberal Country Party farmers, so Field didn't feel the need to offer any concessions. He was an unquestioning supporter of logging and a pulp mill at Wesley Vale and made it clear he thought the farmers were Not in My Back Yarders, NIMBYs.

Robin Gray refused to come, which incensed the locals. Most of them had voted Liberal all their lives and felt that in their hour of need the least he could do was listen. So we set off to Hobart to try to force a meeting with him, and to convince the state ministers about our case. Most of the farmers on the delegation had never been to the parliament, and so we were all dressed up and on our best behaviour for the occasion.

We were waiting to see John Bennett, the minister for the environment, when suddenly his office door flew open, there was shouting and a cloud of feathers filled the air. Another campaigner, having clearly failed to convince the minister to suspend the duck-shooting season, had opened his briefcase jam-packed with feathers and hurled them all over Bennett and his office. This was our introduction to the Tasmanian Parliament.

At the local government level the Latrobe Council was responsible for planning approval. The council showed its hand by inviting North Broken Hill to do the Tasmania-wide launch of its pulp mill proposal at their council chambers. It was a big occasion in Latrobe. CROPS was out in force with protest placards, and many supporters wore gas masks. There were more TV cameras than usual, with statewide media and some mainland journalists in attendance. North Broken Hill's audiovisual presentation was set up, the room was full and the cameras rolled. Without drawing attention to himself, someone seated in the media area got up and left. Shortly afterwards the most vile stench permeated the room. It was ignored at first and then became overwhelming, and the whole event broke up in chaos as journalists, camera crew, sound men, North Broken Hill executives and Latrobe municipal councillors fled the room gagging.

One of our enterprising supporters had made himself a media badge, dressed himself in a manner he thought represented journalists and had taken an old battered briefcase full of rotten duck eggs into the room. As the North Broken Hill presentation started, he stood on his briefcase and walked out, leaving it under the seat. The rotten eggs did their job. Every journalist was given an unforgettable reminder of what hydrogen sulphide smells like, and why no one wanted to live in the prevailing wind blowing from a kraft sulphur-based pulp mill.

Given the council's cronyism, it was hardly surprising that months later, when the final decision on development approval came before council, a quorum could not be had. Seven of the nine councillors had a conflict-of-interest problem, some because their businesses had supported the mill directly, others because they had invested in accommodation for the construction workforce. The final approval decision was then referred to the state local government minister Ian Braid, who exempted the council from the conflict-of-interest provisions and therefore giving it the big tick unamended. This preparedness to excuse blatant conflicts of interest at local government level shocked me at the time, but sadly it has become all too common. The Devonport council was also pro-mill, considering it a great driver of local economic activity. Most of the existing mill workers lived there and expected to get jobs at the new mill.

A public meeting was called to allow North Broken Hill and CROPS to present our cases to the community. The district was divided between urban pro-mill Devonport ratepayers and rural anti-mill Latrobe ratepayers. Tensions were high. In the days before the meeting the mayor of Devonport Geoff Squibb made a monumental error of judgement. He announced that residents of Devonport would be admitted to the hall first, and if any room was available

Latrobe residents could then come in. The millworkers' and farmers' anger threatened to boil over; the police were called to keep the peace and to search everyone as they entered the hall. Whether the police talked sense to Squibb or other council members I don't know, but the directive about attendees was dropped. The searches were not.

Not for the first time I was afraid for my personal safety. There had been tailgating and attempts to run me off the road as I drove home to Ulverstone alone after our regular Wesley Vale meetings. There had been threats over the phone to burn my house down. But being at a meeting was shockingly different. In the same hall where as a small child I had recited poetry in the local eisteddfod I was about to front an angry and potentially violent pro-mill crowd made up of people I knew, who had to be searched for weapons before they came in. As the CROPS supporters were lining up to secure seats, I anxiously waited in the car park for Gerry Bates, who was driving up from Hobart, to join me. We had never met; he was running late, and he shocked me and the several latecomers seeking a parking spot by changing from his jeans and T-shirt into a suit in the middle of the car park while he asked me to brief him on the latest developments. Somehow that broke the tension. It normalised things and made taking the stage less dramatic and intimidating.

The meeting started. North Broken Hill had a sophisticated audiovisual presentation, which no doubt had cost a fortune to make. It had just begun when the projector hissed and died. The company had no backup, and after the usual fiddling around it had to make do by trying to ad-lib and explain invisible graphs and charts to an audience who couldn't make sense of any of that and who rapidly became bored.

We had come without audiovisuals, prepared to argue our case, and we did. The meeting went to questions and answers. North Broken Hill had lined up David Foster, world champion axeman and former janitor at the old mill, to question me. When North Broken Hill later needed a public relations campaign, they promoted him to be a front man. Over time he became an effective advocate for them, promoting logging and the pulp mill and reassuring working people they would get jobs, but he had just started and that night he did not do himself any credit. The company didn't win a trick. As a result I resolved never to rely on audiovisual aids, and I have never done so since. Technology for presentations can never be guaranteed not to fail.

The meeting was heartening, but we had no political support at local or state level apart from independents Bob Brown and Gerry Bates. We needed to sound out the federal politicians, as federal approval was required for the environmental standards to which the mill had to conform. Graham Richardson was still the minister for the environment, so I went to Canberra and invited him to visit Wesley Vale. He agreed. The national media was surprised that he decided to come, but they were largely unaware that I had met him before and we had taken each other's measure.

We organised a big crowd to greet the minister at Devonport's Pardoe airport, which is in direct line of sight of the existing small mill and less than one kilometre from it. Richardson took one look at the crowd of protesters and was immediately open to the idea of stopping the mill. It was not the billowing black smoke pouring out of the pulp mill chimney that won him over: he saw wall-to-wall Liberal voters and recognised an opportunity for the 1990 federal election. To this day I don't know who was responsible for the colour or the timing of that black smoke, but it certainly helped our cause.

Richardson began to leave the airport in a Comcar with Michael Field to tour the district, but before the car had cleared the crowd one of our supporters, Gaynor Ralph, threw herself onto the bonnet. This was a shock all round, and to nobody more than to the minister. She was not injured but Richardson got the message.

Nobody thought that Field showing Richardson around was a great idea. The farmers hatched a plan to get Richardson out of the Comcar and into one of their utes as soon as possible. Now they 'cannot recall' exactly what happened, but Richardson did end up in the back of a farm ute up on a hill overlooking the whole district. The farmers say he had a great time and enjoyed the scones they provided, and from that moment on they put their faith in him.

Graham Richardson and I worked well together. He kept me informed of the latest thinking in Canberra and told me what evidence he needed to make the case for higher environmental standards. In return I told him what was happening on the ground in Tasmania. But other federal ministers remained hostile. With Patrick Johnson, who was working as a field officer for agricultural company Perfecta, I met with John Button to try to convince him of the danger of pollution to surrounding crops. Later Button in a disparaging speech described Patrick as displaying 'Jesuit-like zeal'.

By that time North Broken Hill was effectively running the Tasmanian Government and making fools of its ministers. In an incredible and unprecedented act of hubris the company, who had moved into the Sheraton hotel near the parliament, announced the recall of the Tasmanian Parliament on their own letterhead after a weekend of pursuing the premier around the state in their light aircraft to secure his agreement. Minister for the Environment Peter Hodgman introduced North Broken Hill-drafted 'doubts removal' legislation to lower the company's standards and level of accountability, arguing that these changes made them stronger. The Tasmanian Government had turned the approvals process into a farce.

Tasmanians were sick of political parties being the pawns of big business and sick of the Hydro-Electric Commission and the Forestry Commission deciding what was in the best interests of the state in behind-the-scenes meetings. The community wanted a say in its own future.

As the campaign against the mill gathered momentum and spilled over to the mainland, the only convincing argument North Broken Hill had to support their project was the promise of jobs. Braddon had high levels of unemployment and poor levels of education. Pollution was regarded as the price to pay for jobs. But the jobs in the mines and factories and on the farms had long evaporated, and the economy was in decline. If the promise of jobs was discredited, North Broken Hill knew it was in real trouble garnering community support.

Research helped our cause. I discovered that the prototype for the mill, at Äänekoski in Finland, provided only a few hundred jobs, mostly highly skilled and in the computer centre that ran the mill. The only unskilled jobs were in the wood yard, sorting the timber on arrival. This completely contradicted North Broken Hill's boast of providing full-time work for the unemployed on the north-west coast of Tasmania. Accommodation for single men was to be built in Latrobe – a further admission that most of the work would be in construction and most of those jobs would be taken by people from elsewhere, including a team of pipe-fitters from Korea.

North Broken Hill tried to shore up its jobs argument by opening an employment office in Devonport and encouraging the unemployed to register for work in the mill. It was run by Chris Oldfield, known as 'the Rhinestone Cowboy' by the farmers. The office was another disaster for North Broken Hill, as many who came to register lacked the numeracy or literacy skills to work on a construction site. Keeping the office open and rejecting the unemployed would have eroded support even further, so the employment office closed not too long after it opened.

The media interest in the pulp mill debate intensified. In Tasmania at the time we had relatively concentrated media, with three daily newspapers, three TV channels and about six radio stations. No one anywhere who listened to, read or watched the news could escape hearing about the mill. All three Tasmanian newspapers wrote editorials in favour of it. But we also had statewide ABC radio talkback every day with Sue Becker and an ABC *7.30 Report* based in Tasmania. Both were critically important in airing detailed stories, interviews and comment on the debate, giving scope for exploring the claims and counterclaims of the mill advocates and opponents.

Activist Margaret Wilkinson from Devonport was a regular morning contributor.

Losing the *7.30 Report* from its state bases has been a major blow to community awareness, engagement and transparency of decision-making around the country, particularly for those fighting local environmental battles. The loss has been a boost to those in whose interest it is to keep people in the dark, with scrutiny confined to the sixty-second grab. When you consider what the New South Wales Independent Commission Against Corruption has revealed regarding mining leases, you wonder what a difference might have been made had the local *7.30 Report* been able to report regularly and in detail on what the community knew, as it did throughout the Wesley Vale campaign.

But Tasmania was not where the pulp mill battle would be won or lost. Taking the campaign to the mainland meant more media appearances for national exposure and even more time on the road, showing journalists the area and explaining the issues over and over again. *The Australian* newspaper photo of me standing in front of a windblown tree on the Loanes' property framed the narrative of me as the bête noire of North Broken Hill, the Boadicea of the Bush, giving the false impression that I was a lone heroine in the David and Goliath struggle. But as with every successful campaign, that was as much a media construct as it was the truth. I was certainly out front campaigning full-time, but the team behind me made it possible.

I was not a superwoman. I did not have a predetermined campaign strategic plan or a public relations team or a budget; we worked together and week to week. As a committee we were elected by our community and shared a passion for our cause. Determined to protect our home, we shared everything from information to risk, and no decision was taken without consultation. We made decisions on the run, and part of our strength was our flexibility.

I was enabled to do what I did simply because of the people who washed, cleaned, cooked, babysat, listened and cared. People helped with research and took risks to provide information – such as the luggage handler who let us know whenever any person of interest flew into Devonport. One of the farmers paid to have the clutch in my car replaced; friends lent me clothes suitable for TV; and farmers and their wives gave me meals for the freezer. Mum and Dad and my sister, Gaylene, and her husband, Tony, and my husband's parents, Betty and Rupert, were willing babysitters for the boys, as were my neighbours and friends Jon Paice and Pip Walker. Like them, my husband never wavered in his support for the work I was doing. We were a community determined to do what had to be done. By pitching in, people became activists, empowered and identifying with the cause, taking ownership and pride in our achievement. It was a campaign of volunteers, incredible generosity and trust.

Fundraising brought some wonderful times. People enjoyed themselves socialising in a way they hadn't done for years. We had barbecues at Hop Ground, a historic property at Northdown, spit roasts at the Port Sorell recreation ground and even a New Year's Eve party in 1988 among the hay bales on a farmer's property. On that occasion the Wilderness Society had organised the Great Tasmanian Forest Walk, and so CROPS decided to host the participants for New Year's Eve. We hired a band to play on the back of a truck under a gum tree, and that is when I first met Kim Booth, one of the band members, who later became a state Green MP. Huge barbecues were set up as a tent city grew. The community turned on vast quantities of food and drink. (Meat was plentiful, while the vegieburgers for the visitors were given a wide berth.) It was a huge success. For the first time many farmers met the dreadlocked greenies they had regarded as ratbags, and the forest campaigners had a chance to meet the strange breed of conservatives who were on their side.

When the government moved to fast-track the mill approvals, we held a huge rally in Hobart, with 11,000 people marching to 'Save our State', meaning the state of our democracy and that of the environment. But still both the Tasmanian and federal governments were officially in favour of the mill. It had passed its Tasmanian approvals and by early 1989 the company had begun bulldozing the site. We were in despair, and I asked Bob Brown how he had kept going during the Franklin campaign when he had to face opposition from federal, state and local governments and the dam construction works had begun. I expected some deep philosophical answer and was surprised when he said, 'Keep on campaigning: something will fall out of the sky.' For want of anything better I adopted the same philosophy. Shortly afterwards thousands of dead fish were strewn along the coast as a result of effluent being discharged from the existing Wesley Vale mill. The campaign took off again.

Before the final federal Cabinet meeting about the mill, Graham Richardson took the unusual step of secretly sending one of his staff from Canberra to my home in Ulverstone to discuss every aspect of the project with me and copy all my material. The Cabinet submission was the final throw of the dice. Interestingly it was John Kerin, minister for primary industry, who led the opposition to the mill in that Cabinet meeting; Richardson followed suit. Cabinet decided to continue to support the mill but to require North Broken Hill and Noranda to meet higher standards, to be determined by the federal Environment Department.

And then, on 15 March 1989, I had a quick phone call from Graham Richardson at 10.55 am. 'Listen to the eleven o'clock news,' he said, and rang off. I turned on the radio and heard Noranda announcing that it was pulling the plug on the project. The joint venture collapsed. The mill was dead.

In Australia there was shock all around. State and federal politicians all still proclaimed their support for the project and ran around in circles organising emergency meetings to try to get it back on track. They did not know – though we and Richardson did – that Greenpeace International had applied intense pressure to Noranda in Canada. The Toronto *Globe and Mail* had sent a reporter to Tasmania to photograph the Wesley Vale district, and CROPS people had been interviewed on Canadian talkback radio, so people in Canada knew what Noranda was about to do in Tasmania: destroy a farming community and drive the logging of high-conservation forests. They also knew that Noranda had promised to meet higher standards in Australia than those met by its own mills in Canada. Greenpeace was arguing that whatever standards they were prepared to meet in Australia must be the new benchmark in Canada. Their assertion carried weight, as a major spill from a Noranda mill had seen the closure of a prawn fishery just weeks before. For Noranda the cost of upgrading their mills to the same standard as a new greenfields site in Tasmania would have been astronomical, and the announcement of even higher standards was the last straw. The risk to them had become too great.

CROPS members were jubilant, relieved, exhausted, grateful and suspicious all at the same time. We immediately made our way to the home of Snow and Shirley Thomas to celebrate and were roundly condemned in the local press for rejoicing in what the local chamber of commerce regarded as a tragedy for the towns of Latrobe and Devonport. A public meeting was held in Devonport and the full extent of North Broken Hill's cynical exploitation of the community's need for work was on display. One man said that, because of Christine Milne, his profoundly disabled son would not have the job promised to him had the mill been built.

Within weeks Premier Robin Gray called a snap state election, asking for a mandate to get the pulp mill back on track. I knew I had to stand for parliament. With state Liberal and Labor still supporting the mill, our only hope of keeping it off the agenda for good was to have our own people elected. I decided to stand in the electorate of Lyons, as that was Premier Gray's seat and included Wesley Vale. Bob Brown put together a team of independents: Di Hollister and me from CROPS; Lance Armstrong, a Uniting Church minister and peace activist from Launceston; Gerry Bates from Franklin and himself. The campaign began again in earnest.

The farmers might have been unfamiliar with the ins and outs of political campaigns, but they were pretty handy with a hammer and nails. Soon my election posters were up from one end of Lyons to the other, making an impressive statement about the level of support for CROPS, and demoralising the Liberal Party and Premier Robin Gray.

But we didn't have it all our own way. Supporters of the mill got busy too, and soon the Wesley Vale district was covered in signs and posters. Every night many were vandalised; every morning the farmers replaced them. They soon tired of this and decided on a plan. One decided to hot-wire the poster on his land; it gave him great amusement to watch as the vandals jumped the fence and retreated just as quickly. Others decided to lie in wait in the paddocks for the vandals and have a few stubbies at the same time. We laughed uproariously when we found out they had gone to sleep and didn't wake until the next morning, only to find the signs vandalised again.

On 13 May 1989 I was elected as an independent to the Tasmanian House of Assembly with the highest ever below the line personal vote in the history of the parliament. As I've said, all five independents were elected. The Liberal government of Robin Gray lost its majority. In the Labor–Green Accord signed on 29 May, 'No new pulp mill at Wesley Vale' was specifically listed as a condition of government.

Since then I have often recalled Bob Brown's words, and they have come true time and time again. Just when loss seems inevitable, something unexpected happens to breathe new life into a campaign. I am now an ardent believer in things dropping out of the sky, and I endorse Peter Cundall's words: Never, ever give up.

For me, now holding the balance of power in Tasmania, the battle to transform politics and society had only just begun. I had received a boost of confidence by being named as one of Australia's Leading Women '88 – the bicentennial year – and as a prize I chose a new briefcase made by Adelaide artist Pauline Griffin. You won't be surprised to learn that I turned up to the parliament with that brand-new briefcase, and as I carried it into that bastion of male dominance it was a tangible reminder not to be co-opted and assimilated, but rather to fill it with the campaigning tools to advance the values that had led me there.

# The Case of Port Arthur: Gun Law Reform

OBJECT: *The shotgun belonging to Christine's father,*
*Tom Morris. It remains in the family.*

WHEN I WAS TEN YEARS old, I came inside one Saturday morning
to find Mum crying in the kitchen. Mum was not a particularly
emotional person so I knew that something terrible had happened.
When I asked her what was wrong, she said, 'Mr Kennedy has been
shot.' I was puzzled; the only Mr Kennedy I knew was the man
who came to spray our crops, and I couldn't imagine why anyone
would want to shoot him. But of course she meant President John
F. Kennedy, assassinated in Dallas on 22 November 1963. No doubt
we watched the whole story – the cavalcade in Dallas, the shot – on
the evening news the following day. But what lives in my memory
about the defining news of that decade was the banging of the
flyscreen door as I came into the kitchen and the sight of my mother
crying and listening to the wireless that sat on top of the fridge.

On 28 April 1996 I was having Sunday lunch with my parents
at the farm. We were just enjoying our cup of tea with the TV on
in the background so Dad could watch the football. Then across the
bottom of the screen came a breaking story. There had been a shooting
at Port Arthur and people were dead. I turned to my mother and

asked, 'Where in the world is there another Port Arthur?' because it seemed impossible that it could be our town in Tasmania. But within minutes Premier Tony Rundle rang to say that yes, this had happened in our Port Arthur and I should return to Hobart immediately as all political leaders needed to meet as quickly as possible. As for so many other Australians, the fact that thirty-five people had been shot and killed was hard for me to get my head around.

Like most country kids in the 1950s and 1960s, I knew guns as part of the culture of living off the land. Dad was an excellent shot and took pride in the family history of marksmanship. My great-grandfather William Morris had won the clay shooting championship at Sydney's Royal Easter Show, and Dad was proud that a Tasmanian had shown them how it was done. As I have said, Dad went kangaroo shooting every winter when the cows were dry. On his return he would skin the animals and hang the carcasses on the Hills Hoist clothes line overnight to allow the game meat to mature. As a child I remember the shadows of the carcasses moving across my bedroom wall.

Dad was very proud of his gun. It had a particularly lovely wooden stock shining with the patina of age, and he would polish the wood and metal until they gleamed. His shotgun was a tool of his trade, to put stock down and put food on the table. I was never afraid of the gun; it was never used to frighten or intimidate us. But my sister and I knew to be careful around it. Though it was always unloaded behind the passage door, Gaylene and I were constantly warned not to touch it as it was dangerous. We also knew that if we ever tried to climb up to the ammunition cupboard, we would have been in big trouble. We never did. While it was drummed into us that shooting accidents were deadly, and occasionally there were quiet and coded conversations about someone having taken their own life with a gun, it was not until I left the farm and went to boarding school and university that I became aware that guns were frequently used to intimidate and threaten women and children in their homes.

When I stood for parliament in the large sprawling country electorate of Lyons in 1989, I had some insight into the threat of gun violence in rural Tasmania and how casually it was taken by Tasmanian authorities. When someone took a shot at Bob Brown at Farmhouse Creek in 1986, the offender was charged with discharging a firearm on a Sunday. I was also mindful that when referring to a 'chuck-a-greenie' competition in 1987, the mayor of Esperance Jack Kile was reported as saying, 'Offer the locals $10 a head and we'd soon clean them up.'[1]

I couldn't help noticing that in my predominantly rural electorate of Lyons, few road signs escaped being pockmarked with bullet holes. My supporters put up election posters in paddocks and on fences along the major roads. One day I came around a corner and there was one of my posters with a bullet hole between my eyes. It is incredibly chilling to know that someone has lined you up in their gunsight and fired to kill. Then my office received a series of letters with a bullet hole drawn on the forehead of my newspaper photo and red-biro drops of blood. The police found the letters were being sent by a young man in Beaconsfield with a mental disability. He had a gun licence and access to his father's gun storage cupboard. The police were not prepared to prosecute but agreed to cancel the gun licence and warn his parents of the consequences if he continued to use a gun.

Once elected in 1989, we independents moved to protect the community. In 1990 Bob Brown reintroduced legislation that he had unsuccessfully moved three years before to ban rapid-fire, self-loading semiautomatic and military-style weapons in Tasmania, saying, 'This state is ... largely a rural community with a gun culture that goes back to the days of the European invasion. Guns helped cause the near-genocide of the Aboriginal people of this island. Guns were responsible for the extinction of the thylacine or Tasmanian tiger. Guns are today responsible for the majority of suicides in Tasmania. Guns leave us with an unacceptable and tragic level of death and trauma and guns cause too many people, particularly women, to live in fear for their safety ... It is past time that attitudes changed and that this parliament accepted its responsibility to protect the community from the menace of irresponsible gun use.' The legislation was defeated.

After I became the Greens leader in Tasmania in 1993, I introduced and debated gun law reform legislation again. On 24 October 1995 it was defeated once more, with every single Liberal and Labor member of the Tasmanian House of Assembly voting against it. One of the Liberals made the prescient comment, 'Unfortunately every now and then someone does go crazy and that is very regrettable, but the number of times it happens is very rare.' Six months later came the Port Arthur massacre, with the military-style weapons the Tasmanian Greens had been trying to have banned for years.

Between that debate and the Port Arthur massacre, a state election had been held on 24 February 1996, in a poisonous political atmosphere. We Greens posed such a threat to the pro-native-forest-logging and anti-gay-law-reform status quo that both the Liberal and Labor parties ran hard on the need for a stable majority government without us in balance of power. Liberal Premier Ray Groom said throughout the campaign that he would govern as a majority or not at all, but he lost his majority, resigned and was replaced as leader by Tony Rundle so the Liberals could continue to govern in minority.

Michael Field, the Labor leader, had tried to force a referendum to go back to the polls if no party won a majority, and he said he would prefer to be in Opposition than to be in a minority government with the Greens holding the balance of power. This was the only time I know in Australian politics when an Opposition rejected the chance to form government. Having done so, the Labor Party went all out to paint the Greens as supporting the Liberals.[2]

In the days following the election we were constantly, ruthlessly attacked. The media and the Labor Party were hunting in a pack for a photo of Tony Rundle and me together, illustrating this supposed collusion. The business community, dominated by loggers and miners, wanted another election. Tony Rundle sought a meeting to discuss how a minority government might work but did not want to risk being seen with me. In the end we met to talk in a Devonport churchyard among the mourners after the funeral of a mutual friend, Peter Gilham. No one noticed.

It was in this poisonous situation that the massacre at Port Arthur ripped Tasmania apart. We all went into deep shock. People scrambled to find out where their children or parents or friends were. As the number of dead and wounded rose, there was an overwhelming sense that any of our loved ones could have been among the dead. Tasmania is a close-knit community; everyone seemed to know someone who had been there that day visiting or working on site or who had been killed, wounded or emotionally scarred.

As I lay in bed trying to think of words that would express what I was feeling and have any impact, I knew that right across the state other people were also lying awake: people feeling insecure, despairing or angry, frightened for the future in Tasmania; people praying for some insight; people crying; and others just staring into the dark. My mind was filled with the images that came to symbolise this tragedy, not only for all of us but for the world: the father who lost his whole family; the child dying in her mother's arms; the people sitting at the tables with cameras and bags just having their lunch, suddenly confronting death; the small rectangle of dry sticks beneath the tree where the little girl's body fell; the couples who had begun to enjoy their retirement; the women pushed under the tables by their husbands; the young man who threw himself in front of his wife and three-month-old baby; the Camp Quality puppeteers; the woman who yelled the warnings; the tourists including a seven-month-pregnant woman huddled in a cottage on the site not knowing whether the gunman would burst through the door at any moment. These images are so powerful because they convey a picture of all of us: ordinary people doing ordinary things.

Amid that whirlwind of carnage and emotion, Tasmania's Cabinet met early the next day.

The details of the disaster were still unfolding. The national media had arrived, the global media was on its way and it seemed that the eyes of the world were upon us. The premier, the leader of the Opposition and I met in an extraordinary Cabinet meeting. We were briefed on the latest details of the dead and wounded, the capacity of the hospitals to cope and the incredible efforts and bravery of the emergency services, but the main item on the agenda was to discuss an appropriate response. Tasmania's Liberal and Labor parliamentarians didn't know what to do. Opposed to gun law reform, they had to do something, but what? There were suggestions about better enforcement of existing laws, but it was clear to me that anything less than gun law reform and a ban on rapid-fire, self-loading, military-style weapons was inadequate and unacceptable.

I put my case strongly and was listened to, because everybody present knew that I had extraordinary leverage: only months before they had all refused to ban the weapons that had now killed thirty-five people. With the world's media outside they knew I would not be afraid to say that they had blood on their hands. Interestingly I was supported by Ron Cornish, a Liberal minister with whom I had clashed because of his entrenched opposition to gay law reform. I had forgotten that before he came into politics he had been a policeman and was therefore more sympathetic than most to banning guns. Twenty-four hours after the tragedy we announced that rapid-fire military-style weapons would now be banned, and that we would form a tripartite committee chaired by Liberal Minister for Justice John Beswick to determine the details.

Before parliament met the following morning, Premier Rundle invited Michael Field and me to join him in visiting the hospital to offer support to the wounded and thanks to the staff. Michael Field decided not to attend. I felt I owed it to the people to go, though I knew that my being there would fuel the simplistic 'Liberal Green government' narrative that some in politics and the media were so anxious to establish.

By the time we got there, many of the mainland families and friends of those who had been shot had arrived. Once they were reassured that the injuries of those they loved were not life-threatening, they became angry. We stood at the end of beds and faced a fierce barrage of questions. What sort of government has such poor security? Why weren't we doing more? Why had it taken so long to get help? Why did he have so many guns? What sort of state is this?

I have always regarded the professionalism of the medical staff that day as nothing short of superhuman. They were nursing not only the wounded but also the man who had shot and killed people they knew, and wounded others. As for us, two weeks earlier a Liberal premier and a Greens leader couldn't have been seen together; now we stood shoulder to shoulder.

We left the hospital and returned to the parliament to support a motion of condolence.

Speaking to it, I said, 'We have watched the generosity of spirit in the community, on the Tasman Peninsula, throughout Tasmania and throughout Australia, as people offer spiritual and practical support and reach out to each other. Now, as legislators, we must do the same ... As Tasmanians, the greatest expression of condolence and sympathy we can offer to the families and friends of those who have died or have been wounded is to ensure that their suffering and death have not all been in vain.' For me that had to mean gun law reform.

Parliament rose for a week as a mark of respect and so a state memorial service could be held. Early in the morning on the day of the Hobart memorial service, only three days after the massacre, we three party leaders flew down to the Port Arthur site to join Prime Minister Howard, Opposition leader Kim Beazley and Democrats leader Cheryl Kernot. They wanted to visit the site to lay a wreath before returning to Hobart for the service. Tony Rundle, Michael

Field and I sat in silence in the back of the helicopter, ready to take off; my stomach was churning. Nothing in my life had prepared me for what we were about to do. We were flying down to meet people in my electorate – some of whom I knew and some I didn't – who were grieving, trying to make sense of the senseless. We were going to witness the Broad Arrow Cafe still bloodstained and taped off and we had to be strong, we had to rise to the occasion, to be the people to be leaned on.

No one was saying anything like this, so I did. I told the leaders I knew we needed to make things better and not worse; that I didn't know how I would cope, whether I would be strong enough to handle what we would be facing. I suggested that when we landed and started meeting people, the premier should go first, then Michael Field and then me, and as each one of us found it hard to go on, we should fall back and let the next one step up. To this day I wonder whether, had there been three men in that helicopter, any one of them would have admitted his vulnerability and made a plan, or whether they would have pretended everything was under control.

It was a beautiful day. The Tasman Peninsula looked stunning from the sky, and as we came in to land I couldn't help thinking about the sheer beauty of the place in contrast to the blood that had been shed there. You can't visit Port Arthur without its history seeping into you. The misery of the 12,700 convicts who had been locked up and brutalised there is palpable. Another act of barbarism had shed more blood, added another layer. Then we landed. What I remember is raw, gut-wrenching, sobbing grief, twisted handkerchiefs and stoicism. We had words pent up inside all of us, held back as if saying anything would break the dam and they would all come flooding out.

Then we returned to Hobart for the state memorial service in St David's Cathedral. It was packed. John Howard, the prime minister of only five weeks, said, 'This is an event that has shaken the core of the country in a way that no individual crime has done in my lifetime.' Thirty-five candles were lit, one for every man, woman and child who had been killed. Two thousand people gathered on the footpaths and lined the streets. The enduring mental snapshot I have of that day is of Walter Mikac, father of Madeline and Alannah, husband of Nanette – all of whom died – clutching three Dutch irises, staggering from the cathedral under the weight of his grief.

We in the Tasmanian Parliament, consistent with what we had decided the day after the massacre, swung into action. Our tripartite committee met on 2 May to determine the detail of our gun law reform proposal. Peg Putt joined me to represent the Greens. Michael Field was joined by David Llewellyn and the government was represented by John Beswick. The reforms were strongly argued. We Greens took our cues from the Gun Control Coalition led by Roland Browne, and we secured a number of further concessions, but not a ban on automatic and semiautomatic handguns as we had hoped.

When parliament resumed on 7 May, John Beswick introduced a *Prohibited Guns Order 1996*, acknowledging that it was timely for us to further regulate and control semiautomatic guns. He then introduced the *Guns Amendment Bill 1996*, saying, 'We are moving towards a safer Tasmania through these amendments, and I believe that it is significant that all parties have formed a united front to make it so. By our actions here today we place severe restrictions on the availability and use of semiautomatic guns by prohibiting most guns in that class. This bill further limits the availability, use and disposal of automatic weapons by dealers and collectors, as well as placing a total limit on collectors' permits for automatic weapons. It also includes an important provision to eliminate magazines of greater than the permitted capacity which are capable of being fitted to certain guns that are not prohibited but would be in that class if larger magazines were fitted to them ... I can forecast at this time that other amendments to the Act will be forthcoming on the basis of agreement reached by all parties. Other discussions to be held at the Australian Police Ministers' Council in Canberra on Friday may also lead to new directions in gun control throughout Australia. It can therefore be expected that there will be further and more extensive legislation in the near future to implement the remaining areas of agreement between the parties and any measures that are agreed upon to bring about national uniformity in gun laws ... I do wish to express my appreciation of the support given by both the Australian Labor Party and the Greens in the way this matter has been approached.'

I said, 'In supporting this bill I want to pay tribute to my former colleague in this House, now senator-elect Dr Bob Brown, and to the Coalition for Gun Control in Tasmania and in particular Roland Browne. While I have no intention of engaging in recrimination because the enormity of what has happened makes that style of politics part of the politics of the past, what I do intend to do is to thank the people who maintained their faith that changes could be made to gun laws, that ultimately people would recognise that it would be necessary to remove the density of firearms from within the Australian population, in particular the Tasmanian population, and indeed to tighten up on who could have weapons, under what conditions and for what purpose.'

I pointed out that the admirable cooperation between the parties had been a function of the balance of power, an example of how such a situation can lead to a chosen consensus.[3] So before John Howard chaired the Australian Police Ministers' Council to negotiate national gun law reform, Tasmania had already taken national leadership, banned those weapons unilaterally and indicated a willingness to go further if that was what the federal process determined.

While I have always condemned much of what John Howard did in government, not least taking Australia into a war in Iraq based on a lie, I have always given him credit for having the courage to move on gun law reform nationally. It was a great step in the national interest. What is rarely acknowledged is that his action was enabled and facilitated because the Tasmanian Parliament gave him the platform to do so before he met with state police ministers to push for change. I remain proud of the role the Greens played over many years and in the balance of power to make Australia safer by driving gun law reform and being ever vigilant to maintain those laws.

Our tripartite committee continued to dissect and debate additional reforms, some proposed by the Police Ministers' Council and some by we Greens. We all continued to advocate for the reforms to an often hostile electorate, but for the most part MPs who did not agree with the bans respected the confidentiality imposed on them by their party leaders and did not fuel opposition through the media.

As the gun laws took effect, guns were handed in by their thousands; one day we all went out to the foundry to see them dropped into a furnace. With all their capacity to threaten, kill and maim, these guns were reduced to bars of metal.

There was an incredibly moving and powerful memorial service at the Port Arthur site, but the one that haunts me was held at the Botanical Gardens in Hobart, at which three Scottish fathers spoke. Sixteen children and their teacher had been shot at a small school in the Scottish village of Dunblane on 13 March, only a month before the Port Arthur massacre. These bereaved parents reached out to us from one end of the planet to the other, calling for a ban on all deadly weapons including the handguns that had taken their children's lives. Having small children of my own, I stood outside the Conservatory and cried. Even now, I cannot visit the Conservatory without wondering what has happened to those Scottish families.

Dad never said much about gun law reform; his gun was not in the prohibited category. I still remember his unspoken gut-wrenching grief when a stroke took away his ability to sight it. But the depth of his feeling on the matter never left him. Not long before he died in 1999, he put a codicil on his will to prevent me as an executor from having anything to do with his gun. It still remains in the extended family.

It is more than twenty years since the Port Arthur massacre, and thankfully a whole generation has lived without a mass shooting in Australia. But we have to be vigilant. Former prime minister Tony Abbott, in an act of utter reckless negligence, did a deal with Senator David Leyonhjelm to lift the ban on the import of the Adler A110 lever-action shotgun, which has similar firepower to banned pump-action varieties. Under Prime Minister Turnbull, state premiers decided in December 2016 to lift the ban but reclassify the weapon and restrict access to it. Handguns remain a big problem. While automatic handguns are banned in the United Kingdom, they are now the weapon of choice in Australia for drive-by shootings and for criminals generally. In the Senate while I was leader, Greens senator Penny Wright worked hard but unsuccessfully to secure a ban on automatic and semiautomatic handguns. Surely such a ban is not beyond us.

Gun law reform in Australia was hard fought. On all sides of politics and at kitchen tables in homes across the country people debated it and accepted it. Some, like my father, didn't say much, others were grudging in their acceptance, and still others embraced it wholeheartedly. But it was done. It has been a wonderful reform for the country. It upsets me greatly to watch a new generation of parliamentarians – who have never had to deal with a massacre or are apparently unmindful of violence against women – be prepared to negotiate so easily to wind back gun laws as if they are incidental in the scheme of things. They are not. The Port Arthur massacre and the consequent debate reframed the place of guns in our culture. There must be no going back.

For so many of us brought up on the land in the 1950s and 1960s, with fathers who had no jewellery, special books or artefacts, guns were the only things of sentimental and monetary value those men thought they had to pass down through the generations. Most of those guns never had to be handed in or ended up in a furnace, but their owners identified with the owners of those that did. As a woman from the bush and as leader of the Greens in Tasmania and nationally I understood, better than the majority of my fellow parliamentarians, why the debate over gun law reform cut so deep. But I also understood what my dad and the farming fathers of my dad's generation didn't. The really valuable thing they had to pass on was not their guns. It was their connection to the land.

# 6

# Pride

OBJECT: *PFLAG T-shirt worn by Christine to the 2013 Gay Mardi Gras parade, Sydney. It is now part of the Museum of Australian Democracy Collection.*

IT WAS THE 2013 GAY Mardi Gras parade in Oxford Street, Sydney. Thousands of spectators lined the streets, music blared, people danced and pranced, supporters were calling out, banners hung from buildings, people on balconies raised their glasses to toast us as we marched – the parents, families and friends of lesbians and gays (PFLAG). I was excited, energised and above all proud: now I knew why these were called Pride marches. My son Tom and I were marching together, both of us beaming, and it felt good to be part of something so positive, so appealing, so praiseworthy, so out there.

I'd spent the previous few hours in the marshalling area meeting people, getting organised, watching the final touches to the floats and marvelling at the way Mardi Gras now attracted the armed forces and the police as proud participants. With the last of the make-up and glitter applied and costumes sewn, stapled or glued on, we were under way. A young man painted blue from head to toe leaped over a hedge and rushed up to me. That's how I first met the wonderful LGBTIQ advocate and football player Jason Ball: Beyond Blue meeting Green.

I thought how amazing it is to have seen the campaign for LGBTIQ rights in Australia evolve from the cruel ugliness of the last quarter of a century into such a reaffirming positive force. Young people all over the country don't get what the fuss is about, but of course many young LGBTIQ people certainly do. Every day they live with the hurt and rejection that discrimination visits upon them. Just weeks before I had been in Toowoomba as a panellist on ABC TV's program *Q&A* when a question came from a young man, visibly shaking as he stood in front of his home-town audience to talk about gay rights. His trepidation was a powerful reminder that what is not even noticed anymore on the streets of Sydney or Melbourne remains a reason for rejection or discrimination elsewhere.

I chose to wear the PFLAG T-shirt and march with PFLAG rather than be on the Greens or the Marriage Equality float because I wanted to reach out to that young man, and to young LGBTIQ people everywhere, and let them know that as the mother of a gay son and as the first leader of a federal political party to march in Mardi Gras, I too get it and I embrace them. I wanted to say: 'You are not alone.' But I also wanted to show my son how proud I was of him. I wanted to call out to other parents of LGBTIQ people: 'Stand up with and for your kids. Be proud of them.'

For all the bonhomie and celebrations of the night, the laughter, the partying, the celebrities rubbing shoulders in the VIP area, I still had a knot in my stomach, a reminder that Mardi Gras is political. It is not just a big night out and a tourist attraction in Sydney. It started as a political statement from those who marched for gay rights in 1978, and it still is. It is deeply frustrating that we were still marching for marriage equality in 2013, let alone 2017 when it should have already been legislated.

After the 2010 election the Australian Greens entered an agreement that saw Julia Gillard retain the prime ministership. Public opinion was with us to legislate marriage equality, but Labor was divided between those who were opposed under any circumstances and so wanted a conscience vote and those who saw this issue as a matter of discrimination that needed a binding vote. The issue was to go to the Labor National Conference in December 2011, and expectations were building that at last Labor might change its platform and make the policy binding. But as the pro-marriage-equality activists were organising behind the scenes, so too was the Shop, Distributive and Allied Employees Association (the Shoppies Union or SDA), led by arch-conservative Catholic Joe de Bruyn.

This union representing retail workers is one of the largest in Australia, and de Bruyn controlled it with an iron fist. MPs and senators preselected as SDA union members form part of the factional deals of the SDA and oppose marriage equality as a bloc or risk their preselection. Because the SDA delivers a bloc vote in the leadership ballot, Prime Minister Gillard knew that her leadership would not survive if the SDA withdrew its support.

To make sure that marriage equality was not endorsed at the Australian Labor Party (ALP) conference, de Bruyn worked with Jim Wallace and the Australian Christian Lobby, a far-right extreme anti-gay organisation. Their plan was for Julia Gillard to sabotage the vote by announcing beforehand that she would support a conscience vote on the issue but not marriage equality as a binding party policy. They knew this would split the vote by forcing members who supported Gillard but not her position on marriage equality to choose between ending discrimination or voting against the prime minister and further destabilising her leadership.

The prime minister moved the motion for a conscience vote herself. By 208 to 184, Labor voted to allow its MPs to discriminate against same-sex couples. Those opposed to marriage equality could then proceed with this change to the Labor platform, knowing a conscience vote if taken in the parliament would not have the numbers to win.

The party platform changed and the result was spun as a great win for marriage equality, with campaigners rejoicing at the ALP change of heart. To this day I think they were wrong. What had been secured in 2011 was no change for the foreseeable future – extended to 2019 by the 2015 ALP national conference. Worse still, it legitimised the idea that a conscience vote in the parliament is appropriate in dealing with issues such as discrimination. We have had to use the conscience vote over time, but at some point it has to stop. It is not okay. Human rights are human rights. Discrimination on the basis of race, religion, gender, sexuality or disability is wrong and unconscionable. It is not a matter for an opinion poll. Would you have a conscience vote or plebiscite on whether to discriminate against women? But that is where we landed in Australia: in 2016 we came perilously close to deciding whether or not LGBTIQ people can marry according to the whim of the public.

Remember the Brexit count, when the United Kingdom voted in a referendum to leave the European Union? Watching on my computer as the vote was being counted, I was surprised by my emotional investment in the outcome. As a global citizen sitting in faraway Tasmania I was horrified that the European Union, the most successful peace project to come out of the Second World War, was coming unstuck before my very eyes, all because of a vote that should never have happened and the hubris of one man, British Prime Minister David Cameron. At that moment a tweet crossed the screen in front of me. It was obviously directed at those Remain voters who were horrified by the Yes vote: 'Now you know how it feels to have the whole country deciding on your future.' It was from an LGBTIQ person in Australia.

David Cameron and Malcolm Turnbull have this in common: neither gave much if any thought to the social consequences of their decisions because they thought their pro-Remain and pro-gay marriage positions would get up. So they thought they were safe in indulging the right-wing elements of their parties. Did Malcolm Turnbull even stop to think about the personal costs and consequences of the plebiscite for the LGBTIQ community in Australia, their families and friends? As he holds his grandchildren and talks of being a trustee of their future, does he think about how he would feel if one of them was LGBTIQ and denied equality? I doubt it.

He just couldn't see that former prime minister Tony Abbott proposed a marriage equality plebiscite in the first place to destroy the unstoppable momentum for a parliamentary vote. Abbott wanted to take the issue off the agenda for the 2016 election and to buy time to organise to defeat it. That is exactly what happened. Abbott and his right-wing backers such as Eric Abetz, Cory Bernardi, George Christensen and Matt Canavan took a calculated gamble that they could defeat the momentum towards marriage equality, just as Prime Minister John Howard had done decades before in holding a referendum on Australia becoming a republic. The design of the question and the rules can divide and conquer. Malcolm Turnbull, who led the pro-republic campaign, should have known that.

As we know, the bid to hold a same-sex marriage plebiscite was defeated in the Senate in November 2016. I cannot bear to think of the pain that would have been inflicted on LGBTIQ people everywhere if it had proceeded. At the time some assumed the world had changed and the vote in favour of gay marriage would be successful, just as it had been in Ireland. I understood their optimism; I too had felt it at Mardi Gras and in rallies around the country and badly wanted to think things had changed enough. But having walked into a Devonport meeting with the inspiring High Court judge Michael Kirby in 1994 and watched people spit on his beautiful black coat, having feared for the personal safety of gay activists who attended a meeting in Ulverstone in 1990 where people chanted 'Kill them, kill them, kill them', I was – and am – not so sure. Knowing about the relationship between the Australian Christian Lobby, the SDA, the Exclusive Brethren and the Liberal and Labor parties, one thing is for sure: the 'No' campaign would have been vicious, divisive and cashed up.[1]

And so it was from those campaigning for the No vote in Turnbull's $122 million non-binding opinion poll. Turnbull's clinging to the Coalition leadership at the expense of LGBTIQ people is only delaying the inevitable: marriage equality will become law in Australia. A parliamentary vote is required to end discrimination of any kind and to remove the definition of marriage in the *Marriage Act* – that it is between a man and a woman – that John Howard inserted in 2004. The best way to secure that outcome is to work with the Greens. Worldwide in the more than ninety countries where Green parties exist, ending discrimination of any kind is a strongly held principle such that every Green in any parliament will support marriage equality every time.

~

WHEN I WAS FIRST ELECTED as member for the seat of Lyons in 1989 as part of Bob Brown's team of independents, decriminalising homosexuality with its twenty-one-year jail term was part of our platform. When we achieved balance of power, we pursued Labor to act on decriminalisation as part of the agreed reform agenda cited in the Labor–Green Accord. Labor insisted on a conscience vote for ALP members. They were internally divided and cowed by the horrific fear campaign run by the state and federal Liberal parties and the churches and bolstered by two anti-gay groups formed in June 1989: For a Caring Tasmania (FACT), and Concerned Residents Against Moral Pollution (CRAMP).

With AIDS being labelled a gay disease and the community fear being constantly reinforced by the Grim Reaper ads on TV, Health Minister John White came up with the idea that gay law reform be buried in a health bill and sold as addressing AIDS.[2] We found it offensive because it would reinforce the AIDS stigma and heighten discrimination rather than remove it, but for the sake of getting reform at all we reluctantly agreed. The government bill passed the Lower House with decriminalisation provisions intact, but when it hit the Legislative Council the decriminalisation provisions were removed. The debate in the Legislative Council was appalling, with calls to run homosexuals out of Tasmania, to reintroduce the death penalty for them and at the very least to jail them.

The campaign for decriminalisation went all the way from Tasmania to the United Nations Human Rights Committee, which in 1994 found that Australia had breached its obligations under the International Covenant on Civil and Political Rights. For the first time, a UN treaty body had recognised discrimination on grounds of sexual orientation as a human rights violation. Gay rights advocates in Tasmania had made history.

We often think historic breakthroughs happen in other places, but this set Tasmania apart and brought global focus to gay rights advocates Nick Toonen, Rodney Croome and the stalwarts of the Tasmanian Gay and Lesbian Group, including Richard Hales and Miranda Morris. Twenty years later UN Human Rights chief Navi Pillay described this as 'a watershed with wide-ranging implications for the human rights of millions of people. Since 1994, more than thirty countries have taken steps to abolish the offence of homosexuality. Some have enacted new laws providing greater protection against discrimination on grounds of sexual orientation or gender identity. And in many parts of the world, we have witnessed a remarkable shift in public attitudes, in favour of greater acceptance of gay and lesbian people.'[3]

With the UN decision in 1994 momentum continued to build in Tasmania for reform. All other states in Australia had already decriminalised homosexuality, but in Tasmania a majority Liberal government and an extremely conservative Upper House refused to act. However, the Labor federal government did. It passed the *Human Rights (Sexual Conduct) Act (Cwth) 1994*, which in the event of a legal conflict would have overruled the Tasmanian legislation. But owing to legal uncertainty about some of its provisions and Ray Groom's government's refusal to repeal the Tasmanian legislation, the Tasmanian Gay and Lesbian Group lodged a case with the High Court to get a clear ruling in November 1995. Gay law reform was a key issue in the 1996 Tasmanian state election three months later. It resulted in a hung parliament, with the Liberals becoming a minority government in which the Greens, with no written agreement, held the balance of power.

I introduced my *Criminal Code Amendment Bill No. 2* on 15 May 1996. No doubt as a result of the mounting pressure on the Tasmanian Government because of the pending High Court case, the Liberals decided to permit a conscience vote. For the first time since 1990 we had a chance of securing a majority in the Lower House for gay law reform. Halfway through the committee stage I received a note from Labor's Judy Jackson saying I needed to filibuster as she had lost the Labor numbers and needed time to get them back. David Llewellyn and Michael Polley were strong opponents and had been lobbying Labor members to oppose. If I ever needed a definition of flying by the seat of the pants, that was it. Meanwhile activists in the Tasmanian Gay and Lesbian Group were lobbying every MP to keep the numbers.

Finally we got to the vote. One crucial person we needed for the numbers was Liberal member Bob Cheek, who was supportive in principle but had not made up his mind. Thank goodness for his children. He told the chamber, 'I come from a fairly conservative background, a farming background really, I guess, and football teams and all the rest; the sort of people who dislike homosexuals and love telling poofter jokes, no offence to the people over there. Even my family is split down the middle. I actually went home for a quick meal tonight and there were differing views over the situation. My son, who is in his early twenties, as I was going out the door said, "Dad ... Dad, don't let us down." They were words, I guess, that meant a fair bit to me. I think that it is probably symptomatic of the younger generation, who will not put up with prejudice.'

He voted for the bill, which passed the House of Assembly 24–8 with three abstentions. Then the Legislative Council debated it.

The debate took place only a few weeks after the Port Arthur massacre. Jim Wilkinson MLC, who handled my bill in the Upper House, said, 'Inadvertently discrimination occurred against a partner of one of the victims, a gay man, Andrew Mills. Because it was not known that Andrew Mills and David Capper were a couple, David Capper was notified of his friend's death by telephone and not in person with counsellors present, as was the practice with other partners. He was at home alone when he received the phone call. It is against this background that this bill to decriminalise homosexual acts between consenting adults in private comes before the House.' Quoting Michael Kirby's words, he added, 'It will be a terrible indictment of the moral sense of this part of Australia if the land be beautiful but the hearts of the people are cold and full of injustice ... We in Australia have come a long way in the perception of human rights, even in my lifetime. Respect for the basic human rights of homosexuals in Tasmania is a further step which must now be taken. The political leaders of Tasmania should take this step. Not so much because of a decision in Geneva. Not out of fear of Canberra's actions. But because reflection upon their moral obligation to a minority of their fellow citizens demands it. Justice requires it.'

The dissenting views were very strong. Extremely conservative MLC George Shaw said that homosexuality was addictive behaviour: 'The more one is exposed to it the more the perversion comes to dominate one's life, much like cocaine or alcohol.' Tony Fletcher, leader of the government in the Upper House, said, 'At an earlier stage I said that in my opinion the homosexual lifestyle was a lifestyle for losers. Quite a number of people rang me up and challenged me about that comment ... but I still [believe] it is a lifestyle to choose and, while I recognise that there are some enormous talents among people who identify with their homosexuality ... their deaths and the HIV/AIDS virus and their lifestyle are inextricably linked, I believe. So it is not for me to condone or to promote the homosexual lifestyle. I believe it is wrong, but I believe that the law at the moment in Tasmania is such that homosexuals or adult people of either sex acting in private with consent are not criminals and we ought to amend our criminal code in Tasmania to reflect that ... the law has already changed in the federal jurisdiction. That jurisdiction is superior to ours and that law is superior to our law and therefore we ought to put our law right to properly reflect that.'

The bill was voted down, 8–6.

At the beginning of 1997 Premier Rundle and I met without advisors to discuss the year. He wanted his legislation passed and in particular his Budget, and he asked what I really wanted. I told him I wanted my bill for gay law reform to be passed. Having already given the Liberals a conscience vote, he agreed that if I could get a private member's bill through the House of Assembly again, he would instruct the leader of the government in the Upper House to get it through the Legislative Council. We had a deal. However, he said I would have to find a way to allow some of his most high-profile and outspoken members to save face, given some of their appallingly homophobic arguments. Former premier Ray Groom was attorney-general and fiercely opposed to decriminalisation, as was former federal member and then member for Denison Michael Hodgman. They had argued that my bill would result in Tasmania being overrun with paedophiles; Michael Hodgman even accused me in the parliament of being 'the mother of teenage sodomy'.

I came up with the idea of a committee of experts working with parliamentarians as a mechanism to break parliamentary deadlocks. In the days following the Port Arthur massacre we had had a tripartite committee to work out the details of gun law reform. It had worked up to a point, but there was no mechanism to break deadlocks on matters of contention other than numbers. There had to be a better way.

I invited the secretary of the Department of Justice, together with the University of Tasmania's Professor Kate Warner, later Tasmania's governor, to a meeting in Parliament House with Attorney-General Groom, among others, to tease out his concerns about decriminalisation leading to paedophilia. Professor Warner had already provided a paper to the Tasmanian Parliament on the merits of the bill, and Groom had nowhere to go. At the press conference following the meeting, to save his face I said the issues had been resolved and would be clarified by amendment. There was no need for amendment, but we all agreed that an amendment would enable the attorney-general to stop his accusations of paedophilia and so allow other Liberals who wanted to support the bill to do so. It was effectively a smokescreen that provided a way forward.

The bill passed and went to the Upper House for consideration. True to his word Tony Rundle instructed Tony Fletcher, the leader of government business, to get the bill through. On 1 May 1997 the Upper House voted to repeal the anti-gay laws in Tasmania, and the bill came into effect on 13 May. Gay law reform would have happened eventually as a result of a High Court case, but it was made possible in 1997 because the Greens had balance of power and used it to enact change.

Throughout Tasmania the news spread fast. Activists descended on Parliament House; the success was the culmination of so much work and pain, highs and lows for so many. Tasmania had gone from having the worst laws in the country to having the best. It was a moment that changed Tasmania. It broke the glass. Tasmania could now be progressive.

I went to find Tony Fletcher to thank him and took a box of D'Anvers chocolate truffles as a gesture of appreciation. He was cold and dismissive, and refused the chocolates. He said he had supported the bill to bring Tasmania into line with the Commonwealth; he had used his position to drive it to a vote as the premier had required. He had even made some positive remarks about the reform being a significant move forward for Tasmania. But it was clear he did not regard it as something of which to be proud.

A few years later I was at a small celebration dinner in Hobart at which Justice Michael Kirby was the guest speaker, reflecting on the struggle for Aboriginal and gay rights in Tasmania. I had not forgotten the spittle on his coat years before. I have also never forgotten his speech because of the dignity and intelligence of the man; the soaring oratory and resonance of his voice as he recited Oodgeroo Noonuccal's poem 'Song of Hope':

> Look up, my people,
> The dawn is breaking,
> The world is waking
>   To a new bright day,
> When none defame us,
> No restriction tame us,
> Nor colour shame us,
>   Nor sneer dismay.[4]

I felt the same sense of joy as I marched with Tom in Mardi Gras and again when Rodney Croome was chosen as Tasmania's Australian of the Year in 2015 and I went to Canberra to be there when his Member of the Order of Australia was presented. I was so proud. It was such a far cry from the days when he had been an English student of mine at Devonport High School, from the days of the 'kill them' chants of 1989. He could have left Tasmania but he didn't; he stayed to change the culture. And, together with a courageous group of campaigners, he did. They achieved for themselves and so many others pride in Tasmania, a deep sense of connection, belonging and recognition. I have given my PFLAG T-shirt, together with the rest of my T-shirt collection, to the Museum of Australian Democracy because it represents the courage and activism of those who dared to stand up not only for equality and human rights, but for their families.

There is a tiny graveyard in New Ground, near Port Sorell in north-west Tasmania. It was land taken up by people breaking new ground as settlement spread in the colony of Van Diemen's Land. In it, in a direct line of sight to Mount Roland, are buried Rodney Croome's forebears and my own. My great-great-grandfather John Morris (1805–1885) had a son William who married Rodney's great-grandmother Annie Elder Aitken. They are all buried there, proud Tasmanians. Perhaps nothing and everything is inevitable. Perhaps Rodney Croome and I were always destined to break new ground.

> To our fathers' fathers
>   The pain, the sorrow;
> To our children's children
>   The glad tomorrow.[5]

# 7

# Demolishing Democracy: Dirty Tricks

OBJECT: Conspiracy *sculpture by Tasmanian artist Gerald Makin.*

DURING THE 1989 TASMANIAN ELECTION campaign Bob
Brown and I attended many fundraisers for our team of independents.
At one such fundraiser I noticed a piece of sculpture by Tasmanian
potter Gerald Makin called *Conspiracy*. I suggested to Bob that a dark,
closed sculpture of two men standing huddled together stitching
things up perfectly personified the relationship between the Liberals
and the Wesley Vale pulp mill proponents North Broken Hill. Bob
generously bought the sculpture for me as a present, and it has sat on
my bookshelves ever since.

When I look at it, I remember the saying that the more things
change, the more they stay the same. That sculpture could have
been the cover of the Carter Royal Commission report conducted
after the 1989 election that saw Edmund Rouse, the owner of
Gunns Kilndried Timbers, jailed for attempted bribery and the
premier Robin Gray described as having acted 'deceitfully and
dishonestly'.[1] As the Tamar Valley pulp mill and the campaigns to
save the magnificent old-growth forests raged, the sculpture came
to represent, for me, John Gay of Gunns Pty Ltd and the Labor
government of Paul Lennon.

Over the years the sculpture continued to personify contemporary politics. As the Tarkine rose to national prominence, with the miners replacing the loggers as the biggest threat to the world's largest tract of temperate rainforest, it reminded me of the Australian Workers' Union and the mining industry, as well as federal ministers Tony Burke and Greg Hunt as they rejected Australian Heritage Council advice and gave mining the big tick. Now I see Adani and the Turnbull Liberal and Palaszczuk Labor governments cosying up to facilitate the biggest coalmine in the world, ignoring its potential impact on global warming and the Great Barrier Reef.

As well as symbolising politicians prioritising the demands of their unions, parties or corporate donors over the public interest, *Conspiracy* explodes the idea that Australia is a democracy. This morphing into plutocracy is a major factor in the disillusionment with politicians and democracy itself. Government by the wealthy has always been there, but now the takeover is almost complete; voters are fed up with their elected representatives acting to enrich themselves, their political parties or their corporate donors through development approvals, exemptions, subsidies, and blind eyes turned to compliance with and enforcement of the law regardless of social or environmental cost.

Campaigners everywhere could put names to the faces of elected representatives and big business representatives getting together to advance the cause of business. It is so common that the rush towards the revolving door between business and politics has become a stampede. Of the 538 lobbyists registered by the Department of Prime Minister and Cabinet in 2016, 191 were former government representatives.[2] What makes politicians attractive to the corporates is that they understand and have access to the inside workings of political parties, so business can directly influence those in power. Cases in point are Martin Ferguson leaving his position as minister for energy in the Gillard government and going to the Australian Petroleum Production and Exploration Association, or Ian Macfarlane leaving his role as minister for industry and science and going to the Queensland Resources Council to promote coal and gas. Trade Minister Andrew Robb left Parliament in 2016 after negotiating the China–Australia Free Trade Agreement and began consulting for a Chinese billionaire almost immediately. Former Liberal senator Helen Coonan and Labor minister Mark Arbib are now with Packer's Crown casino and Consolidated Press Holdings, respectively. But the media report of former Queensland Labor premier Anna Bligh joining the Bankers' Association early in 2017 as federal Labor was considering a Banking Royal Commission says it all: 'Does Anna Bligh have what it takes to stop a royal commission into the banks?'[3]

It can work the other way too. Gary Gray went from director of corporate affairs at Woodside Petroleum to contest the seat of Brand in Western Australia for the ALP. Labor desperately needed a big resource company in Western Australia to back it against John Howard's assertion that a Labor government would create risk for the mining boom. Woodside did so. Following the ALP's election victory in 2007 and Gary Gray winning the seat, Prime Minister Kevin Rudd appointed him parliamentary secretary for regional development and northern Australia.

Cosying up to business is one thing, standing up to vested interests is another. Strength and resilience are required in the face of combined corporate and political power. I have been arrested trying to stop the Road to Nowhere in the Tarkine, and arrested and jailed during the Franklin blockade. But far more frightening was the time when I was a newly elected MP and the police rang to tell me I had received a death threat, the first of many. They advised me to organise for my two boys to stay elsewhere and told me they would be keeping me under observation for the night. The next day a plainclothes officer followed me to work and sat in the foyer of my office for the day. My boys have never forgotten being picked up from primary school by the police to prevent them going home.

As whistleblowers also know, these are the consequences of taking a stand in Australia. But you can either give in to intimidation or stand against it and go on. Knowing what the forces opposing you will throw at you helps to build resilience and develop coping strategies, as well as to anticipate what might come next and name it. That's why I am telling these stories. Hopefully they will help other people, and women in particular, to come to know their strength and better understand the lengths to which those who oppose you will go. Information is power, and bringing things out into the open is a great political disinfectant. A conspiracy sculpture on the bookshelves is a good reminder.

By 1993 that sculpture definitely represented Premier Ray Groom's Liberal government and the logging industry, which was in uproar because the Labor–Green Accord had put in place a review of native forest logging, with a view to the federal and Tasmanian governments proposing an extension of the Tasmanian Wilderness World Heritage Area to include the high-conservation-value forests. The logging industry leaned on minority Labor Premier Michael Field to renege on an undertaking to the Greens and to the Tasmanian Parliament not to proceed with legislation that would give the loggers the resource security they demanded. His capitulation to the forest industry and to big business and its consequences is legendary. Having lost our confidence, he went to a state election that he lost spectacularly.

At the behest of the logging industry the Liberal majority government of Ray Groom made it a criminal act for people to protest in the public forests. When the 1993 federal election was called, the logging industry was determined to make sure there were no more World Heritage proposals and no forest protection gains for the environmentalists.

The Tasmanian Greens had preselected paediatrician Dr Judy Henderson to be our Senate candidate. She was an exceptional person. A medical graduate of Sydney University, she had spent a decade in Nepal heading up paediatrics at the Kathmandu hospital and walking the villages of Nepal inoculating children against childhood diseases. She came to Tasmania after the Franklin River campaign and as an expert in overseas aid and development was the national deputy director of Community Aid Abroad. The polling suggested that she had a good chance of winning and could possibly have held the balance of power in the Australian Senate.

Just before midday on 11 March 1993, two days before the election, a railway employee found an apparent bomb on the railway line adjacent to a logging yard at Black River in far north-west Tasmania. Two passing cars reported a nearby 'Earth First' sign to police and to TasRail. Ray Groom – without any evidence – said, 'It is most regrettable that some more extreme elements of the conservation movement may be willing to use the threat of violence to pursue their cause.'

In the parliament that evening I made it very clear that the forest industry had been actively campaigning against the Greens: now we had an unidentified explosive device. 'I put to you, Mr Speaker, who has greater access to explosive devices: conservationists wandering around or people in industry?' I asked, pointing out that this could easily have been a stunt to discredit the conservation movement two days before a federal election. But the following day *The Advocate* ran a front-page story headed 'Railway Bomb: Environment Group Linked', pointing the finger at the 'international eco-terrorist group Earth First'. All the TV election eve Tasmanian news bulletins showed police scouring the area for evidence of the ecoterrorism that had hit Tasmania. The media, forest industry and Labor and Liberal politicians, still without a shred of evidence, sent a loud and clear message: environmental radicals from Earth First were about to take criminal action to destroy the forest industry.

Judy Henderson narrowly missed out on a Senate seat. The 'bomb' was found to be ammonium nitrate, used by local farmers and loggers to blow up stumps in land clearing. A second device nearby had wires and batteries bound by cloth tape, but could not have been detonated. The Earth First sign was written on a sheet and without their trademark exclamation mark. In the investigation that followed – as with every case of so-called 'ecoterrorism' throughout the 1990s – Tasmania Police could find no one responsible. Years later a memo from Victoria Police's Counter Terrorist Intelligence Section (CTIS) was obtained by Friends of the Earth through a Freedom of Information request. Written in July 1993, just four months after the 'bomb', the CTIS memo noted that 'the device is considered [by Tasmania Police] to be an elaborate hoax and they have not ruled out the possibility that it may have been placed there by loggers in an attempt to discredit the Green movement'.[4]

To this day no one has been held to account for placing a bomb on the Black River bridge. A cynical election frame-up had done what it was designed to do: stop the Greens from getting a senator elected and frighten Tasmanians into thinking that the non-violent direct action that characterised all environmental protests had been jettisoned in favour of radical violent action.[5] To excuse Tasmania Police or to think the Black River bomb was a random malicious idea thought up by the local forest industry would be wrong and totally naive. The tactics were imported by the loggers from the USA Wise Use Movement in the battle between environmentalists and loggers over the fate of Australia's high-conservation forests, not just in Tasmania but all over the country.

The Forest Protection Society, a national logging industry group, was set up in 1987 to counter the environmental movement in the forest debate. It shared a postal address with the National Association of Forest Industries, and its fact sheets said that logging rainforests was the best way to protect them. It modelled itself on the USA Wise Use Movement, whose rallies often featured log-truck convoys brandishing yellow ribbons and parading through towns in the heart of Oregon's timber country, or circling the state capitol buildings with horns blaring. The tactic was copied here. In January 1995, when the Keating government decided not to renew some export woodchip licences and to exclude loggers from areas of native forest in Tasmania, New South Wales, Victoria and Western Australia, 4000 loggers and a huge log-truck convoy surrounded Parliament

House in Canberra. Ron Arnold, the chief of Wise Use, has said, 'Citizen activist groups allied to the forest industry are vital to our future survival. They can speak for us in the public interest where we ourselves cannot. They are not limited by liability, contract law or ethical codes. They can provide something for people to join, to be part of, to fight for.'[6]

As Tasmanian Greens leader throughout this period I became increasingly frustrated that in spite of all the adverse publicity directed towards environmentalists, Tasmania Police could never find anyone responsible for any so-called 'ecoterrorist' activities, but had no problem with levelling blame at the conservation movement. The tactic of evidence-free accusation was repeated time and time again throughout the 1990s and right up to 2012, with incidents frequently preceding elections or visits by federal ministers.

Accusations of tree-spiking – driving a spike into a tree to either stop the tree being felled or destroy the blade in the sawmill – were powerful weapons against the Greens and environmentalists. By an amazing coincidence, out of all the logging sites in Tasmania, a tree spike was found at the very one to which Forestry Tasmania and the Tasmanian Government took federal MP Ian McLachlan during his inspection of the Southern Forests. In 2012, in another spectacular coincidence, Labor Premier Lara Giddings told a heated pro-forest rally in Huonville that she had seen tree spikes and believed that complaints about them had been made to the police – who, yet again, found nobody responsible. She was later forced to apologise for linking acts of vandalism to environmentalists.[7]

Logging machinery was often vandalised and burned in Tasmania's Southern Forests, and every time it happened Giddings' mentor Paul Lennon stormed into the Tasmanian Parliament demanding that the Greens immediately reveal what we knew about the incidents. At the time it was widely rumoured that the vandalism was the result of an internal dispute between logging contractors, but none would say so for fear of retribution. The reward for information leading to a conviction was never claimed. The logging industry was happy: the damage to the environment movement had been done, and the insurance industry paid out.[8]

During the time of these allegations the federal government was compensating the loggers in Tasmania. In my experience, no group of people has ever received more money from the public purse than the Tasmanian native forest logging industry. They were paid to come into the industry, paid to leave it, subsidised to re-enter it and compensated to leave again. They were subsidised to buy machinery and log trucks, and compensated when they sold them. The corrupt process to which the federal Liberal and Labor governments turned a blind eye was exposed during a Senate inquiry I instigated. But it continues to this day, with Tasmania's magnificent high-conservation-value native forests destroyed by subsidised native forest logging yet again, and the Liberal state government now in the High Court seeking to defend yet more draconian anti-forest-protest laws.

The use of intimidation through Strategic Litigation Against Public Participation (SLAPP) suits was a hugely stressful, expensive and time-consuming tactic against protesters opposed to the Gunns pulp mill, but it backfired dramatically when adverse corporate action destroyed Gunns itself. Nevertheless, having to 'lawyer up' to fight campaigns or defamation actions as governments look the other way is now commonplace.

Intimidation against anyone who donates money to environmental advocacy or Green politics is another weapon in the arsenal of the corporations and their Liberal and Labor apparatchiks. They oppose any independent commissions against corruption and nobble any that are established. They refuse to engage in serious donations reform, and keep their own donors hidden via donations to third parties such as the Free Enterprise Foundation[9] but have the temerity to attack anyone who acts legally and discloses donations. People who donate to a specific environmental project, perhaps buying a particular area of land, are tolerated, but not those who give money to raise awareness of government or corporate action destroying the environment or who back legal action against them. As a result, fundraising has become a core activity for a wide range of environmental groups and environmental law centres, restricting and detracting from their ability to do the work they are established to do.

Nothing infuriated the Liberal Party more than the $1.6 million donation by Australian philanthropist Graeme Wood in 2010 to help the Australian Greens win seats in that year's federal election. In spite of the millions donated to the Liberal and National parties over the years from corporate donors to secure Coalition seats, they could not stand it when, under the rules they refused to change, a generous and committed conservationist made a substantial donation to us.

The following year a woodchip mill in the east-coast town of Triabunna came up for sale. Gunns were selling the mill and there were two potential buyers: Aprin consortium, who sought to establish their own export woodchip operation, and Graeme Wood, who wanted to close it down. Bob Brown and I were in favour of the Wood bid because we had campaigned against the export woodchipping industry and advocated the closure of this mill for more than a quarter of a century. But from July until November 2011, senators Abetz and Brandis alleged that 'this case approaches the borders of corruption', arguing that we supported the closure of the mill purely as a favour to Graeme Wood, and that all our Senate questions and speeches opposing woodchipping had been purely expedient. It was a blatant lie.

The Liberal Party moved a motion referring us to the Privileges Committee to investigate us for contempt of the Senate, carrying the penalty of six months in jail or a huge fine. It was carried with the support of the Liberal, Labor and National Party senators. Senator Brandis was a member of the Privileges Committee but he refused to recuse himself, in spite of his statements alleging our guilt and the matter of procedural fairness. He eventually resigned when he recognised that he would be ultimately forced from the committee if the matter ended up in the High Court.

The committee reported in March 2012 that we had no case to answer. However, it had been a successful vexatious effort to defame us over the intervening four months and generate as much adverse publicity as possible. It also defamed Graeme Wood, a generous and decent person. The committee refused to award costs to us, arguing that we would not suffer substantial hardship in paying the costs of representation. For the Australian Greens it had long-term ramifications. The Liberals made it clear to all people who might want to support the Greens – for as long as political donations remain legal – that they risk having their name and reputation dragged through the mud for months by senators Abetz and Brandis.

Unless you have had your integrity and honesty impugned in such a baseless, public and profound way and faced months of uncertainty about the outcomes and the costs, you cannot imagine how hard it is to wake up every day and keep on doing your job – how hard it is not to become bitter about the ruthless and cowardly accusers who, when proven wrong, just shrug it off and do the same thing to someone else. The treatment of Gillian Triggs as president of the Human Rights Commission is another more recent example. But as difficult as it is for individuals and environment groups, the greater damage is to Australia's democracy and the integrity of our public institutions. How do you persuade good people to stand for public office when they risk personal denigration? How do you persuade people that the parliament and its processes have integrity when they can be misused in such a grossly unfair way?

The last Senate inquiry I instigated before I resigned was into tax evasion by big corporations, especially multinationals. It highlighted the fact that these corporations that make multibillion-dollar profits redirect them to jurisdictions overseas and pay no tax here in Australia. I wanted to demonstrate how they receive billions in subsidies and make large political donations to make sure this continues. They are on massive corporate welfare from the public purse paid for by governments slashing payments to the unemployed, single parents and pensioners so their corporate mates remain happy. This is corrupt.

In 2013 in New South Wales the Independent Commission Against Corruption (ICAC) exposed the corrupt relationships between government ministers and the coal and gas industries, showing that mining and extraction licences had been granted illegally. But the licences were not cancelled, and the farmers and communities concerned suffered and protested, only to have Premier Mike Baird legislate to have the farmers and environmentalists arrested, not the licence holders. As Australian Greens leader I moved for a national ICAC, a move not supported by the large political parties. You don't have to wonder why.

Other dirty tricks used to attack environmentalists and defeat conservation campaigns evolved over time. One such trick is to use an environmental argument to defeat the environmental outcome being sought. Using exaggerated claims of platypus deaths to prevent the restoration of Lake Pedder was the first; promoting native forest logging to make way for plantations as solutions to global warming, and talking up 'clean' coal or coal seam gas are merely the latest.

Rescuing stranded assets by attacking and undermining their successors (for example, defending coal by disparaging wind farms) was part and parcel of the Abbott government's attacks on the Renewable Energy Target, the Australian Renewable Energy Agency and the Clean Energy Finance Corporation. They used the public relations 'Coal is good for humanity' materials produced by PR firm Burson-Marsteller for the fossil fuel industry in the United States. And Tony Abbott and his Cabinet became their echo chamber to such an extent that when Australia hosted the G20 meeting in 2014, Joe Hockey set aside time for the Burson-Marsteller material to be showcased, and known sceptic Bjørn Lomborg was invited to the presentation. Later Australia suffered the insult of our government cutting back funding for science while trying to facilitate a home for Lomborg in one of our universities. Fortunately protests from academics and students alike destroyed their plans. Following the South Australian energy blackout in September 2016 Prime Minister Turnbull carried on the assault, attacking renewable energy and promoting gas regardless of the facts.

As a review of the electricity grid and the National Energy Market rules is undertaken, it is no surprise to watch big oil, coal and gas try to stop the necessary changes and impose new costs and charges or regulatory measures on individuals and communities who are trying to become 100 per cent powered by renewable energy. The weak low emissions target in the Finkel Review is a case in point. Deliberately lower than the US, UK and EU, it is a political fix designed to accommodate coal, but even it is a step too far for the Coalition.

We have even got to the point that when citizens prove in court that ministers and governments have failed to uphold the law, these ministers and governments retrospectively legislate to change it. The Federal Court's determination in the 2006 Wielangta case that the Regional Forest Agreement did not exempt loggers from protecting threatened species under Commonwealth law was a victory for all of us who had been campaigning against native forest logging, but the win was short-lived. The Commonwealth and Tasmanian Governments legislated in 2007 to make the meaning of the word 'protection' dependent on a decision of government, not actual evidence.

While in most aspects of life I agree with the adage that if there is a choice between a conspiracy and a stuff-up to explain a contentious situation, choose the stuff-up every time, I cannot endorse it in Australian politics when we have a disproportionate dependence on resource-based industries, a supermarket duopoly, only four major banks and four major accounting firms, and highly concentrated gambling and media ownership. They effectively determine how the country is run.

If we are to take back power from the corporations, and reinstate our democracy, that means electoral reform. We need to introduce proportional representation at every level of government. The big business lobby loves majority government, which they say is stable and delivers business certainty. But next time you see someone from the Liberal or Labor party or the Business Council of Australia on television telling the community to back any party that can win a majority in an election, ask: 'Stability and certainty for whom?' Not for the community, not for the environment, not for future generations, but for big business and their backroom deals.

Their worst nightmare occurs when no single party has all the power and decisions have to be made on the floor of the House; it means that backroom deals can come unstuck. It is why prime ministers rail against the Senate, where, without government majorities, scrutiny is applied. This is the basis for the longstanding and ruthless campaign by Liberal, Labor and big business against minority governments, especially those in which the Greens hold the balance of power. Regardless of the facts that the legislative and reformist credentials of those governments are better than those of governments commanding a majority – and I cite the Field and Rundle governments in Tasmania and the Gillard government nationally – the fear tactics continue unabated, fanned by the media dominated by Murdoch.

That is why I keep my *Conspiracy* sculpture in full view. It is a salient reminder of the challenges and costs of standing up for the public interest in Australia. It embodies all the tricks of the conspiracy trade. But right near it on the bookshelves are E. F. Schumacher's *Small Is Beautiful: Economics as if People Mattered* and *Good Work*, which is its powerful antidote:

> We must do what we conceive to be the right thing and not bother our heads or burden our souls with whether we're going to be successful. Because if we don't do the right thing, we'll be doing the wrong thing and we'll be just part of the disease and not a part of the cure.[10]

It is a statement of what those who would take power from the people fear most: the courage of people, communities everywhere and political parties like the Australian Greens who will not put up with these tricks, who defy them, shine a light on them, who won't be bought and will never, ever give up.

8

# Being a Woman in Politics

OBJECT: *The 1989 Labor–Green Accord document,*
*with doodles by Christine's son.*

I WAS LUCKY AS A CHILD to be surrounded by strong women. My mother went back to teaching when I went to school; all my teachers bar one were women. My mother's sister Barbara had a job as a stenographer in Hobart. When I went to boarding school, she would drive me home for weekends and tell stories of life in the office. The nuns at St Mary's College insisted that girls could do anything and would brook no excuses. When I went to university, five of us who had been taught by Betty Parsons went back to Wesley Vale Area School to have our photo taken with her. She was immensely proud that five country children, including three girls, and all from the same year group, had made it to university. At university I lived at an all-women's college, where I competed in the intercollege debating team and was elected president in my final year in 1973.

When I went out teaching, I had some terrific female role models, including vice-principal Noreen Stubbs and senior mistress Betty Paterson at Devonport High School. While teaching there, I took exception to the male staff drinking with local principals at the Devonport Gentlemen's Club instead of joining the rest of us for drinks at a local hotel on a Friday night. I couldn't believe that in 1975 there were still establishments that put a sign on the door saying 'No Ladies Beyond this Point'. It was my introduction to the ways of the 'boys' club'.

I had no doubt that women were equal to men and just as capable. My life choices up until the Wesley Vale campaign affirmed that equal capability. So life in politics came as a shock. I was convinced that I had to stand for election in 1989 to represent the opposition to the Wesley Vale pulp mill. Even though this was the worst time in my life to go into politics – I had two small boys at home – I felt I had no choice; I don't think I could have lived with myself if I had baulked at the final hurdle. Because you have to be away from home so much, there is never a perfect time for anyone – male or female – with children to go into politics but as long as women continue to identify as the primary carer, the burden of responsibility falls more heavily on them. When I stood for the Senate in 2004, my children were grown up, but my mother was ageing. The beginning and end of life are the times when women feel most needed, and most guilty and deprived if they are not there for those they love. Just when you are feeling that at last you can do things for yourself, you realise that it is not that simple. It boils down to this: if you thought too much about the logistics of going into politics as a woman, especially with children, you would probably never do it.

Whichever way you look at it, we have a political system designed when men governed wherever and whenever they chose, and women stayed home. For men parenting was secondary; for women being a parent was primary. Organisational work structures reflected that, and in politics not a great deal has changed. Female politicians bring their preschool children to Canberra for sitting weeks, but male politicians don't. The crunch comes when the children go to school. It is now the organisational structure more than the culture that makes being a mother in politics so difficult, and that is what needs to change. Is there a way to organise national politics that does not separate parents from their children? Finding an answer is critical to greater female participation in politics.

I chose to stand in Lyons because it was where my family's farm was and where the pulp mill would be built. It was also the electorate of Premier Robin Gray. Running in Lyons was regarded as a huge risk. During the campaign I received a phone call from Labor minister Graham Richardson, who in a panicked tone told me the polling showed that I would lose. He was, of course, worried about his reputation if I was defeated; if Labor were to win federal government the following year, Green preferences were crucial. If I had known what I now do about politics, I would have gone into a panic: Richardson would not have called me had the situation not been looking dire. But ignorance is bliss. On the basis of no evidence other than the number of signs I had in paddocks and the success of local meetings, I reassured him that things were on track for victory.

I knew nothing about what it meant to be in politics, little about Lyons and nothing of what it would mean in practice to represent it. Lyons was the geographically biggest electorate in Tasmania at that time, covering both the east and west coasts and extending as far south as Sorell and as far north as Latrobe; it took days to cover. I hadn't realised, and no one explained, that I would not only be away when the parliament sat but also in the electorate much of the time too. I came to love its dispersed communities and landscapes, but the travelling was hard work and being away from home never got easier.

My large group of community activists was heartening and supportive. These people are frequently women who are not in the full-time paid workforce and who have decided to fight for their community. Many others who support the cause have work commitments that preclude them from full-time campaigning, so the bulk of the effort is left to the women working from home. But while community activists might well have the brain, the capacity and the will to run a campaign, they usually have no money. They are often at home with their children and participate in the paid workforce part-time or not at all. They don't have the clothes, the transport, the childcare, the income to do what they need to do, but they find a way to do it anyway. They are the backbone of all Green movements, and I salute them.

Until the night of the election I had no idea what the result would be. We had no polling; there was no planning for the following day. But I won! We held an election-night party at the Argosy motel in East Devonport, and we were all ecstatic.

Although I knew my success would be monumental for my family, I didn't really think through what it meant. I had a community to serve, a pulp mill to stop, and a family with a husband and two little boys who were the centre of my life. Thomas was four years and nine months old and had started kindergarten at the beginning of the year, and James was weeks away from his third birthday. During the Wesley Vale campaign my husband Neville, who was teaching full-time, managed to help me look after the boys and keep the house ticking over. We had help from family and friends: Gaylene would arrive to look after the boys, cook, clean and iron. My parents and parents-in-law were always ready to help. I would drive into the farmyard, drop the boys and head off for interviews or meetings, always confident that the boys were being well looked after. But my election meant I was going to be away from home for quite a lot of the time. I really didn't know how I would manage.

I had to make permanent arrangements. We lived in Ulverstone on the north-west coast and the Tasmanian Parliament was a four-hour drive away. Parliament sat for three days at a time, requiring me to leave at 5.30 am on Tuesday mornings and get back in the middle of the night on Thursdays so I could be there when the boys woke up on Friday morning. My newly elected colleague Di Hollister and I travelled together and shared a flat next door to Bob Brown in Waterworks Road, Hobart.

Neville and I decided that he should take leave from the Education Department so we would have one parent at home full-time. Only those who have made this difficult decision, especially in this age of job insecurity, really understand how incredibly difficult it is. For Neville to take leave from teaching was hard and lonely, especially at a time when being a 'stay at home dad' was practically unheard of. For me it was gut wrenching to walk out of the house and leave my little boys behind for days on end, only to face a male-dominated, testosterone-charged parliament seething with resentment against me.

Before a woman becomes a parliamentarian, she is usually regarded as a good person, a community activist, a professional person, a teacher, a good mother, a role model even – and the day after, she ceases being a person. I had won 'women in leadership' awards, but the day after the election, in the eyes of many people, I became a self-serving scumbag, one of those pollies on the take at the community's expense. Although nothing about me had changed, everything had. People looked at me differently.

If as a female MP you assimilate and become co-opted into being one of the boys and clearly have no intention of changing anything, then you are fine, but criticism and personal attacks become constant if you are one who rocks the boat. I dealt with the barbs by deciding to ignore criticism from those whose opinions I generally did not respect but listen to those I did. It is a means of staying sane without becoming arrogant.

Friends really matter. I had a wonderful circle of female friends and confidantes outside politics, including my fellow Greens candidate Di Masters. Those women kept me grounded, supported and nurtured. They had known me well enough and for long enough to know when and how to help me. They looked out for me as a person, not as a parliamentarian.

Although Neville and I tried to make sure that the boys didn't suffer, I inevitably missed many of their special days in primary school. This was a time when the idea of personal leave from parliament to attend a school function was unheard of, let alone taking time off to have a baby. The fact that women can now take maternity leave from parliament is a big indicator of how far things have progressed for women in the past twenty-five years. But at the time we Greens held the balance of power: no one could afford to be away for any vote. The Labor government and the Greens had eighteen members between us, and the Liberals had seventeen. On one occasion numbers were so tight that the Liberal Party brought one of its members from his hospital bed to be present for a vote.

I remember the emotional turmoil intensely. My only sister, Gaylene, aged thirty-eight, died suddenly of a pulmonary embolism in August 1990. When I heard the news, I was in Hobart, about to attend a tense meeting with the Labor Party because of my private members' bill to save some schools Labor had announced it would close. I drove by myself to the north-west coast, in tears all the way. The following days remain a blur of funeral arrangements, the funeral itself, my parents, Gaylene's husband and daughters, the questions my boys kept asking. It was a deluge of shock and grief.

I wanted a pair, as the parliament was to sit a few days later. This is an informal arrangement between the government and Opposition parties when one MP agrees to abstain from voting while a member of the other party needs to be absent from the House due to special circumstances. The Liberals said they would not give pairs to Independents, except in exceptional circumstances. But in a discussion between Bob Brown and the Labor Party it was decided not to ask for the pair as it was thought Robin Gray would not honour it and would bring the government down. The choice between being with family when we really needed to be together and risking the government falling for the lack of my vote was about the hardest I could have been asked to make. So lacking in trust, so mean-spirited was that parliament that four days after the funeral I was back.

And still I was being torn in two. When James in kindergarten was chosen to play Christopher Robin in the Christmas concert, I helped him practise his lines for A. A. Milne's poem *Vespers* at home. But I wasn't there to see the performance, though everyone said James was a perfect Christopher Robin. His teacher gave me a photo. He doesn't remember all this, but I have never forgotten. On another occasion Thomas came home very excited about a day when mothers were invited to school. He was so disappointed that I couldn't come. His grandmother Betty Milne went with him, and they had a wonderful day together. There is a photo of the occasion in his Grade One presentation book. And during the 1992 election campaign, when he was five, James was hospitalised in Hobart with osteomyelitis. I had no choice but to leave him by day and return to the hospital at night. I had to be bright and cheery at campaign meetings and functions when I was worried sick and they were the last places I wanted to be.

All this makes me sad to think about even now: maternal guilt, let alone Catholic guilt, never leaves you. I rationalised all this, as mothers in my situation often do, by hoping that when my boys grew up they would think that the sacrifices we had all made were worth it; that together we had done our bit to save Pa's farm and sustain an environment locally and globally in which it was still possible to be dazzled by nature and in which they and their generation could breathe easily, enjoy clean water and uncontaminated food, and look forward to living in a safe climate.

In truth I was the one who missed out. The boys were loved and cared for. They developed a close relationship with all their grandparents and became accustomed to meeting lots of different people and enjoying their company. They rode donkeys up at Seaview Farm; they were with me on the day that the Douglas-Apsley National Park was declared. They were regulars in the parliament and at electorate meetings from one end of Tasmania to the other. They learned great life skills. They saw gender equality in action and were part of history being made. Recently I found a copy of the Labor–Green Accord among my papers. It has a child's writing and doodles through it; I must have given it to one of the boys to draw on to keep him amused at a meeting.

It sums up the highs and the lows of my political life in those years: Wesley Vale saved; the Tasmanian Wilderness World Heritage Area massively expanded; schools saved; and a child seeking the attention of a distracted mother. This is the same child, my son Thomas, who now credits a number of his professional skills to the years he spent observing and learning to communicate with people as he accompanied me in the electorate.

In part the knowledge that I had missed out on so much helped make my decision to retire in 2015 a whole lot easier. James and his wife, Shannon, announced they were having a baby due in July 2015. All the feelings of those years bubbled up and I knew I didn't want to miss out the second time around. I wanted to be there, as a 'present' grandmother.

I tell these stories to demonstrate the turmoil of a life with a public and a private face. When you see parliamentarians on television or in the media generally, you can only know how much they choose to reveal. Everyone in politics makes decisions about how much of themselves they show to the public. You never know what is going on inside, and if you ask in a quiet moment you may be shocked at the burdens they are carrying.

Losing your seat in an election is a difficult time for any parliamentarian as the sense of rejection at the hands of the people you have tried hard to represent is very personal, public and intense. Nothing prepares you for it and it is often impossible to return to the profession you once enjoyed, especially if the professional skills required have changed in the time you have been in politics. Your staff lose their jobs, your re-elected former colleagues continue with their careers, your friends are getting on with their lives and you are left to work out who you really are and what you want to do after years of being defined by the job.

For me in 1998 it felt very personal and spiteful, coming as it did on the back of a change to the electoral system designed for that very purpose. I struggled to readjust and my father died during this period.

And in that milieu, my marriage ended.

I met my partner, Gary Corr, when he was doing pro bono legal work relating to protection of the Tarkine for Senator Bob Brown. In 2014 he became gravely ill in Sydney with septicaemia and a massive liver infection. He was rushed to hospital in a high-dependence ambulance, and when we arrived doors were flung open, trolleys raced, staff crowded and questions flew. As he was being assessed in Emergency, I was standing by the bed in a state of shock. The next thing I knew, one of the hospital's public-relations staff approached me to ask what I wanted to say to any questions from the media. Another patient or a visitor in Emergency had already taken a photo on a mobile phone, and the word was out. I asked that it be confirmed that it was my partner, that I was there and nothing else. It was touch and go whether Gary would survive or withstand the surgery. This was the week leading into the horrific Abbott first Budget. I was under enormous pressure when the government released its slash-and-burn Budget, as the Greens were still in balance of power. I knew that whatever we supported would get through and what we didn't would be scrapped.

Gary came out of intensive care and returned to the ward on the Sunday night, and I flew to Canberra the following morning to face a huge parliamentary week. He gradually recovered, thanks to the extraordinary skill and care of Dr Koroush Haghighi and his team at Prince of Wales hospital in Sydney, to whom I will be forever grateful. I was emotionally and physically exhausted. Between media interviews and meetings I was on the phone to the hospital.

I had to prepare the Greens response to the Budget and deliver it on Thursday evening before flying back to Sydney on Friday morning. Emma Bull, my chief of staff, and the staff team worked themselves to the bone to look after me and to get the job done. Rachel Siewert redoubled her efforts in the Senate chamber and Richard Di Natale was a godsend. As a doctor he helped me understand what was going on with Gary's illness. I prepared and delivered a Budget Reply speech of which I was proud.

I could have gone public with what was going on, but I didn't. I couldn't have coped with people engaging with me on a personal level. As a woman I had always dealt with public life in compartments, behind a shield. The terms of engagement with people in the parliamentary workplace were friendly, civil but formal. If that shield were pierced, I would have been an emotional wreck and genuinely unable to do my job. But the second reason I didn't talk about Gary's illness in that Budget week of 2014 was that critics of the Greens would have said it was a cynical attempt to avoid scrutiny in a particularly difficult political situation. I didn't want to give them the opportunity.

From day one of my political career in 1989, I had decided not to talk about the trials of being a young mother in parliament. It had huge personal interest value for the media and would have been an electorally popular thing to do, but I knew enough to be sure that allowing your children to be used to positively reinforce your image is not a good decision. When I see people in politics with their children reinforcing family values or softening their image or highlighting women in politics or similar, I worry for the children. If anything goes wrong for them, they risk having it spread across the nation's media. In my experience if you keep your family life private, the media respect that choice. If you don't, then you are all fair game.

Besides, in 1989 there were very few women in Tasmanian politics. Women were expected to fit into the system, not the system to adapt to a different way of seeing or being in the world. Many MPs and members of the community thought that women should be home looking after the children and cooking the dinner and not 'abandoning' their families. Any reference to the difficulties of public life would have resulted in being told to 'Go home then'.

It was bad enough being constantly told to smile more by male parliamentarians and journalists. This implies your role is to be pleasant and decorative; it is unattractive for women to be serious. Looking too serious was a constant criticism during my whole career. When the charge of excessive seriousness was levelled at Hillary Clinton there was uproar, with recognition that accomplished women in their own right should not be reduced to pretty faces. People asked whether anyone had told Donald Trump to smile more. I thought: at last!

To make way in politics in the 1990s you had to be strong, forthright and able to withstand the barbs. Bullies see vulnerability a mile off, and any discomfort or emotion would have been considered signs of weakness. Bob Hawke could cry and be a hero for showing his feminine side, but if a woman had done the same thing she would have been considered not up to the job. Fortunately I had learned at boarding school many years before how to hide emotion. I would never let the nuns see what I was really feeling, and I showed nothing to those bullies in the Tasmanian Parliament. The Senate was a cakewalk by comparison.

The Tasmanian Parliament in 1989 was an incredibly hostile, angry, vengeful, white-male-dominated place. The Liberals were angry that they had lost government and that Labor with thirteen seats had displaced them because of an agreement with the Greens. Abuse was hurled across the chamber at Di Hollister and me; we were called 'political sluts' 'in bed with the Labor Party' and 'political prostitutes', among other choice expressions. I was horrified. That kind of language and behaviour would never have been tolerated at home, in the farming community or in the high schools where I had taught, but in the parliament they were fine, it seemed.

I was mocked for suggesting that on-farm tourism would be a good idea to supplement farm income. 'Mrs Milne and her jam-led recovery' resounded around the chamber. When I spoke strongly against a matter in debate, Leader of the Opposition Michael Field responded, 'Mrs Milne can stamp her feet all she likes ...' On it went, week in and week out.

There were no facilities for families in the Tasmanian Parliament in 1989. If your children came to the parliament, the public areas or your tiny office were the only available places for them to go. I argued for a spouse and family room with a lounge suite, a television set, a fridge and tea- and coffee-making facilities. It was eventually provided, but a few years after I left it was disbanded. I also worked to get the sitting hours changed to be more family-friendly, and that is a lasting legacy.

Being thoroughly professional, informed and across the issues engenders respect and makes it harder for the men to undermine you, despite all their insults. They are okay with women they regard as feminine and soft or who are ineffectual, but they are personally challenged by a woman who is their match or better. They cannot stand a woman who stands up to them. Like the bright girl in the class, she must be brought down a peg or two.[1]

The role of celebrity in politics is to bring women down a peg or two. Celebrity affects women in politics much more than men. For the most part, serious, respected female players are sidelined in favour of the vacuous, or those prepared to play at being vacuous, while serious respected men are still centre stage. It is disastrous not only for women in politics but also for women in the media, and especially for older women.

I made my career about the issues, not about me. I didn't want to get on *Dancing with the Stars* or breakfast TV talking about my children or my relationships or my home or my make-up simply because that is what people now want to know. If I had to have a makeover to be featured in women's magazines, I was better off not being there. My media and communications teams tried hard. They argued that as leader, if I wanted to get more 'soft' media coverage, I had to give more of myself and my family and relationships. Whenever I gave in and agreed to put my toe in the water, I found it highly uncomfortable, even stressful. I would rather write and deliver several Budget Reply speeches than be on Annabel Crabb's *Kitchen*

*Cabinet* again, despite her efforts to make me feel at ease. But people liked the program for all the reasons I didn't; it was about me as a person and not me as the flagbearer of an idea.

Having spent decades in politics keeping my personal and professional lives quite separate and maintaining a strict focus on the issues so as to be respected and effective, why would I want to sacrifice my last vestige of privacy? I had always remembered Margaret Whitlam saying that she never wanted to be Gough's handbag, and she wasn't. Why would I expose my family by making them political props?

Over the years I noticed that I am not alone in this. Women in politics already personify hard work or they wouldn't be there, and diversity by virtue of their gender. They don't need to be framed by a partner and children to be multidimensional. Men on the other hand soften and broaden their image by appearing with their families. If wives, husbands, children or partners want the publicity and that works out well, that's fine. But for many women in politics their sense of self doesn't require framing with a partner and children. Their partners and children don't need or want it either. Women's equality will be enhanced when we see and judge parliamentarians as individuals and not as a family package.

The questions asked of a female politician about her partner are vastly more offensive than those asked of her male counterpart. Shock jock Howard Sattler put to Prime Minister Gillard on radio that her partner Tim Mathieson was a closet gay. Can you imagine any shock jock putting a question like that to any male prime minister about his wife or partner?

I am frustrated that as more women are being elected to politics after decades of campaigns for equal representation and equal rights, what they have to say is still deemed to be less wise or important than the words of men. Older men – especially older white men – are respected as wise elders in society and in the parliament. They are the 'fathers' of the Senate or the House of Representatives. It is a complete joke when you listen to a lot of what they say. So many represent an era of white male privilege, social injustice and ecological destruction, whereas older women who have fought that privilege all their lives are regarded as old and past it, and should get out of the way.

If we as women abandon the substance of what we have to say for the sake of popularity and profile, there will be no drivers for change in parliaments. If we fail to stop the slide into Hollywood, we will see women elected to parliament but we will not see advances on common decency, on addressing women's rights, family violence, global warming, the environment, inequality, pay parity, marginalisation, housing, superannuation gaps, childcare, overseas aid – and the list goes on. Power with purpose is what women want, and celebrity careers undermine that.

Being elected is the start of the journey, not the destination. Frankly, the grind and stress are not worth it if being a parliamentarian is all you aspire to achieve. In the early 1990s Lara Giddings was the youngest woman ever elected to parliament in Tasmania. In her inaugural speech she said that all she had ever wanted to be was a member of parliament and now she was. She voted to reduce the numbers in the parliament, which saw many women, including her, lose their seats. She went on to become premier of Tasmania, but to deliver what was never clear. In the later years of her career she took a stand for voluntary euthanasia, and that stand for something she believed in will be the policy reform campaign for which she will be best remembered as a parliamentarian.

Compare the treatment of Australian women in politics with the treatment of Hillary Clinton or Elizabeth Warren in the USA, or German chancellor Angela Merkel. In Australia looks, clothes and age are given much more attention and therefore are seen to matter more than intelligence or ideas. As Julie Bishop said about Julia Gillard in 2007, 'I don't think it's necessary to get dressed up in designer clothing and borrow clothing and make-up to grace the cover of magazines. You're not a celebrity, you're an elected representative, you're a Member of Parliament. You're not Hollywood and I think that when people overstep that line they miss the whole point of that public role.'[2] What a difference a decade – and being in office – makes. Julie Bishop has now become Hollywood. Her public role as foreign minister is now overshadowed by her Armani suits, $30,000 ball gown and role as an A-lister in corporate marquees. I have no doubt she would say that her higher profile gives her more influence, but the question remains: influence to do what?

It is said that if only we had equal representation of women in parliament, politics would be better and kinder. I support equal representation because it is fair that half the population secures half the seats. But women – even those in business and politics who have made it against the odds – are not necessarily feminists or role models for the advancement of women's rights or a better, kinder world. This is because they are bound by the same party lines as their male counterparts. Julie Bishop and Bronwyn Bishop, Fiona Nash and Connie Fierravanti-Wells, Julia Gillard and Tanya Plibersek all voted to cut financial support for single parents just as readily as their male counterparts. They will defend locking people in camps in Nauru and Manus Island. When it comes to support for the Adani coalmine, the only point of difference is whether it should be subsidised.

This is why I was less enthusiastic than most about Prime Minister Julia Gillard's misogyny speech. Like women everywhere I was pleased that she had ripped into Opposition leader Tony Abbott. I too had been disgusted by the 'Ditch the Witch' and 'Bob Brown's Bitch' signs and the fact that Bronwyn Bishop, Sophie Mirabella and Fiona Nash were happy to stand under the signs and say nothing.

But for all her talk about supporting women, Gillard had, on the morning of the misogyny speech, cut financial support for single parents. There was cognitive dissonance between what she was saying to Tony Abbott and the women of the world and what she had just voted to do. Entrenching the marginalisation of women is not the action of a feminist prime minister. Nor was her decision to extend the Northern Territory intervention and deny Aboriginal women control over their own incomes. Nor was her decision to abandon guardianship of unaccompanied refugee children so that they could be sent to offshore detention.

I was, and remain, proud that Australia has had a woman as prime minister. Julia Gillard will be held up as a role model for girls around the country for a long time, and so she should be. Her dignity in the face of extraordinary insult and her consultative leadership style are long-lasting legacies. But her prime ministership was a lost opportunity for the rights of women, refugees, Aboriginal people and the LGBTIQ community.

~

THE PROCESS OF FIGHTING TO open up the two-party system to accommodate diversity, equal female representation and multi-party politics, to cement commensurate institutional structures as a norm, continues. It is the job of every Green parliamentarian to keep it up, no matter how hard – but for women it is hardest of all.

When asked by women for advice about whether they should go into politics, I say: regard it as one huge opportunity in a life of activism, but only do it if you have a clear idea of the changes you want to make. What is the point of being there if you are only making up the numbers, or for the salary or the perks? Consider the logistics of where you live and where the parliament is located and make appropriate choices. Don't do it as simply a career choice, because it is not worth the sacrifices if it is only about your own advancement. A very clear and compelling purpose makes being an MP not only worthwhile but incredibly fulfilling. You will have done what you knew in your heart you ought to do.

Remembering that there is never the perfect time, consider whether it is the right time in your life, and if you have options to consider it at a better time, then do that. As so many women have said, you can have it all but not all at the same time. If you don't have other options, it depends on how important the issue is to you given the disruption you will experience. Consider a timeframe: how many years do you want to devote to it? Even if you don't stick to it, it is good to have a point at which to reflect.

Think about how much of your private life you are prepared to give to the public. In this age of social media and celebrity perhaps this seems a dated idea, but if you don't think about this and plan for it, your personal relationships will be compromised. Discuss with those closest to you the parameters of their involvement. If they don't want to be involved, dress in white or have their history of addiction or illness discussed on television, you need to know where to draw the lines.

Ask for help with the support you need to enable you to stand for election or to do the job. If it is childcare, housework, gardening, shopping, time to visit ageing relatives, transport or money, then ask those who you are representing in the party or those who ask you to stand how to meet those needs. If that is not forthcoming, go back to the question: What ought one to do? You might still stand, but you will do so with greater insight and resilience.

Finally, believe in yourself. Women are the equal of men anywhere, any time. As the nuns used to say, 'Girls can do anything.' Never forget it. It is an enormous privilege to have the opportunity to change the world from a position of elected public office. To create or grasp that opportunity for yourself and the women who come after you and to use it should not be dismissed lightly. Don't give up on the idea because it seems too hard. Try to find a way to make it work for you.

And when you get there, never forget the women at the gates. It will be from standing on your shoulders that they scale the wall.

# 9

# In Praise of Knitted Berets

OBJECT: *A Knitting Nannas Against Gas beret,
given to Christine in June 2013 by Jenny Leunig.*

I LOVE THE KNITTING NANNAS. They are gutsy women of the land, the backbone of rural life. Those of us who were brought up in the country, who married into the country or who chose it, know them already. They are our sisters, neighbours, friends and relatives. They are our forebears and our daughters. We share the sensations and the memories of sight, smell, taste, touch and sound that centre us and take us back. In our mind's eye we can still see the wind making waves in the wheat, hear the cows' gentle rhythmic chewing, taste the dust and feel the companionship of an old dog on the porch.

But another element connected to country is just as deeply ingrained: women's experience of country. It is sharing and loving all that is familiar on the land outside the farmhouse while at the same time looking after the inside, the home and the family. This means making a home, finding ways to make ends meet, feeding and clothing the family, saving water, getting the kids to school. It also means putting on a brave face, dressing up to go to town or church, all the while worrying and weeping silently about the state of the family finances. The men work outside as the milk or beef prices collapse or the harvest fails, but it is the women who watch the bills mount and the overdraft inch perilously close to its limit and keep this knowledge to themselves, protecting everyone else for as long as possible. The unassuming and selfless strength of women on farms and in rural communities has enabled life on the land in Australia to endure.

This strength is intergenerational. In my childhood, life 'inside' meant the old copper in the laundry, the sewing machine and remnants of cloth, odd balls of wool and bottles of buttons. It was books of handwritten recipes and the inviting smell of cakes in the oven. It was the rarely used 'good' cups, saucers and plates in the buffet and the fire in the kitchen. It was the farm books, literally lined exercise books accompanied by the accounts, punctured by a wire stake. And while the modern kitchen, laundry, home office, computer and online purchasing have replaced the old technology, the tasks remain the same.

Women work to protect these things and their families, and the Knitting Nannas are part of that long, long activist tradition. They describe themselves as a group of women in their prime of life, who appear to be mild, middle class and conservative, and who make their presence felt in the war against unconventional gas mining, other forms of non-sustainable energy and rapacious greed. They use the common stereotype of the sweet little old lady to lull their opponents into a false sense of security. The idea of the Knitting Nannas is that of the iron fist in the soft fluffy yellow glove – there aren't many scarier things than a forthright woman in her prime.

Most people have heard about the women knitting while watching guillotine beheadings during the French Revolution, but I didn't know that they gathered and knitted there as an act of defiance against the past and emerging regimes. Among the things they knitted were red caps: symbols of freedom and citizenship. Having been initially heralded as Mothers of the Nation for their protests against the shortages and high prices of food, their rowdy and unpredictable behaviour made them a threat to the new revolutionary regime, so they were denied the right to political assembly. They gathered together and knitted these caps to make their point.

The Knitting Nannas, denied the right to say 'no' to coal seam gas on their land and in their community, defiantly but legally and peacefully knit in their own Place of the Revolution, outside offices of corporations and members of parliament and Parliament House itself.

The yellow and black knitted beret, the product of their own labour, is their badge of freedom and citizenship. I love the fact that the berets are knitted by hand, a skill passed down through generations of women to express love of family and community, combined with a sense of place and defiance of the forces that seek to undermine it.

I first met the Knitting Nannas Against Gas (KNAGs) in Lismore, in the Northern Rivers area of New South Wales, in April 2013. The previous year a group of local people concerned about coal seam gas had distributed leaflets of invitation to a public meeting at which Greens MP Jeremy Buckingham and others would be speaking on the threats posed by the industry. They expected that between fifty and 200 people might turn up: 800 did.

Jenny Leunig, a sixty-eight-year-old grandmother, was one. Until then she had not taken too much notice of politics, believing that no government would permit the development of industries that would be seriously bad for people or the environment. She was shocked by what she heard and so, when another meeting was arranged a fortnight later to organise people into action groups, she attended. As with many women, she thought she had little expertise to offer so did not volunteer for media, photography, IT or logistics. But she had the time to sit peacefully as part of a rally or sit-in, so decided to join the non-violent direct action group.

This group met over several months with little progress beyond talking about what might be possible. Two women decided to start things off by going and observing what was happening first hand, and they took their knitting. These women, Clare Twomey and Lindy Scott, had the idea of making knitted berets part of the protest, from a hero beanie knitted for Davey Bob Ramsey, the first local to be arrested for locking on to machinery at Shannon Brook Ponds, and shoved into his hands after his 'not guilty' verdict. Jenny designed the berets – yellow and black to express solidarity with the Lock the Gate movement against inappropriate mining and in support of sustainable solutions for food and energy production – and has subsequently knitted hundreds. The Nannas knitted not only berets but also chain sleeves to stop blisters for protesters locked on to machinery or gates, long lengths of knitting to prevent machinery access through gates and fences, and yellow and black triangles and cushions to support protesters forced to sit for long periods of time.

For three years, every Thursday, they would pull up portable chairs outside the office of New South Wales National Party MP for Lismore Thomas George and knit. They chatted to passers-by about the danger coal seam gas posed to land, groundwater and rivers. I was delighted to be there as leader of the Australian Greens to join with them and to don the beret. I offered them the Australian Greens' support in the federal parliament and urged them to never, ever give up. They didn't.

The movement grew rapidly, as it empowered older women to come together to become actively involved in standing up for protection of the environment everywhere and against crony capitalism, corruption, cruelty and environmental destruction. It is fantastic to see genuine participatory democracy in action. Soon there were Knitting Nannas groups all around the country. When one of the Knitting Nannas from Lismore went back to the United Kingdom to visit friends and relatives, she took the documentary film *Gasland* with her and the story of the Knitting Nannas. The idea took off, and now there are Knitting Nanna loops in England.

I joined the Knitting Nannas in Toolangi, Victoria, as they knitted for the Great Forest National Park and against the logging of high-conservation native forests in the Victorian Southern Highlands. I was with them in Hobart's City Mall as they knitted to save refugees from the cruelty of Australia's offshore detention camps on Manus Island and Nauru. I stood with them when they joined a group of about sixty anti-coal seam gas protesters who, when locked out of Parliament House, staged a four-hour sit-in at the front door in June 2013. They were there to support independent Tony Windsor, Senator Larissa Waters and the Greens in securing a 'water trigger' for coal seam gas projects and to give landholders the right to prevent mining companies from entering their land. The water trigger protest was successful, but the *Landholders Right to Refuse (Gas and Coal) Bill 2013* to ban mining companies entering land was defeated by the combined votes of the Liberal, National and Labor parties.

My fellow Australian Greens senator Larissa Waters and I were given a warm reception at the sit-in. Jenny Leunig was there with a bag of berets to give to parliamentarians who had the courage to oppose coal seam gas. She had recently had a hip operation, and so, rather than stay home, she had a T-shirt especially made, with 'No to CSG, Yes to Clean Water' on the front and 'Handle with Care, New Hip Installed' on the back. Larissa and I were delighted when Jenny presented us both with KNAGs berets she had knitted. We wore them proudly right there and then at the front door of the Australian Federal Parliament.

When I became leader of the Australian Greens in April 2012, one of my top priorities was reinvigorating the party's conversation with rural and regional Australia. From the Wesley Vale campaign onward it had been obvious to me that people who live on the land have a great deal in common with the Australian Greens. With the Clean Energy Package to come into effect two months later, the climate crisis and its effects on rural Australia hitting hard and the scare campaign of Tony Abbott in full swing, that conversation needed to be had sooner rather than later.

Wherever I went in Australia as the newly elected leader, I found that people were concerned about sustaining the land and river systems on which our food production is based, about coal and gas mining on productive agricultural land, about serious breaches of biosecurity and the spread of invasive species, and about promoting Australian-grown and made products. They were worried about the extent to which big agricultural corporations, the supermarket duopoly and the agrochemical industry had taken over the politics of the agricultural and horticultural sectors, dividing and ruling food producers. They loathed the fact that the Liberal, National and Labor parties were in the pockets of the coal and gas industries. I was not surprised, given that Mark Vaile, a former leader of the National Party and deputy prime minister of Australia, became chairman of Whitehaven Coal, operating one of the largest open-cut coalmines in Australia.

Farmers protested long and hard against the Whitehaven mine and were supported by people from all around Australia. We Greens raised their issues in both the New South Wales and federal parliaments, but to no avail. A blockade was mounted to try to stop the mine and to save the Leard State Forest, the biggest remnant of natural bushland on the almost entirely cleared Liverpool Plains.

When I went to the blockade with New South Wales Greens MP Jeremy Buckingham to thank people for taking a stand to protect the climate and our biodiversity, I had the privilege of sitting and talking with nonagenarian Bill Ryan, who was later arrested together with more than a hundred other protesters. When he was arrested, he said, 'I'm now 92 years of age and I was a veteran of the second world war. I served in the Kokoda campaign in New Britain. I thought what we were fighting for there was proper democracy. But I've learned that was not the situation. The government doesn't listen to the people, and this mine is a good example. There were over 300 submissions against the mine, and one submission for it. But it was approved. [...] Something is wrong. We're faced with a catastrophe. I owe it to my grandchildren, and I owe it to all children. I was willing to put my life on the line in the second world war, so putting my body on the line here is a small inconvenience.'[1]

He was right. Liberal and Labor state and federal governments permitted the coalmine in spite of glaring inadequacies in the offsets Whitehaven Coal had proposed. Offsetting allows developers to compensate for what they are bulldozing by protecting areas supposedly containing the same species of vegetation and habitat that they are clearing. Any analysis will show that it is a developer's scam and a biodiversity disaster.[2] Overwhelming evidence was presented that showed the critically endangered white box woodland was being offset with stringybark, which would not provide habitat for several nationally threatened species.

Whitehaven was permitted to purchase additional property to supposedly meet its offset obligations, and the mine proceeded. Federal Minister for Industry and Science the Hon. Ian Macfarlane MP, representing Prime Minister Tony Abbott, officially opened the mine in September 2015. Whitehaven laughed all the way to the bank. Miners around Australia took note that the *Environmental Protection and Biodiversity Conservation Act*'s teeth were rotten. The Leard forest has now been bulldozed for coal, even though it was home to 396 native species, thirty-one of which are threatened, including the barking owl and the koala. The critically endangered white box gum grassy woodland has been cut down to 0.1 per cent of its original range.

In spite of what farmers had been told about environmentalists being their enemies, I was determined to demonstrate to them that I wanted to protect the land and water for future generations as much as they did. Neither farmers nor the Greens want it sold off to foreign governments via wholly owned subsidiary corporations. To this day I am frustrated by the failure of governments to recognise the wisdom of environmentalist Lester Brown. He has written that food is the new oil, arguing that as the world warms and food crops fail because of floods and droughts and fires, land and water constitute the new gold. Just as the race for oil has led to conflict in so many parts of the world, so the race for control of food-producing land and water in an age of global warming will be equally hard fought.

In 2008–09 there was a world food crisis caused by global warming. Grain crops failed because of drought and fire in the breadbaskets of Europe, Australia and the USA. Some countries including Vietnam and Brazil responded by banning the export of grain crops such as rice and wheat. The shortages sent the price of bread in the Middle East soaring; this was one of the triggers of the Arab Spring. The first public rebellion was in Tunisia, and it began with people marching carrying baguettes.

It was a wake-up call on global warming's impact on food production and political stability worldwide. China, Saudi Arabia, Qatar, South Korea and several other countries realised that no matter how much money they had, in future they might not be able to buy food on the open market if countries defied World Trade Organization rules and banned the export of grain. So they began land grabbing. Government-owned corporations started buying huge areas of agricultural land and water licences around the world with the specific aim of trading in world markets when times were good but sending the food directly back to their own countries when grain was in short supply. This is not trade as we have known it; rather, it is outsourcing food production. It has even reached the stage where Pakistan advertised land for sale with a security force to protect it. Conflict is a few extreme weather events away. Such a policy of selling land to foreign governments also leads to vertical integration; local workers lose out as the new owners bring in workers under specific visa categories.

Responding to this new phenomenon, I instigated a Senate inquiry into foreign ownership of agricultural land in Australia. The evidence given by a Qatar government-owned corporation was compelling. But even when the representatives of Hassad

Foods – having spent more than $100 million buying agricultural land along the eastern seaboard – admitted in 2011 that the purchases had been made to secure a food supply for Qatar, the Labor government was not persuaded to change the rules. Already one-third of Western Australia's water licences are owned by foreign interests; no one knows how much land is owned by foreign corporations as the rules governing the information required by the Foreign Investment Review Board are weak. Several times in the Senate I tried, with the support of Nick Xenophon, to secure support for a private member's bill to severely restrict the sale of land, but every time it failed as the Liberal, National and Labor parties denigrated the attempt as xenophobic. The failure of the Liberal, National and Labor parties to recognise global warming as a game changer for food security and their refusal to put the lens of climate-change impact over foreign policy and Australia's engagement with the world is a big mistake. Furthermore, at a purely practical level, once water is privatised and land sold, it is hard to buy it back, even when you need to do so to save ecosystems. The fate of the Murray River is proof of that.

But I didn't only want to talk to farmers about keeping the land in Australian hands; I also wanted to discuss ideas for keeping people on farms and maintaining the viability of rural communities. This meant talking to them about the potential of renewable energy to become another 'crop' in their rotation, and about changes a warming world would bring. Some crops and stocking rates that they had maintained for generations would no longer be viable because of changed weather conditions, but others might be. Changing varieties, anticipating the spread of disease and pests, and reducing stocking rates were needed. Soil carbon had been sold as a climate-mitigating money-spinner. I wanted to tell them that it wasn't going to be a silver bullet but nevertheless building carbon in the soil was not only good for the soil but would also improve water retention as rain became more unpredictable.

I also wanted to sell the financial and ecological benefits of the Greens' Carbon Farming Initiative. By pursuing landscape-scale ecosystem restoration and carbon storage that linked reduction of greenhouse gas emissions to improving the degraded state of the natural world, farmers would earn money and improve their land at the same time. I wanted to let farmers know how they could benefit without the ineffectual planting of monocultures characteristic of Managed Investment Schemes. I wanted to reassure them that any projects that caused adverse impacts on water availability, biodiversity or land access for agricultural production would be on a Negative List.[3]

It was a well-thought-out package, and the Liberal and National parties condemned it publicly and relentlessly. But, after all their objections, when the vote was put to the Senate, they didn't vote against it and let it pass on the voices. They knew it was good for rural Australia. Once in government the only part of the Clean Energy Package that they wanted to keep was the Carbon Farming Initiative. They then debased it and morphed it into their Emission Reduction Fund, the mainstay of the failed Direct Action policy.[4]

Going out to the bush has done as I hoped it would: opened doors to new conversations and new options. It has reduced the hostility that was often there before. Local action groups such as Knitting Nannas and the Lock the Gate movement are growing, and they recognise the role played by the Greens in helping protect the interests of rural communities.

The Greens are winning seats in rural councils and state rural electorates across the country. Even the National Farmers' Federation in late 2016 accepted that global warming is real, and a new organisation, Farmers for the Climate, has formed. Building an alliance for climate action and environmental protection with people who live outside the cities is happening. There is a move away from the policy platform of the large political parties and their corporate donors of 'dig it up, cut it down, ship it away, if it moves shoot it and if it doesn't build a road into it'. Other options are now being explored and implemented, but it is a slow process.

Years before I went into the Senate, I learned that when it comes to rural Australia, it is not environmental policies that prevent people voting Green but social and economic policies. Over cups of tea at kitchen tables across the country, after amicably discussing climate change and coal seam gas or trade agreements or ownership of agricultural land or invasive species, people would say to me, 'Why don't you just stick to the environment? Then we could vote for you. Why do you want gay law reform and marriage equality and drug law reform? Why do you argue for more funding to public schools and less for private schools?'

But just as views about farming change as one generation replaces another, so too do social views. Marriage equality is now supported in rural Australia, although life for young LGBTIQ people in the bush can still be very hard. The community and the police have realised that the law-and-order-focused 'war on drugs' has failed and that treating the issue as a health issue is appropriate. The tried and true Murdoch press, far right and Liberal political party scare campaigns against the Greens' drug policy, delivered like clockwork at every election, might well have outlived their usefulness. As the *Sunday Age* deputy editor Michael Coulter wrote in 2015:

> The truth is the war on drugs has filled our jails, enriched the worst among us, wasted scarce police resources and blotted up millions of dollars that could have been far better spent. It has been an unmitigated disaster and it needs to stop.[5]

The social conservatism of rural Australia and the asset-rich, income-poor nature of many households have stopped people voting Green, not our stand on renewable energy or climate action. Succession planning, funding for old age, property settlements post-divorce and boarding school fees are big issues outside the cities. No matter how logical the arguments or how fair the proposals, people who own land are vulnerable to fear campaigns telling them that they will be the losers in any moves to address wealth inequality.

When push comes to shove, farmers will admit that the Greens and some independents are the only ones who will stand up for them against the mining and gas vested interests in the Liberal, National and Labor parties. They know their future on the land depends on our being there. They want us in parliaments for that purpose, but they are still reluctant to vote for us. They gamble that other people will put Greens into parliaments to protect their environment and vote instead for others who they think will better fund private schools to keep boarding school fees down, or keep the live animal export trade in business. It is a conundrum.

But if you want to change a culture or a country, you have to lead and convince people to change with you. You need to sit and talk with them, just as the Greens and the Knitting Nannas are doing. If you are only chasing votes, you never effect change. All you do is follow and merely reinforce and exploit the status quo, as the National Party does, and that does not serve the environment or the community well. By denying global warming and promoting coal and gas the National Party is destroying livelihoods in rural Australia.

Groups such as Knitting Nannas and Lock the Gate are authentic sparks of democracy fighting back against the plutocracy Australia has become. They gave people on the land a strong, loud voice at a time when they were feeling powerless, and they still do. They have provided a safe space in which people have been enabled and empowered to be proactive beyond their property boundaries and to stand up for the land and water precious to them and to future generations. They have been successful in stopping the expansion of coal seam gas in northern New South Wales but, as importantly, they have restored dignity and instilled courage into the ground-down. They have tapped into the deep well of country women's strength and resilience and have achieved what they set out to do. They are the 'iron fist in the soft fluffy yellow glove', forthright women in their prime and of their time.

That's why I gave my Knitting Nannas beret to the Museum of Australian Democracy. I hope over time Knitting Nannas berets will become to the history of land and water what the baggy green is to cricket. Whereas the latter is the highest honour in Australian cricket, being selected to play for your country, the Knitting Nannas beret deserves one of the highest honours in conservation as it represents self-selection to take a stand for country, for the land. Knit in and knit on, Nannas.

# 10

# Climate in a Bottle

OBJECT: *Two bottles containing water from beneath the Ross Ice Shelf and Terra Nova Bay in Antarctica, given to Christine in 1998 by Corey Peterson.*

IN AUGUST 1998, WHEN I was facing the loss of all Green seats in the Tasmanian Parliament because of the change in the electoral system masterminded by the Liberal and Labor parties, a parcel turned up in the mail. It contained two small bottles of water collected beneath the Ross Ice Shelf and Terra Nova Bay in Antarctica by scientists on board the icebreaker RVIB *Nathaniel B. Palmer*, a US research vessel. They were accompanied by a note: 'Just remember that deep waters can carry quite a punch half a planet away ... you are acting locally but being watched globally ... Cheers and Good Luck, Corey Peterson'. The sender, Corey Peterson, is a sustainability expert who was on the *Nathaniel B. Palmer* expedition.

Sending the water was Corey's personal gesture, recalling my remark in 1989 that the rest of the world was watching Green politics as it emerged in Tasmania. But at another level, it was a salient reminder that Tasmania's back door, the Southern Ocean, packs a punch half a planet away. Not only does it store more heat and carbon dioxide than any other region, it is the place on the planet

149

where all the ocean basins connect, and it is the cold, dense Antarctic bottom water that drives the world's ocean currents. Antarctica is also where the nutrients from the deep ocean are brought to the surface, underpinning the productivity of the oceans and the marine food chain. Those two bottles of water spelled all this out. Disruption in politics was required locally and globally to act quickly and decisively on global warming to prevent disruption of those ocean currents and the dire consequences for people and for the marine food chain.

It was just what I needed to be inspired and to refocus on the big picture. I had been appointed to Australia's first ever Greenhouse Gas Council in 1990 and in the same year to the United Nations Global 500 Roll of Honour for my work protecting forests. The shine was taken off that experience when I found that Margaret Thatcher had also been appointed as a Global 500 Laureate for her action in relation to greenhouse gases. At the awards ceremony I wrote a protest letter signed by the majority of the recipients in which we called on her to accept the stance of the British Government as being inadequate to date in curbing carbon dioxide emissions – in the same week her environment minister, Chris Patten, was blocking the European Commission calls for stabilisation of carbon dioxide emissions at 1990 levels by the year 2000 – and to commit to a significant reduction in greenhouse gases by 2000.

That protest letter demonstrates how well informed we were in 1990 about the speed and seriousness needed to respond to the science of the 'greenhouse effect', as it was called – and how far we have regressed since then. It marked the beginning of the political machinations of the fossil fuel industries and their political representatives to create doubt, to deny and to delay. Their success has been to the detriment of us all. The science is now overwhelming but there is less clarity in the public mind about the issue now than there was then.

So it was that within weeks of the democracy-destroying 1998 Tasmanian election I attended COP4 (the decision-making body of the Conference of the Parties to the United Nations Framework Convention on Climate Change) in Buenos Aires to ramp up my work towards stronger worldwide political action to address global warming. Thereafter I attended the annual COPs on a pretty regular basis until the Paris Agreement was negotiated in 2015. Global warming became my passion because I reached the conclusion that, unless it was addressed, all life on Earth was threatened; nowhere was safe and no species or protected area was beyond its reach now and into the future.

Climate conferences have their own rhythm. In the first week negotiators reach a point so that when their ministers arrive for the second week, decisions can be made. There is usually a huge climate civil society march, which for many years coincided with marches in countries all around the world, all designed to bring pressure to bear on decision-makers as they arrived. In Copenhagen in 2009 the airport had huge signs showing the aged faces of presidents and prime ministers saying in 2020, 'I'm sorry, we could have stopped catastrophic climate change, we didn't.' Prime Minister Rudd's face was among them.

Another feature is the breakfast meeting of parliamentary members of the Global Greens. Many of my Green colleagues globally are not only members of parliament but also government ministers on national delegations, and excellently placed to provide informed advice on the state of the negotiations and the role Australia is playing. In Lima in 2013 Australia was once more working to rort the accounting rules on land use, land-use change and forestry: the hallmark of our negotiating strategy from the signing of the Kyoto Protocol in 1997 to the present. I raised the issue with my European colleagues and asked them to object. They came back saying that the European Union was fully aware of what Australia was doing but had its own problems with Poland. If they raised the issue of Australia's bad behaviour, they might lose some of the European countries from the agreed EU position. They had their eyes fixed on finalising the rules in Lima so that the road to Paris the following year would be less fraught. Australia got away with it because the EU had bigger fish to fry.

After taking my seat in the Senate in 2005, I attended COP11 in Montreal, where the Kyoto Protocol was ratified without Howard's Australia or Bush's USA. Australia had held the rest of the world to ransom when the Kyoto Protocol was negotiated in 1997, arguing for an increase in emissions of eight per cent over 1990 levels by 2012 when the rest of the world took a cut: it added insult to injury by refusing to ratify.

In Montreal I was privileged to deliver the statement from the International Union for the Conservation of Nature to the United Nations on the impact of global warming. The walk up to the podium was one of the proudest and most nerve-racking moments of my life. I talked of the impact of global warming on nature and the species going to extinction. As I walked off the stage and down the stairs, I wished Dad had still been alive and that Mum could have been there with my children. It had been a long road from Wesley Vale to the United Nations. Back at home my speech was barely reported. The Howard-controlled Senate remained scornful and mocking of the very idea that climate change was happening and that humans were in any way responsible.

Frustrated by the lack of coverage about the seriousness of what was happening, in 2006 I produced a pamphlet, based on the research of climate scientist Dr Melanie Fitzpatrick, for distribution in Tasmania, demonstrating the impacts of global warming already evident in my own state. I thought that if people read about what was happening on the east coast instead of the Arctic, it might have greater impact. Eastern Tasmania has some of the fastest-warming ocean water on Earth, warming two to three times faster than the global average. It is the end of the magnificent ecosystem of giant kelp forests that has characterised the east coast of Tasmania for millennia.

I also highlighted the fact that the famous Tasmanian leatherwoods in the Southern Forests are flowering at a different time and out of sync with the orchards in the Huon Valley and so farmers will now have to pay beekeepers to bring their hives to facilitate pollination. I pointed out that on the Central Plateau the rare and endangered cider gum is on the way to extinction as minimum temperatures rise. For the farmers I noted the risks that certain sleeper weeds and insects may become invasive as those temperatures rise and also the impacts of reduced chilling hours on production for certain varieties of fruit trees. People didn't really believe all this.

Australia was still resisting ratifying the Kyoto Protocol, and Prime Minister Howard was using his absolute control of both the Senate and the House of Representatives to block any Senate inquiry into the effects of global warming. Twice, supported by the Nationals and the National Farmers' Federation, they defeated Greens efforts to inquire into climate impacts on agriculture. The Nationals' Barnaby Joyce declared climate science to be undecided while Queensland National Ron Boswell famously said in the Senate, in response to the likelihood of a 1.1-metre sea-level rise in a century, 'Being someone who has spent his life in boats since I was a kid, I haven't seen any sea-level change.'

In 2006, just ahead of the COP in Nairobi, British economist and academic Sir Nicholas Stern stated that climate change is the biggest market failure of all time and that strong early action is cheaper than the cost of not acting. His speech had a huge impact, with the prime minister of tiny Pacific Island nation Tuvalu asking – in the light of the evidence on sea-level rise, displacement of people and the huge humanitarian cost of not acting – 'Who will take my people?'

The climate rally in Nairobi was incredibly moving; people had travelled on the backs of trucks for days to get to the city to tell their stories. One such story was of a woman whose village had suffered horrendous drought. They needed the water from the village well for themselves and their livestock but the wild animals were dying of thirst and so came into the village, where they were regarded as dangerous and killed. She also spoke of growing tensions between tribal groups over access to water. This was the first time I gained real insight into the likelihood and scale of global warming causing conflict and displacing people and species within and across borders.

In 2007 UN Secretary-General Ban Ki-moon described the war in Sudan's Darfur region as the world's first climate change conflict because changed rainfall patterns meant water scarcity. That has intensified to the point where mass starvation and death of people and wildlife are now commonplace. In March 2017, 257,000 people were internally displaced in Somalia because of water scarcity and 4300 crossed the border into Ethiopia. Thirsty elephants are being shot at waterholes in Kenya because they can drink up to 190 litres of water at a time. I came home from the Bali COP and began work on producing 'Re-energising Australia', a comprehensive policy document setting out the climate emergency and advocating for serious action in every sector of government.

I attended the 2009 Copenhagen conference as a member of the Women's International League for Peace and Freedom global delegation. Thousands of NGOs came from every corner of the planet, and the memory of the march through the city on a freezing day will stay with me forever. We were a sea of humanity, some in traditional clothes, others dressed as polar bears, still others singing and dancing. We were all willing the political players to reach a legally binding agreement.

It didn't happen. At the last moment President Obama flew in and tried to cobble together a top-down political deal with willing 'important' political players including Prime Minister Rudd – but the Chinese were not playing ball either in the top-level meeting or on the plenary floor. The final deal offended the whole culture of the United Nations Framework Convention on Climate Change (UNFCCC), in which genuine consultation and consensus were valued, and so it was rejected. Apart from trying to impose an agreement from on high, President Obama's deal took no account of the fact that while the USA had been focused on the Middle East, it had not been watching China increasing its influence in Africa and the Pacific via vast investment and overseas aid. China didn't need to say anything. In a process where one vote one value applies, where the vote of Tuvalu is equivalent to the USA, African countries and the small island states had the numbers to refuse to ratify the deal.

~

IT WAS 8 NOVEMBER 2011 and I had just had one of the best days of my parliamentary career. We had made history when the Senate adopted legislation to implement an emissions trading scheme to address global warming. I was both exhausted and excited, having negotiated and shepherded the legislation through the Senate for the Greens. It had been a long haul over many years. Then an email landed in my inbox; after some preliminary congratulations, the writer and vice-chancellor of James Cook University Sandra Harding asked why I was wearing a polar bear badge in the newspaper photographs and not one representing an Australian animal.

I thought, 'Oh for goodness' sake, why can't people just for once be pleased?' I decided to ignore it but then I checked out the sender and decided to reply. I wrote back pointing out that what I was wearing was an artwork, a brooch by Léa Stein, not a badge. I explained that I had deliberately chosen to wear the polar bear brooch for the debate because polar bears are the globally recognised symbol of global warming. They rely on the Arctic sea ice for hunting, breeding and travelling. With record temperatures in the Arctic, the ice is melting and retreating earlier in the spring and refreezing later in the autumn when eventually the temperatures drop. The changing pattern of ice habitat threatens their ability to feed, find a mate and raise cubs. There is nothing sadder than knowing that polar bears are drowning because of the loss of Arctic ice.

However, the critic of the polar bear brooch was not deterred. She told me she could produce a badge featuring an Australian white lemuroid ringtail possum, and that I should wear it to highlight the plight of tropical species far more endangered by global warming in the short term than polar bears. I agreed to wear it at the UNFCCC in Durban in 2011.

The beautiful white lemuroid ringtail possum used to make up about forty per cent of the population of possums that live in the cool misty rainforest above 1100 metres on Mount Lewis in tropical north Queensland. It was featured in the campaigns to protect the Wet Tropics in the 1980s. Biologist William Laurance, distinguished research professor at James Cook University, wrote:

> much has been written about how global warming will affect the colder parts of the planet – the polar and boreal regions, glaciers, and alpine mountains. In fact, some of the warmest places on Earth, especially tropical rainforests, could also be intensely vulnerable to climate change ... many people are unaware that tropical species – particularly those specialised for cool, cloudy mountaintops – are often sensitive to hot weather ... as temperatures rise mountaintop specialists have nowhere to go. Their populations will wither and shrink and potentially disappear altogether.[1]

While recognising the impacts of global warming on polar bears, he pointed out that creatures living near the poles have adapted to seasonal swings in temperature, whereas tropical zone species are thermal specialists adapted to a narrow stable temperature range. He added that tropical species endangered by global warming probably outnumber their polar counterparts by 1000 to 1.

He illustrated the point by referring to the mass death of a colony of giant fruit bats in New South Wales on 12 January 2002 when the temperature soared to 42.9 degrees, eight degrees higher than the average summer maximum:

> The fruit bats normally just doze in the treetops through the day but on this afternoon they were fanning themselves, panting frantically, jostling for shady spots and licking their wrists in a desperate effort to cool down. Suddenly when the thermometer hit forty-two degrees the bats began falling from the trees. Most quickly died. The research team led by Justin Welbergen counted 1453 dead from one colony alone.[2]

The same thing happened in February 2014 when 45,500 fruit bats died in a single day as temperatures in Queensland rose to 42–44 degrees. In December 2016 young bats started dropping out of trees in large numbers. The mothers had flown off, and the babies were not attached. They gradually dropped lower down the trees as they starved to death until they fell out. The causes were thought to be the El Niño weather pattern and loss of food and habitats as more land is cleared. Over the weekend of 14 February 2017 south-eastern Australia was the hottest place on the planet. The mercury hit forty-six degrees, and thousands of bats fell dead to the ground.

Steve Williams and his team, also of James Cook University, specialise in the study of the impacts of global warming on tropical wildlife. They concluded in 2009 that species extinctions will increase dramatically if temperatures rise more than two or three degrees and that most of the wildlife found only in North Queensland will be wiped out entirely if temperatures rise the four to six degrees that is projected in the absence of a global concerted effort to restrict the rise to less than two degrees. By 2016 Professor Williams had observed that many endemic birds of the Wet Tropics are experiencing retracted ranges and have already moved uphill with only one degree of warming. He told me that the only other population of possums

(*Hemibelideus lemuroides*) not on Mount Lewis has had to move higher up the Atherton Tablelands; at 1000 metres you can find the animals but there are none in what used to be the lower part of its range below 700 metres. It is not a good sign for the diversity of life in the tropical forests. Once at the top of the mountain, there is nowhere else to go.

The white lemuroid possum was thought likely to be the first mammal globally to be driven to extinction solely by global warming, but that sad place has now been taken by a small rodent, the Bramble Cay melomys (*Melomys rubicola*), which lived only on a single low-lying island off the eastern Torres Strait. It was last seen in 2009. It is likely to have been driven to extinction by sea-level rise and ocean inundation, destroying its habitat and killing many individual animals.

The white lemuroid ringtail possum is not far behind. In late 2005 a severe heatwave hit the Mount Lewis region, coinciding with a failed wet season. Without misty cloud cover the possums could not withstand the heat and died. The survey conducted afterwards found only four possums, but since then there has been a very slow recovery. But with more extreme and more frequent heatwaves predicted as the world warms, it is only a matter of time before such an event coincides again with clear skies, and that will prove fatal for the white lemuroid possum on Mount Lewis.

Having agreed to take the badges to Durban and feeling devastated by the realisation that the possums' extinction was looking me in the face, I began wondering if Léa Stein would design a white lemuroid possum brooch, not just because it would be beautiful but for global distribution as a way of raising awareness of the fact that global warming combined with habitat loss from mining and logging, urban expansion, commercial agriculture and invasive species will send one-third of all species to extinction by 2050. Stop for a minute and take that in.

Though Sandra Harding had delivered a badge to commemorate

this magnificent creature, I put to her the idea of a Léa Stein brooch and asked for her assistance in having the university prepare and translate into French the work of their researchers and provide a high-quality image so I could send them to Stein. I talked to Léa Stein's agent in Australia, Bruna Harrison of Harlequin Jewellers in Sydney, and put the idea to her; she was enthusiastic. Bruna told me that Léa, now in her eighties, is a recluse but still produces two designs a year. She does not use computers and has to be approached in person, so Bruna agreed that if information and a photo could be provided, together with a letter from me, she would give them to Lea on her next buying trip to Paris. Léa told Bruna that she would consider it.

A year went by, and I had given up thinking that anything would come of the idea. Then I heard from Bruna, who had been in Paris and could report that Léa had been working on the design but was having trouble with the tail. Finally the brooch was completed, in six different variations of texture. Three hundred were made available for early release in Australia before the global release in 2015. We were all incredibly excited that our project was about to materialise, and were quite blown away when we saw the brooches for the first time – a badge had been transformed into a stylised and stylish artwork. The brooch was launched most appropriately at the Global Tropical Biodiversity Conference at James Cook University in Cairns in 2014.

I had been invited to deliver a keynote address there, and it seemed appropriate to bring together the Australian team who had made the brooch happen and the scientists on whose work we relied, and to celebrate as a group. It is a modern example of the age-old ways women work, in families, communities and life in general. This was a tale of four women: a French artist, a university vice-chancellor, a small business proprietor and an Australian Greens Party leader, working together and combining our ideas, our skills, our nous and our networks to produce something beautiful, meaningful and multilayered.

When I wear that brooch, it is a statement that at the poles and in the tropics, our fellow species, which we have known and loved, are on their way to extinction. I have a granddaughter who will be thirty-five in 2050. According to modelling of business as usual provided by Dr Sophie Lewis at the Australian National University, the global land temperature will have increased by just over three degrees from my birth to when my granddaughter turns thirty-five. I grieve that she will know silent and empty places where polar bears, white lemuroid possums, orangutans, elephants, giraffes and a myriad other species on land and in the oceans once lived. Although the Great Barrier Reef will already be dead, just how empty and silent the seas and those landscapes become depends on us. It is why I will never stop being a campaigner to address global warming, environmental degradation, overpopulation and over-consumption, and I will never stop standing up to the governments and corporations that continue to drive them.

In Durban in 2003 at the World Parks Congress, I was invited to go to the wild coast of South Africa to see where an Australian company, Mineral Commodities Limited (MRC), was set to develop a sand mine against the wishes of the local community, who were campaigning against it. There was no road into this beautiful landscape and so we used tracks worn by local people. When I arrived, apart from a few hens scratching around a hut, there was nothing moving. No birds, no animals, no nothing. I asked my guides why it felt so empty. They said that food was so scarce everything had been eaten out. I was profoundly moved by the desperation, the loneliness and the loss.

Over a decade later I read about the murder of local activist Sikhosiphi 'Bazooka' Radebe, who had been leading the campaign against the mining operations of MRC in South Africa. The company denied any involvement, but at his funeral the chief of the local tribe said, 'I am blaming the government because the government gave permits for those Australians while people were saying "no" to the government.'[3] This is the story of the planet.

We are living in the Anthropocene, a period in the Earth's history in which we humans have altered all the systems that support life on Earth. We are destroying the habitat that we and our fellow creatures need to survive. We live on a finite planet, yet we behave as if an increasing global population can continue to consume the Earth's resources from forests and fisheries to fossil fuels at an accelerating rate and nothing will change. When I was born in 1953, the global population was 2.5 billion; it is now over seven billion, and by 2050 it is projected to be more than nine billion. If everyone consumes at the current rate of those of us in the developed world, why would we think that anything other than a reduced number of humans will have a place to live? When you add to that the impact of invasive species and overlay it with global warming, changing the climate and threatening food and water security for everything from plankton, plants and insects to reptiles, birds, animals and humans, you cannot escape the fact that we are living in the sixth wave of extinction and destroying our own home.

The Antarctic bottom water collected over recent summers is warmer and fresher than my samples from 1998. No one knows when the tipping points that disrupt the ocean conveyor belt, the thermohaline conveyor, will be crossed. There is no time to lose.

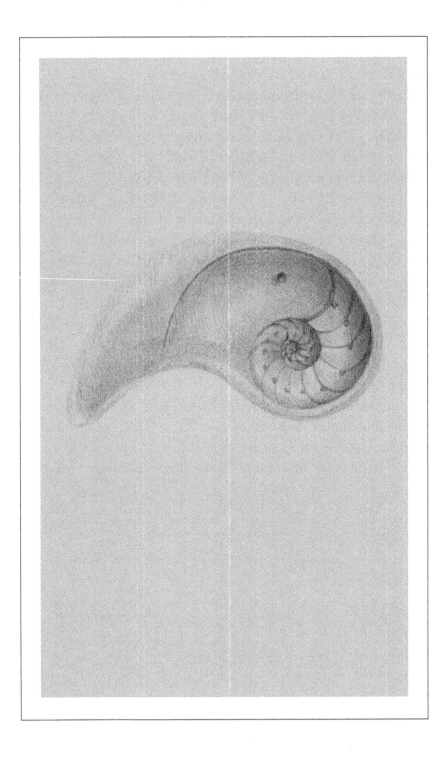

# 11

# Global Citizenship and World Heritage

OBJECT: *Sliver of nautilus shell and a South Pacific pearl encased in perspex, given to Christine by the government delegation from New Caledonia following the World Heritage listing of their coral reefs.*

WORLD HERITAGE LISTING is a vital conservation tool. It delivers global oversight and is the only thing to guarantee long-term protection from the vagaries of Australian changes of government at state or federal level. It was crucial in saving the Franklin, and by 1989 Australia had listed the Great Barrier Reef, Kakadu Stage I, the Willandra Lakes, Lord Howe Island, Gondwana Rainforests, the Wet Tropics of Queensland, and Uluru.

And, of course, the Tasmanian Wilderness World Heritage Area. How this was expanded is a lesson in real politics. In 1990 discussions between the Tasmanian Labor government and we Greens over the area to be protected became intractable as Labor, the Mines Department and the Forestry Commission objected to virtually every additional hectare under consideration. Federal minister Graham Richardson became increasingly frustrated and said, 'Draw a line around her hand,' and a staff member obediently did so. That is how the initial boundary of the expanded wilderness area on the west coast, south of Macquarie Harbour, was determined. I wished I had had bigger hands.[1]

In 1998, following lobbying from the Mirrar people and the Australian environment movement, UNESCO sent a mission to Australia to examine the likely consequences of the Jabiluka uranium mine on Kakadu, a World Heritage-listed property. The report concluded that severe ascertained and potential damages to the cultural and natural values of Kakadu National Park would be caused by Jabiluka and recommended that the project not proceed.

The significance of this issue as a World Heritage test case cannot be overemphasised. When a place is inscribed on the World Heritage list, it is recognised as having outstanding universal value to humankind, and it then becomes the responsibility of the state party to the World Heritage Convention to look after it for the whole world. No more degradation of the site is permitted beyond that which existed at the time the property was listed, and when the degrading activity ceases, the state party has a responsibility to rehabilitate the area. While the site remains under the control of the state party, its management is scrutinised by the World Heritage Committee, which meets once a year and consists of the representatives of twenty-one countries that are signatories to the Convention. If a property is being damaged, it can be listed as World Heritage In Danger.

This is the global leverage the Convention brings to bear. The In Danger listing was developed to try to assist developing countries to protect their cultural and natural heritage when they could not financially afford to do so. It was never envisaged that a developed nation would fail to protect a site. It was not meant to be a global sanction; rather it was supposed to be a mechanism for a global offer of help. But for developed countries it has now become a politically embarrassing source of shame.

The Australian Government went into a panic about the possibility that there could be an In Danger listing for Kakadu. Determined that it had to be avoided at all costs, they immediately set up an interdepartmental committee overseen by the Department of Foreign Affairs and Trade to fight it. The government succeeded in having the recommendation watered down. Australia was now required to submit a detailed response pending an extraordinary meeting of the World Heritage Committee at UNESCO to determine whether or not to list Kakadu as World Heritage In Danger.

The meeting was of intense interest to governments and conservationists around the world. It was seen as a test case for the World Heritage Convention and Committee. Although I had lost my seat the year before, I remained intensely committed to the protection of World Heritage sites so I travelled with Alec Marr, the national director of the Wilderness Society, and Ben Oquist to the World Heritage Committee meeting at UNESCO headquarters in Paris, where the issue would be decided. We worked with Lincoln Siliakus, who had done so much to organise legal support for the protesters during the Franklin blockade years before, and who was living in Paris and fluent in French. We lobbied the ambassadors to UNESCO and provided them with all the photographic evidence they needed of the damage being done to Aboriginal people and the environment as a result of the existing Ranger mine and the risks posed by the new Jabiluka mine.

While conservationists the world over are always up against the odds, we are continually working to help each other. I therefore set about contacting people who might be able to help persuade their government delegations to the World Heritage Committee to support us against the Australian Government. One such person was Hungarian János Vargha. After he had campaigned against the Nagymaros dam on the Danube, a change of government had seen him rise to the position of environmental advisor to the prime minister. When Alec and I could get nowhere with the Hungarian delegation, who pretended to speak no English, I contacted János. It was amazing. Overnight the whole delegation became fluent in English, and the following morning they were at our disposal to help.

We ran a strong media strategy and gained considerable profile, with articles appearing around the world. We had supporting commentary from the International Union for Conservation of Nature (IUCN) and the International Council on Monuments and Sites, which had both recommended the Jabiluka In Danger listing. The overwhelming concern of the committee was the impact on the Aboriginal people and their land. To plead their case, Yvonne Margarula, a traditional owner of the Mirrar people, had travelled to Paris with a delegation including Aboriginal spokesperson Jacqui Katona. The media was intensely interested in their position and reported widely that the Mirrar people wanted an In Danger listing for the property.

The Australian Government delegation was led by Roger Beale and Kevin Keeffe, who embarked on a charm offensive. They hired the room next to the main committee room and constantly invited the Aboriginal delegation to meetings and discussions, leaving the doors open so that passers-by could witness the care and concern they had for the Aboriginal people. The committee members therefore had difficulty believing that the government had not conducted proper consultation with the Aboriginal people at home. The behaviour of the Australian Government delegation belied the fact that they had failed to provide mapping of the sacred sites on the mining lease and had never completed a cultural heritage management plan. They wanted to convince the Aboriginal people that the government had had a change of heart and would now do everything to accommodate them – subject to the Aboriginal people not having any discussions with the environmentalists. As a result the Mirrar changed their position and no longer supported an In Danger listing. The Australian Government had got what it wanted: approval for the mine – which would damage a World Heritage Area – and no global condemnation.

The committee was clearly relieved that they did not have to take on a developed country such as Australia. Conditions were imposed on the Australian Government including the mapping of sacred sites on the Jabiluka mineral lease, the completion of a cultural heritage management plan and a comprehensive package of social and welfare benefits for all the Aboriginal communities of Kakadu. Progress reports were also required regarding the provision of detailed information about the scale of the existing Ranger mine and the proposed Jabiluka mine. The Australian Government was jubilant; we were devastated. As the decision was read out, I looked across the room at the Aboriginal delegation standing with the Australian Government delegation and wondered if the committed and dignified and courageous elder Yvonne Margarula, who spoke no English, had really been told and fully understood what was going on.

It was a critical moment for the credibility of the Convention. Alec Marr said on ABC news that he felt the World Heritage processes and the independence of the committee had been compromised. He added, 'We'll focus all our energies now on our corporate campaign and I would urge all Australians to become involved in this campaign.' I said the decision set a dangerous precedent for protected wilderness areas around the world, indicating that:

> World Heritage Areas are open for mining, tourism and
> whatever exploitation people want to have in them,
> providing the government of that country's got enough
> money to browbeat the members of the committee
> into that decision ... It is a vote of no confidence in
> the scientific advisory panels to UNESCO and I feel
> absolutely ashamed that the Australian Government ...
> as a result of a multimillion-dollar lobbying campaign,
> has so seriously undermined the integrity of the World
> Heritage Committee itself, and indeed the Convention.

The protests continued; the corporate campaign escalated. When Rio Tinto took over North Limited and acquired the Jabiluka deposit, it decided that because of the community opposition it would not proceed with the mine, and commenced a rehabilitation program. We learned a valuable lesson. No matter what the Convention said, no matter what expert advice the advisory bodies gave, the World Heritage Committee was still susceptible to political pressure.

Alec Marr suggested that I should run for election to the Global Council of the IUCN as a representative of a non-government organisation (NGO). As the world's premium environment policy organisation and the official advisory body to the World Heritage Committee, it was a critical role at that time as we needed to make sure that the IUCN was reinforced against pressure from state party members such as Australia. Membership of IUCN is from both government and NGO members, arranged into two houses. Each region of the world has three council positions, with Oceania represented by someone from Australia, New Zealand and the Pacific Islands. To be elected, you had to secure a majority of votes in both houses.

Prime Minister Howard and the Tasmanian Government were equally horrified that I might be elected to such a prestigious and influential body. The federal government decided to run a candidate against me in the election to be held at the IUCN Global Congress in Amman, Jordan, in 2000. John Tanzer of the Great Barrier Reef Marine Park Authority was the government's candidate. I worked hard to contact governments and NGOs all over the world and ran on a platform of action to address global warming, protect forests and strictly uphold the provisions and protections of the World Heritage Convention.

The Australian Government knew I was likely to win the votes in the NGO house but sent out Australian ambassadors around the world to try to persuade governments to vote for its candidate. I was not naive about the extent to which the Department of Foreign Affairs would horse-trade global positions and exert influence. 'If you back our candidate, we will support yours for other UN positions' is a standard government modus operandi, often sweetened by

LEFT: Christine with her mum, June Morris, at a family birthday party, 1955.
RIGHT: Christine and her sister, Gaylene, 1956.

Christine and Gaylene on the Clydesdales, 1957.

The poster signed by Christine in commemoration of her 1983 arrest while protesting the Franklin Dam. Constable Hyland, on the right, is the officer who arrested her. The poster is part of the Museum of Australian Democracy Collection.

ABOVE: Speaking out in opposition to the Wesley Vale pulp mill, Launceston 1988.

RIGHT: James Milne, Wesley Vale farmers' protest, 1988.

Election night 1989 with parents, Tom and June Morris. Christine was elected to the Tasmanian Parliament as one of The Independents' team of five members.

Neville, Christine, James and Thomas at Cradle Mountain, 1988.

Bob Brown with Thomas and James at the opening of the Douglas-Apsley National Park, 1990.

LEFT: Neville, Christine, James and Thomas in the tally room on the night of the 1998 Tasmanian election.

BELOW LEFT: Gunns Protest, 2004.

BELOW RIGHT: Speaking at the United Nations Climate Change Conference in Montreal, 2005.

Christine and Thomas, PFLAG, Sydney Mardi Gras, 2013.

ABOVE: Australian Greens senators Larissa Waters and Christine with members of Knitting Nannas Against Gas outside Parliament House, 21 June 2013.

LEFT: Christine with Bill Ryan at the Leard State Forest Blockade protesting Whitehaven Coal, 2014.

An asylum seeker self-immolates in 'Not Drowning', by Cathy Wilcox, 2016.

Brenda the Civil Disobedience Penguin, by First Dog on the Moon.

Christine speaks at the National Day of Climate Action in Queens Park in Brisbane, 17 November 2013.

With James, Thomas and Gary on her final day as the leader of the Australian Greens, 6 May 2015.

Speaking at the Global Greens Congress in Liverpool, England, March 2017.

Christine with her granddaughter Eleanor, August 2017.

additional offers of aid; witness the governor-general's 2012 tour of Africa on behalf of the Australian Government to try to secure votes for Australia's election to the UN Security Council.

Once we arrived at the venue, Alec Marr and Virginia Young (strategic campaign coordinator for the Wilderness Society) swung into action and organised a global team of NGOs to help campaign for my election. Globally the word had spread that Australia had gone rogue as a result of its campaign against the Kakadu In Danger listing, and so people were willing to help. We had huge support from Greens MPs in various European countries and from many NGOs who wanted a strong environmental activist elected. The Sierra Club from the USA, the Royal Society for the Protection of Birds in the UK, the Ecological Society of the Philippines, and Ancon from Panama all offered critical support.

But as we feared, government representatives from several countries told us they had been instructed from home to vote for the Australian Government candidate. The Howard government's diplomatic efforts had borne fruit. They had also sent a team of people at taxpayers' expense to support their campaign and had brought multilingual pre-prepared pamphlets to distribute widely.

On the day of the election I was pessimistic; I couldn't see how we could win enough votes. I chose not to go to the hall where the results of the ballot were read out and stayed in a cool area beside a small fountain. Suddenly Alec appeared, grinning and gesticulating wildly. I had not only won a majority in both houses but had also topped the poll in the NGO house and came second in the government house. All the governments of South America had voted for me, and the German Government representative's support had also been crucial. His government had agreed to support the Australian Government with its vote, which he did, but he held proxy votes for many EU government organisations and some countries that had not attended and had not issued voting instructions. He voted them all for me. I had been elected to the Global Council of IUCN.

I was stunned, excited, grateful and overwhelmed all at once. It was a huge honour and responsibility, as well as a great opportunity to shore up IUCN, defend its independence and influence global environment policy, drive World Heritage listing in our region and improve the rollout of environment policy in Oceania. I was determined to use the opportunity to maximum effect.

I was given a small glass globe by IUCN, which sits on my bookshelves under a beautiful photograph of a shy albatross. The globe is beautifully crafted and spins smoothly on its base. It is a source of joy and foreboding, and a call to action.[2]

Hardly had I returned from Jordan than the Australian Greens hosted the first meeting of the Asia Pacific Greens in Brisbane, as part of the preparation for the first Global Greens Conference to be held in Canberra in 2001. I caught up with Bob Brown, who had a present for me: a beautiful Helen Kaminski designer raffia hat complete with a navy ribbon. I thanked him and put it on my head before asking where he got it. He had no hesitation in telling me that he had retrieved it from a rubbish bin at Brisbane Airport, and wasn't it a great find. I should have known better than to so readily put a Bob Brown gift on my head; years before he had presented me with a silver bangle to add to my much-loved collection. After I had pulled it over my wrist, I asked where he had bought it, only to be told he had retrieved it from under a dead pig on the Bracknell tip.

One small delegation had come from New Caledonia representing an NGO, Corail Vivant. Its members pleaded with us to help them save their coral reefs. New Caledonia has the second largest barrier reef system in the world after Australia's but it is also the world's fourth-largest nickel deposit. They had horrific photographs of the mines destroying tropical forests and the impact of the tailings on the coral reefs. I put to them that World Heritage listing might be a way forward. I was now in a position to help, and the Australian Greens formally voted to work to secure the listing.

I secured funding through two foundations, one in Australia and one in the United States. I joined forces with the Mineral Policy Institute, an NGO working to protect communities from mining ventures around the world, to administer the funding. This meant that a local person could be employed in New Caledonia to work with the Kanak people towards this listing. It was daunting at first; I am not a fluent French speaker, had no contacts in New Caledonia apart from the three delegates and knew that New Caledonia had no environmental protection laws at all. The French Government had seen to that when it granted Nouméa partial autonomy in 1998.

As New Caledonia was still under French jurisdiction in foreign affairs and in budgetary terms, I decided to start with the French Government. Greens MP Dominique Voynez was minister for the environment, and I went to Paris to see her. She was supportive and set the nomination in motion. When she resigned, she was replaced by another Green, Yves Cochet; through his efforts in January 2002 the French Government submitted the nomination. My French Green colleagues and I knew this lacked the necessary detail, but if we had waited to complete the documentation there might have been a change of government or ministry and the opportunity would have been lost.

Once a nomination is made and accepted by the World Heritage Committee Secretariat, it stands unless withdrawn by a future government. We spent hours explaining what listing the New Caledonian coral reefs would mean for the environment and the opportunities for joint management by Kanak people. The scientists supported the listing but argued it should include the terrestrial environment as well, because of the significance of its Gondwanic remnant vegetation. New Caledonia was recognised as one of the ten biodiversity hotspots on the planet. I agreed but realised this would not be politically possible; the French Government would have withdrawn the nomination if its capacity to expand its nickel mines had been affected. The strategy had to be to secure a marine listing, and then seek a stage two nomination for the terrestrial environment.

Through IUCN I was working to address the fact that Oceania had very few World Heritage-listed properties compared with other regions. We desperately needed to bring to the world's attention the beauty and vulnerability of our region in the face of global warming and pressure from overfishing and forestry and mining ventures. UNESCO and IUCN held several regional workshops to raise governments' awareness about the World Heritage Convention. To that end I attended the Global Biodiversity Forum meeting held concurrently with an Oceania Regional IUCN meeting in 2002; while there with my IUCN regional councillor counterparts Wren Green and Suliana Siwatibau, I began lobbying for an Oceania Regional Office of IUCN. It was finally opened in Suva, Fiji, in 2006.

At the same time I was working in IUCN to head off the mining industry's push to open up all protected areas to mining. In 2002 at the World Summit on Sustainable Development, IUCN and the International Council on Metals and Mining jointly decided to seek the best balance between protecting important ecosystems and the social and economic importance of mining. I was immediately suspicious because of my Australian experience, and we thrashed out the terms of reference at later council meetings. The decision was subversion by stealth: within all the talk about better biodiversity reporting and rehabilitation was a review of mining and protected areas legislation. The council said we would not tolerate the weakening of any environmental protection legislation. The full extent of its potential to undermine protected areas became apparent at the World Parks Congress in Durban in 2003: in a draft document, all categories of IUCN protected areas were to be opened to mining in some capacity.

We organised. I made a strong plenary speech opposing any mining in protected areas, and Alec Marr reminded delegates about the sacrifices of people such as Ken Saro-Wiwa, the Ogoni environmental leader who, having exposed Shell's pollution and collaboration with the military regime in Nigeria, was murdered in 1995. Now IUCN was dealing with Shell as if they could be regarded as a responsible corporation. We won the day: the laws relating to mining in protected areas were not relaxed. But thirteen years elapsed before the matter was finally put to rest. At the IUCN Congress in 2016 mining and all industrial activity were finally ruled out in World Heritage areas.

In the meantime, the Australian Government had used an extraordinary meeting of the World Heritage Committee to try to remove the section allowing for the In Danger listing of a World Heritage area without the consent of the state party involved. The government and the mining industry had not forgotten Jabiluka and were determined to free themselves up for mining anywhere. World Heritage protection worldwide would have been undermined if they had succeeded.

So off to Paris I went again as part of the IUCN delegation to stand up for the operational guidelines and oppose Australia's efforts to weaken them. I linked up again with Lincoln Siliakus and once more we walked the corridors of UNESCO lobbying ambassadors. The committee decided to retain the power to list a property as In Danger without the state party's consent. This decision came back to bite Australia when the World Heritage Committee considered putting the Great Barrier Reef on the In Danger list. Australia sent out the diplomatic corps once more: at the 2014 UNFCCC meeting in Lima, Julie Bishop spent as much time heading off the In Danger listing as she did in talks on the climate.

Australia once again succeeded in avoiding the In Danger listing, and it had the UNESCO report 'Destinations at Risk: World Heritage and Tourism in a Changing Climate' censored to remove any mention of the Great Barrier Reef. But nature is blind to such political skulduggery. The Great Barrier Reef is dying because of global warming, with areas stretching hundreds of kilometres now dead, killed by warming and more acidic seawater, and the Turnbull government and the Shorten Labor Opposition still support the opening up of Adani's Carmichael mine, the largest coalmine in the world, in the Galilee Basin. You cannot be serious about addressing global warming if you support coal mining and coal-fired power.

~

IN 2006 I VISITED NEW CALEDONIA, having been elected as a global vice-president of IUCN, to meet with government officials, Kanak leaders and NGOs to advance the nomination process. I visited villages and was honoured to be presented with a New Caledonian flag representing the independence movement by one of the traditional owners. I attended a formal meeting of the Council of Chiefs where they voted to support the World Heritage nomination. I also exchanged lengths of cloth as a cultural welcome to country ceremony; the Museum of Australian Democracy now has the colourful length of cloth resplendent with pineapples and a miniature woven replica of a traditional dwelling.

The final step to World Heritage listing was the development of a detailed management plan. Through the Australian committee of IUCN I sought the help of the Great Barrier Reef Marine Park Authority, which had developed a world-leading management regime, but they did not have sufficient funds or government backing to offer assistance. However, the Australian Institute of Marine Science, through the efforts of Clive Wilkinson, a coral reef expert and author of *Status of Coral Reefs of the World*, offered several places to New Caledonian people in one of their reef management capacity-building workshops. UNESCO's World Heritage Centre, the French Government and the New Caledonian Government, the Kanak leaders, IUCN, the NGOs and Bruno Van Peteghem, Rick Anex, Jacky Mermoud, Didier Baron and the ever-committed Jacques Boengkih finally secured agreement on the detail of the boundaries and the management plan.

In 2008 the 'Lagoons of New Caledonia: Reef Diversity and Associated Ecosystems' was inscribed on the list at a World Heritage Committee meeting in Canada. I raised the money to allow several Kanak leaders to be there, but was disappointed not to be able to be there myself. After an eight-year campaign it would have been wonderful to share the joy of the Kanak people and of the NGO campaigners as their reefs received global recognition and protection.

I was delighted when some months later a delegation from New Caledonia made an official visit to Australia and came to Parliament House. In my office they made a formal presentation of a sliver of nautilus shell and a South Pacific pearl encased in perspex in recognition of the role I had played in securing World Heritage protection of their coral reefs. It is a treasured possession, a reminder of the beauty of nature and what can be achieved when people who care reach out to one another around the planet and do the hard work necessary to protect it.

~

I COULDN'T BE IN CANADA for the 2008 World Heritage meeting because of the Tasmanian forests. As IUCN vice-president I had backed the push by the Huon Valley Environment Centre and the Wilderness Society for a UNESCO mission to examine the management of the Tasmanian Wilderness World Heritage Area, to see the wholesale destruction of the tall wet eucalypt forests still not protected in one of the great temperate wilderness areas on Earth. Richard Flanagan's essay 'Paradise Razed', published in the United Kingdom in *The Telegraph* and updated in the *Monthly* as 'Out of Control', became the defining statement on the tragedy of Tasmania's forests and the cronyism and corruption that had seen Gunns take control of over eighty-five per cent of logging in Tasmania.

Together with the Wilderness Society's Alec Marr and Geoff Law, I attended the World Heritage Committee meeting in Christchurch in 2007 to lobby for sending a mission to Tasmania. We hoped to finally secure the protection of the forests of the Weld, middle Huon, Styx, Upper Florentine, Counsel, Western Tiers, Mersey and Meander valleys, and the Tarkine. We wanted to see protection for not only the giant trees and temperate rainforests but also the wild rivers, threatened wildlife, limestone caves and ancient Aboriginal heritage.

These magnificent forests had been deliberately excluded from the Tasmanian Wilderness World Heritage Area when we Greens negotiated the expanded boundaries in 1989. The Field Labor government was adamant that it would back ongoing logging of native forests in spite of IUCN having supported their inclusion in the Tasmanian Wilderness World Heritage Area in 1988. The forests were cut out by drawing the boundary above the tree line on the slopes of forested valleys, resulting in a boundary line resembling a dog's jagged teeth. IUCN recognised that the politically motivated boundary undermined the ecological integrity of the property and called on the Australian Government to work towards the inclusion of these forests. Twenty years later we were in New Zealand still working to that end.

Our efforts were rewarded: UNESCO's World Heritage Committee sent a monitoring mission, including a representative of IUCN, to Tasmania to report to the Canada meeting in 2008. The mission ignored the many scientific reports on the high-conservation values of the forests, gave limited time to the environment groups and spent most of its time in Tasmania in the company of Forestry Tasmania and the government. It backed the forest industries and recommended no change to the boundaries. It overturned decades of research, campaigning and IUCN recommendations.

As an IUCN vice-president and Tasmanian environmentalist, I was appalled. So too was the World Heritage Centre at IUCN. Together with David Sheppard, the head of the centre, I argued that the report should not be submitted to the World Heritage Committee with

IUCN's imprimatur and that it should reiterate IUCN's previous science-based recommendations, gathered over twenty years. David Sheppard held his ground under immense pressure. IUCN's logo was removed and its delegation to the Canada meeting went to oppose the mission's report. It was clear that my presence would have been too incendiary, given my dual role as an Australian Greens senator and an IUCN vice-president. I didn't want to give the Australian Government the opportunity to try to discredit IUCN's global reputation by suggesting that it was acting politically and not on the basis of science, so I stayed home.

World Heritage listing of the Tasmanian forests seemed a long way off. But the campaigns continued and grew in intensity throughout the Gunns pulp mill debacle. Everything we argued about the corrupt relationship between politicians and the forest industry came to pass. Premier Lennon removed the pulp mill from the Resource Planning and Development Commission assessment process at the behest of Gunns and in turn became embroiled in scandals that saw him out of the Tasmanian Parliament.

In 2005 Gunns filed a writ against twenty people and organisations – including Bob Brown and the Wilderness Society and collectively known as the Gunns 20 – for more than $7 million, claiming that they had trashed the company's reputation and caused it to lose jobs and profits. Their statement of claim alleged assault against forestry workers and vandalism. They lost their suit, and the Gunns 20 were exonerated and compensated. The global outrage generated by the lawsuit proved fatal for Gunns; their move to crush the forest campaign instead crushed them. The global market campaigns against Gunns were strengthened by the court case and, when combined with sheer economics, shifted the forest industry into plantations.

The native forest logging industry was in crisis and approached the conservation movement to seek salvation. They knew they would never sell their native forest products overseas as long as they continued to log areas of high-conservation value. So Labor governments in Tasmania and federally set up a 'forest peace process' to be overseen by Professor Jonathan West that would once again seek to balance conservation and industry needs. I hate the word 'balance': when it is used in a conservation and industry context, whether mining, logging or tourism, the environment always loses.

The environmental movement could have stepped up its campaigns to end native forest logging once and for all, or be drawn into a Labor-dominated process that would inevitably lead to a compromise, favouring native forest logging. They chose the forest peace process, hoping that history would not repeat itself and that this time the compromise would favour conservation.

When in 2010 the Australian Greens won balance of power resulting in the minority Labor government of Julia Gillard, Bob Brown and I as Greens leader and deputy pursued Environment Minister Tony Burke and the prime minister to nominate Tasmania's forests as an extension to the Tasmanian Wilderness World Heritage Area regardless of the 'forest peace process'. It was clear that the federal Labor Party, having been bitten so many times in the past by its Tasmanian Labor colleagues and the forestry division of the Construction, Forestry, Mining and Energy Union over Tasmanian forests, saw the two processes as inseparable. The scientific assessments, old and new, found that more than 500,000 hectares of forests warranted protection and greatly strengthened the case for World Heritage listing of Tasmania's tall forests and rainforests, including the Tarkine. But there was no way the federal minister would consider including the Tarkine without the approval of his Tasmanian Labor colleagues, and that was never going to happen.

When I became Australian Greens leader in 2012, I continued to pursue the World Heritage extension. The UNESCO timeframe couldn't wait for the forest peace process to run its course; any proposal to be considered by the World Heritage Committee at its annual meetings in July has to be submitted by February of that year or it will be held over until the following year. A submission for an extension to the Tasmanian Wilderness World Heritage Area, meeting in Phnom Penh in June 2013, had to be submitted by 8 February. Failure to do so would have risked the election of an Abbott government at the forthcoming federal election and the proposal being subsequently withdrawn.

Minister Burke delivered. The nomination of an extended area, including the forests of the Great Western Tiers and those along the eastern boundary – the Weld, Upper Florentine and Styx valleys – was submitted on time. The extension was accepted. Finally Tasmania's forests and wilderness, always as one in nature, were reunited behind a boundary that would protect and afford them the recognition they always deserved.

As we expected, the Liberal government was elected with Tony Abbott as prime minister in September 2013. He campaigned on a platform of removing 74,000 hectares of Tasmanian forests from the Tasmanian Wilderness World Heritage Area, and following his election he attempted to do so. It was humiliating for Australia when the World Heritage Committee meeting in Doha in 2014 dismissed Australia's efforts in less than seven minutes. Geoff Law was there with the Wilderness Society delegation to see the forests remain protected. Alec Marr was there to witness the handsome dividend paid from the investment over the decades of work that he and I and campaigners from all over the world had put into strengthening the World Heritage Convention and its advisory bodies.

The news came through overnight and the Senate was sitting the next day. The Abbott government was debating its bill to devolve all decisions on the environment, including World Heritage properties, to state governments. I asked the government whether it would commit to unreservedly accepting the World Heritage Committee decision and reject any proposal for logging of any kind in the area, ruling out any new bid to reduce the boundaries. Unsurprisingly Senator Abetz, the leader of the government in the Senate, was grudging. He said the government would accept the arbiter's decision but continued, 'I am one of these old-fashioned people who believe in the ballot box, in people having a say about their own bit of land and in having these decisions made locally rather than having an international body overseas determining our future.' If he and Prime Minister Abbott had had their way, the future of Tasmania's precious forests would have been decided in the Tasmanian Parliament. They would have been razed to the ground.

You always think that when you win a forest battle you will be ecstatic, but actually the feeling is excitement mixed with relief and trepidation. The win is not permanent but rather a battle victory in a long war. After so many years of campaigning and struggle, that is how I felt when I heard the news from Doha that the forests were finally safe from the chainsaws.

But the happiness I felt was muted: nowhere is safe from global warming. In 2016 devastating intense wildfires ripped though our World Heritage Area in places never adapted to fire, with the permanent loss of pencil pines and cushion plants. At the same time warmer, more acidic waters have bleached and weakened huge areas of our World Heritage-listed Great Barrier Reef. Habitats thought to be secure behind protected boundaries remain under increasing threat from alpine areas through to the oceans. Species will need to move to track suitable climate conditions for their survival. It is not enough to secure protected areas, we now need to create connected corridors within ecosystems. Action to address global warming is twenty-first-century action to protect places and species that make up the world's heritage. The fight for the wild goes on.

Lincoln Siliakus – that heroic fighter for the Franklin and beyond – died in Avignon, France, in 2015. I sent him a message that his wife, Anne, read to him the day before he died:

> The world is a better, more beautiful place because you
> cared enough about nature to protect parts of it, places of

outstanding universal value that will continue to inspire, nurture and captivate generations to come. The forest giants of Tasmania stand tall in the wild, sway in the wind, remain home to the birds and animals of the forest. They were here before us and will be here when we are gone but their peace and intergenerational serenity, they give. I hope you feel that peace and strength from the forest giants of Tasmania to you, another forest giant in Paris.

Anne told me, 'He smiled and asked me to write back to you "touched to the heart". That was the best gift he received from his dear Australia before leaving us.'

## 12

# What Price Carbon?

OBJECT: *Christine's full set of the eighteen Carbon Pricing Bills that delivered Australia's Clean Energy Package on 8 November 2011, signed by her Green parliamentary colleagues. The set is held by the Museum of Australian Democracy.*

AFTER THE 2013 FEDERAL ELECTION the Museum of Australian Democracy asked me to give them a document – or several – that had been the most significant for me as leader of the Australian Greens. I decided to give them the full set of the bills that delivered Australia's Clean Energy Package. Those bills, which passed the Senate on 8 November 2011, represented a great achievement for the nation, for the Australian Greens and for me. After years of policy work, campaigns, enormous challenges and lengthy negotiations, we had produced and secured the passage of legislation that gave Australia an opportunity to address global warming in a holistic and serious way, and to begin transitioning to a 100 per cent renewable-energy-powered future. The legislation was described by the International Energy Agency as a template for developed countries.

I had kept a full set of the eighteen bills and had them signed by my Green parliamentary colleagues on the day they passed the Senate. When I handed them over to the museum, I was told that

Julia Gillard had given them exactly the same bills. I was surprised but then realised that, in spite of her 2010 election promise 'there will be no carbon tax under a government I lead', she too must have reached the conclusion that history would judge her legacy to be the passage of the Clean Energy Package, which included a carbon price. It's ironic really, since there is no doubt that if Julia Gillard had won majority government in 2010 there would have been no progress on addressing global warming. Gillard's change from rejecting a carbon price pre-2010 to legislating one in 2011 had little to do with the realisation that it was the right thing to do and everything to do with power: it was the price she paid to secure government for Labor and retain the prime ministership in a minority government. Without the Greens in balance of power, it would never have happened.

To understand how this came to pass, some history is needed.

~

IN THE 2007 FEDERAL ELECTION CAMPAIGN Prime Minister John Howard and Opposition leader Kevin Rudd had promised to introduce carbon trading. The Labor Party won, with Rudd having said a few months before that 'climate change is the great moral challenge of our generation'.[1] One of his first official acts as prime minister was to announce at the United Nations Framework Convention on Climate Change (UNFCCC) meeting in Bali that Australia would ratify the Kyoto Protocol originally negotiated in 1997. This was way overdue – it had already been ratified and had come into effect globally in 2005 – but it was welcomed by the world as a major change of direction for Australia: at last, it seemed, we were taking global warming seriously. Prime Minister Rudd received a standing ovation and the TV cameras whirred.

But Australia was already up to its old tricks. The world agreed to constrain global warming to two degrees above pre-industrial levels. Negotiators tried to include a target of twenty-five to forty per cent reduction on 1990 levels of greenhouse gas emissions from developed countries by 2020, so that developing countries could increase their level of emissions as part of their development trajectory. Australia among other countries objected strongly and so the target, while still there, was relegated to a footnote. Journalists should have noted then Rudd's reluctance to align domestic policy with climate science as a sign of things to come.

Throughout 2008 the Rudd government developed its policy of adopting a cap-and-trade emissions trading scheme. Highly respected economist Professor Ross Garnaut, having produced the Garnaut Climate Change Review for Rudd, was very critical of Labor's shifting direction, condemning the complete lack of rationale for 'the overly generous compensation and huge budget impact of the massive compensation offered to energy intensive trade-exposed industries and coal-fired power generators'. He was also worried about the possibility that Labor might take twenty-five per cent emission reduction cuts off the table. He was right.

In November 2008 I was at the National Press Club when Kevin Rudd announced a target of five per cent emission reduction on 2000 levels by 2020, with a possible increase to fifteen per cent if other conditions were met. The twenty-five per cent minimum required by the Intergovernmental Panel on Climate Change (IPCC) was indeed off the table. A group of young activists was at a table nearby and I will never forget their scream of despair and disappointment. They were quickly hustled outside, but my heart went with them.[2] If anyone doubts just how bad Rudd's Carbon Pollution Reduction Scheme (CPRS) targets were, the final nail in the coffin was the assessment by right-wing climate-change-denying journalist Gerard Henderson that Rudd's targets were 'responsible'.

In February 2009, as the Labor government continued to develop its CPRS, more than 500 activists representing 140 climate groups came to Canberra to protest Rudd's five per cent target, and encircled Parliament House. The Australian Greens stood with them.

On 4 May Labor gave another $2.2 billion to big polluters, delayed the start of any emissions trading scheme for another year to 1 July 2011 and announced that the target would now be increased to twenty-five per cent, but subject to strict conditions regarding what the rest of the world must do.[3] But Labor and big business were confident the conditions would never be met.

On 14 May, the day Kevin Rudd's CPRS legislation was introduced into the House of Representatives, the prime minister personally turned the first sod on new coal infrastructure in the Hunter Valley. So much for the greatest moral challenge of our generation.

Labor deliberately excluded the Greens from any engagement with the development of the CPRS. They negotiated this legislation with the Coalition because they wanted 'bipartisan' political cover from the fierce opposition that would be mounted by the miners and big business. After initial introductory meetings following his election, Rudd held no further meetings with Greens leader Bob Brown the entire time he was prime minister. To Labor the Greens didn't matter so long as they had the Coalition votes, and they bent over backward to secure Coalition support.

The Greens knew just how inadequate Rudd's targets were. Whenever we raised in the Senate the IPCC recommendation of a twenty-five to forty per cent reduction for developed countries, they said that if other countries met their conditions, they would increase the target to fifteen per cent and perhaps go higher, but a maximum of twenty-five per cent was locked in: frustrating for us, since twenty-five per cent was the IPCC minimum. For those who argue Labor's ambition could have been increased, it is pertinent to note that in later years, when other countries clearly met their conditions, Labor never raised theirs; they had secured the support of the Liberals for five per cent and they weren't going to change that, no matter what the science said, no matter what other countries did.

In that context, and with the world watching, the CPRS with its unacceptably low target and extreme generosity to the big energy users and coal-fired power generators was put to the Senate for the first time in August 2009. The Australian Greens, with our eyes firmly fixed on the 2009 Copenhagen Summit and with the support of the broad environment movement, voted against it.[4] The surprise for Labor was that the Liberals voted against their own policy as being too strong. Labor should have realised then that Malcolm Turnbull, who had spearheaded the policy for the Liberals, had lost the numbers.

The CPRS had been specifically designed to be weak enough to gain the support of the Liberals under Turnbull so the votes of the Greens would not be needed. It appeased Labor supporters of the resource- and energy-intensive industry unions and was so generous with free permits and compensation that it salved the ire of the business sector. As with the Gillard mining tax, designed for business by business, Labor sought to secure the political win while business made sure it was only marginally impacted. It was the machinations in the Liberal Party that undid this first attempt at the CPRS, not the Greens.

Prime Minister Rudd then had to make a choice, and this is where the mythology of the CPRS comes completely unstuck. He could have chosen to green up the policy before resubmitting it to parliament, to secure the support of the Australian Greens and the environment movement ahead of the Copenhagen meeting. His other choice was to brown it down to make it even more ineffectual in addressing the climate emergency to gain Coalition support. He chose the latter.

A six-week period of intense negotiation followed between Labor's minister Penny Wong and the Liberals' Ian Macfarlane, with lots of supportive 'Penny and Macca' commentary from a media that had already decided it supported whatever deal was agreed between the parties, regardless of its effectiveness in reducing emissions. Huge further concessions were made. More money became available for compensation to polluting industries.[5] The scheme would have permitted 100 per cent cheap overseas permits, thereby failing to drive a transition in Australia. To add insult to injury, there was a further \$1.1 billion to help mining and manufacturing industries adjust to higher electricity costs. The Western Australian, Victorian, Queensland and New South Wales governments began talking about recommissioning old coal-fired power plants and building new ones to take advantage of the bonanza. It was a disaster of a climate policy.

The final deal was opposed not just by the Greens but by all of the environment movement, even the groups Australian Conservation Foundation, Climate Institute and World Wide Fund for Nature who had joined with the ALP-aligned Australian Council of Trade Unions in a Southern Cross coalition to support the original CPRS in spite of opposition from the broad climate movement. Turnbull gloated about the concessions he had extracted for the fossil fuel industry. Rudd was happy he had a deal. Labor didn't care what we thought. Then disaster struck for their strategy. Turnbull was defeated for the Liberal leadership by Tony Abbott by one vote, and the Coalition, by a caucus vote of 54 to 29, determined to repudiate their own deal and vote against it. Bipartisanship, if it had ever existed, was definitely over.

This was Prime Minister Rudd's second opportunity to rethink the strategy in favour of the climate. Labor could have postponed a vote until post-Copenhagen and renegotiated the CPRS with the Australian Greens, but instead they decided to dump the climate and go with a political strategy to wedge the Liberals. Rudd hoped to capitalise on the Liberals' split and further destabilise them by getting Turnbull loyalists to cross the floor to honour the deal, to spite and hopefully undermine Abbott. It was an unsuccessful ploy, with only Malcolm Turnbull in the House of Representatives and Liberal senators Judith Troeth and Sue Boyce crossing the floor in the Senate.

But still we Greens did not give up.[6] After Copenhagen failed to deliver a global agreement, I came home and worked on a compromise to the CPRS that we announced in February 2010 and which Bob Brown and I put to minister Penny Wong at a meeting in Hobart. We were shocked when she rejected the scheme outright, saying she would not even take it to the prime minister for discussion. What we could not have known was that Labor's powerbrokers – Rudd, Gillard, Wayne Swan and Lindsay Tanner – had already decided to abandon climate policy in favour of pursuing a tax on mining profits.

The failure of the CPRS legislation has been cited endlessly by some journalists and the Labor tribe as the point at which the country lost its way in fighting climate change, and the Greens have been blamed for failing to support it.[7] In reality Labor chose to court the Coalition and freeze out the Greens when designing the scheme. The CPRS was bad policy that would not have reduced greenhouse gas emissions. Treasury's modelling showed it would not have driven transformation in the Australian economy towards zero carbon. Instead it would have delayed it because locking in a weak target also locked in a longer life for high-carbon polluting industries, especially as the number of free permits for trade-exposed industries increased, rather than decreased, over time. Because those compensation arrangements delivered 'certainty' to industry to continue high-emission activities, and required years of notice before they could be changed, industry would never have allowed them to be changed without massive compensation. We would have lost the critical decade to 2020 in which global emissions had to peak and then come down. That's why I said it is not just a failure; it locks in failure. As journalists Bernard Keane and Paul Barry wrote at the time:

> Instead of treating climate change as the great moral and economic challenge of our time, Rudd treated it as a weapon with which to wedge the Coalition. Eventually, he wedged them so hard they broke apart – only for Rudd himself to be blasted by the shrapnel. Abbott, having seen Rudd use climate change as a political weapon for two years, had no compunction in simply doing the same back to him.[8]

Labor degenerated into infighting[9] and Rudd was replaced by Julia Gillard, who offered a Citizens Assembly for climate change advice and a promise that there would be no carbon tax. At the 2010 election the Australian electorate had not given either Liberal or Labor a majority. Labor won 72 seats and the Liberals and Nationals 73; each party needed 76 to form government. The election of Adam Bandt to the House of Representatives seat of Melbourne as a Greens MP, together with our balance of power in the Senate, enormously increased our bargaining power.

Strong action to address global warming, including legislating a carbon price, was what the Australian Greens wanted from any prospective government. We put this to Julia Gillard as the price of supporting her to form government, and she grabbed it. She was keen to secure an agreement with the Australian Greens quickly in order to build momentum and put pressure for support on the independents Andrew Wilkie, Rob Oakeshott and Tony Windsor. It was clear that the other independent, Bob Katter, would support the Liberals' Tony Abbott.

From my previous experience in balance-of-power negotiations in Tasmanian politics I knew the value of a multi-party committee plus external experts as a means of securing agreements and ensuring that new ideas and all views would be examined seriously. Without the inclusion of experts, parliamentary committees tend to report in favour of the view held by the political majority, and the rejected views are simply aired in minority reports. I also knew the importance of making sure that the committee must consist only of those who shared the same objective, so that the process was not blown apart by anyone who had joined simply to run interference.

Committee membership had to be open to all parties and independents but only on the condition that they agreed to the introduction of a carbon price as a starting premise. Bob Brown took the idea to Julia Gillard as part of our negotiations for support. She had already been considering a committee of some kind. He also put to her my condition of an agreed starting date for an emissions trading scheme of 1 July 2012. She agreed, but experience has taught me not to be comfortable with an undertaking given privately and verbally; better to get it in writing or at least have a witness. I wanted to hear it directly from the prime minister, so I went to her office. She agreed that a multi-party committee with experts would be established to deliver a carbon price, which would not only be legislated but would come into effect on 1 July 2012. So we had an agreement to introduce a carbon price, an agreed date for it to take effect and a multi-party process to determine the details of the package. The delivery date was not released publicly but was given to Treasury and the Department of Climate Change as the timeframe.

Once this set of conditions was agreed in the Labor–Greens Agreement of 1 September 2010, Julia Gillard enlisted the support of independents Andrew Wilkie, Tony Windsor and Rob Oakeshott and formed government. The multi-party climate committee first met on 7 October 2010 and monthly meetings followed in the Cabinet room, which gave the committee considerable gravitas and confidentiality. All documents produced for those meetings were 'Cabinet in confidence'. The prime minister chaired the meetings and I was appointed as co-deputy chair with climate change minister Greg Combet. The rest of the committee consisted of Treasurer Wayne Swan, Greens Bob Brown and Adam Bandt, and independents Rob Oakeshott and Tony Windsor. Staffers from ministerial offices, Greens' and independents' offices and bureaucrats from across government departments were also in attendance. Labor and the Greens chose two experts each: ours were globally renowned climate scientist Professor Will Steffan and economist and climate policy expert Professor Ross Garnaut. The government chose Rod Sims, a former deputy secretary of the Department of Prime Minister and Cabinet – he left the committee in 2012 when he was appointed as chair of the Australian Competition and Consumer Commission – and Patricia Faulkner, a former secretary of the Victorian Human Services Department and the state's director of Consumer Affairs. She could advise on programs to reduce the impact of carbon-price-related cost-of-living increases on society's disadvantaged. While Rob Oakeshott and Tony Windsor were consulted, they rarely took sides in the case of disagreements.

There were frequent informal discussions between Greg Combet and myself and the prime minister and Bob Brown and our respective staffs. We rapidly developed a good working relationship, and Bob, Adam and I kept our other three Green senators (Rachel Siewert, Scott Ludlam and Sarah Hanson-Young) up to speed with the negotiations, while Oliver Woldring and Ben Oquist worked with Bob and me on the detail. If Greg Combet and I agreed to disagree, the matter was elevated to a negotiation between Bob Brown and the prime minister, often at their weekly meeting. Once a resolution had been found, the decision was taken to Cabinet and the Greens party room and then presented to the multi-party committee for amendment and agreement.

It was both good and bad that Cabinet had decided on decision-making parameters before the committee meetings. It meant that final decisions could be made, but it also meant that Cabinet was used as a constraint on what was possible. If we Greens wanted to amend any proposal to take a more ambitious position that was deemed beyond Labor's negotiating parameters, it meant delay as it had to go back to Cabinet. Taking the proposals to Cabinet also meant that they were frequently leaked to the press.

The media were becoming frustrated that more of the internal workings of the committee were not being made public. In a vacuum of information they will chase any story, relying on gossip and leaks, using the tried and true 'sources close to the government say' or 'a spokesperson close to the Greens says' and so forth. So when in February 2011 the committee formally decided to introduce a carbon price effective from 1 July 2012 with a fixed price for three years leading to a floating price in 2015, Greg Combet in particular was keen to go public.

A major press conference was held on 23 February 2011 in the prime minister's courtyard with all parliamentary members of the committee present. However, while we had the policy and the date, the committee had not come to any agreement on much of the detail: the starting price, the household compensation package, support for emissions-intensive trade-exposed industry or the treatment of the energy sector. We therefore had no answers to many of the media's questions, and we satisfied neither the media nor the opponents of carbon pricing.

It was a mistake to hold a press conference without emphasising the urgency and scale of the global warming crisis, Australia's responsibility to reduce its emissions and the fact that acting sooner would save lives and be cheaper. Instead the focus was specifically on introducing a carbon price. Without the detail about what the price might be and how any impacts on consumers and energy prices might be compensated, wild speculation resulted.

The climate change deniers, fossil fuel advocates, business community, Murdoch press and Liberal and National parties went into overdrive. The Australian Workers' Union declared that Whyalla would be destroyed – a claim taken up by Tony Abbott. The National Party's Barnaby Joyce declared that a lamb roast would cost $100. Deputy Opposition leader Julie Bishop described the announcement as 'a betrayal of trust for the Australian people', quoting Gillard's assertion that there would be no carbon tax under any government she led.

The prime minister was wide open to these attacks. She was not a climate champion and she didn't understand the urgency of acting on climate change. She wouldn't talk about the science. As a Labor prime minister she was focused on trying to reassure Labor voters and the business community that they would be able to manage the changes and that they would be compensated. She wanted to talk prices and compensation, and she did not really explain or understand the critical difference between a carbon tax and an emissions trading scheme.

She could have explained that a carbon tax is a compulsory payment to the government for the purpose of raising revenue, intended to change behaviour, similar to a tax on cigarettes or alcohol. She could then have explained that while a carbon tax might change behaviour and bring down emissions, there was no guarantee that it would do so, as it would not put a limit on greenhouse gas emissions. The aim was to reduce greenhouse gas emissions because of the climate crisis; that was why she was legislating an emissions trading scheme. In such a scheme, the government sets a limit or a cap on the amount of emissions that polluters can emit in a year, and they then trade these permits to pollute within that limit.

Had she done so, she could have refuted allegations that she had broken her word to the Australian people. She could have pointed out that Labor's previous CPRS had a fixed permit price of $10 per tonne for the first year and explained that the emissions trading scheme being designed would similarly begin with a fixed price and would move to a floating price when a decision on the appropriate level, or cap on Australia's emissions, had been decided and legislated. But she did none of those things.

I was watching ABC TV's *7.30 Report* as the disaster unfolded. Instead of highlighting the enormity of the climate challenge, the dangerous impacts of extreme weather events and the vulnerability of Australia to global warming, Gillard focused on electricity prices.

> HEATHER EWART: With this carbon tax – you do
> concede it's a carbon tax, do you not?
> JULIA GILLARD: Oh, look, I'm happy to use the word
> tax, Heather. I understand some silly little collateral
> debate has broken out today. I mean, how ridiculous.
> This is a market-based mechanism to price carbon.[10]

She failed to appreciate the political implications of acquiescing to the false assertion that a fixed price in an emissions trading scheme is the same as a carbon tax, and as a result she gifted the Abbott Opposition a battering ram.

We finally legislated an emissions trading scheme, an ETS for Australia. It passed the Senate on 8 November 2011 and took effect on 1 July the following year. As planned, it had a fixed price for three years and was designed to progress to a floating price in 2015. It was not a tax. A simple read of the legislation makes that perfectly clear. And we know the result: Tony Abbott and the Opposition lost no time in declaring it 'a great big new tax on everything'. This was Abbott's great big new lie about everything and one that we now know, thanks to the admission of his chief of staff Peta Credlin, he deliberately decided to tell.

People ask why Labor and the Australian Greens decided to have a fixed price ETS and did not immediately go to trading with a floating price. The fact is that we had no choice; Labor and the Greens could not agree on the level of the greenhouse gas reduction target.[11] Without one you cannot have a fully functioning cap-and-trade scheme. We Greens were focused on how hard and how fast we could cut greenhouse gases and transform Australian society and the economy, consistent with the urgency of addressing global warming and our global responsibility as a developed country to act first. The ALP was nationally focused on payment and compensation for every greenhouse gas reduction scenario and was prepared to massage the degree of action, the depth of emission cuts and their timing to reduce any political pain. We Greens were not prepared to fiddle around the edges with ineffectual gestures designed for political messaging that would have no effect on reducing greenhouse gas emissions. For us, it all came down to the science of global warming. The solution was to begin with a fixed price and establish an independent Climate Change Authority designed not to second guess the politics, but to provide independent and fearless, scientifically sound advice to determine the cap.

The July 2012 start date was carefully planned to be as politically palatable and well managed as possible. The Climate Change Authority had until February 2014 to recommend a target; the Gillard government did not want to fight the 2013 federal election on the issue of climate. A target recommended post-election in 2014 could be debated and legislated and come into effect in 2015; the subsequent floating price would have had a chance to operate for one full year before the 2016 federal election.

I thought it was a gamble to consider leaving the decision about an appropriate greenhouse gas emissions target to the Climate Change Authority, a statutory body. No matter how well designed such an organisation may be, its integrity depends on the board members appointed by the government of the day, and whether they take global warming and their legislative objectives seriously. We Greens negotiated to choose three board members. The government insisted on choosing the remaining six, including the chair, with the Commonwealth's chief scientist *ex officio*.

Once we had the Climate Change Authority as a mechanism to deliver a climate target by 2014, we needed to agree on a carbon price for the fixed price period. The government insisted Treasury could model only two scenarios. We Greens asked for modelling of a carbon price consistent with a target of 350 parts per million, or 1.5 degrees below 1990 levels, and a second scenario of 450 parts per million, thought to be consistent with two degrees of warming. The Labor Party was adamant. There was no way they were modelling 350 ppm. Instead they said 450 ppm and 550 ppm would be the scenarios. We objected on the basis that 550 ppm was to model a target consistent with more than two degrees of warming. We asked what was the point of modelling a target considerably weaker than the one Australia, as a party to the UNFCCC, had already signed globally.

We refused to agree with Labor's position; Treasury modelling showed a carbon price based on a weak target would not achieve results. As we had pointed out throughout the CPRS, a weak target/ low price does not drive a transition away from fossil fuels and into renewable energy. If Australia was to ever reduce its emissions and stay within its globally just carbon budget, it had to rapidly transition away from coal-fired power stations and establish renewable energy on a large scale quickly. Labor would not budge, and so we proposed a compromise, based on the United Kingdom experience. There they had established a Green Investment Bank to support renewable energy developments. So we said that if the government persisted with modelling 550 ppm, we wanted a $10 billion fund complementing the carbon price to drive the rollout of renewable energy at scale in the short timeframe required by the science. Labor pushed back, arguing it shouldn't just be renewable energy but should include 'clean' energy, but we pushed back in turn to exclude nuclear energy, carbon capture and storage, and burning native forests from any financial support.

The negotiation was complex, with much arguing backwards and forwards over months. It was made more difficult with leaks hitting the front pages of newspapers. The leaks came from Cabinet, highlighting the extent of the opposition to carbon pricing from certain pro coal and gas quarters in the Ministry.

Time was of the essence. The government directed Treasury to model the weaker scenarios and agreed to our proposals for complementary measures. The prime minister understood these were Green gains and so agreed that I would publicly announce the establishment of the Australian Renewable Energy Agency (ARENA) at the Clean Energy Conference in 2011. Martin Ferguson was to remain the responsible minister but the new agency was to be an independent statutory authority with legislated funding and safe from political interference. Although we were never privy to the details, this arrangement had been the cause of a huge argument between the prime minister and minister Ferguson.

The Clean Energy Finance Corporation (CEFC) established to oversee the $10 billion fund was disparagingly called 'Bob Brown's bank'. The institutional architecture of ARENA and the CEFC is outstanding. Between them they covered grants from the earliest stage of research through to pilot stage and commercial rollout. ARENA was predominantly a grants funder and the CEFC was a debt and equity provider. When the CEFC began making a profitable financial return, the profits would be channelled into ARENA to fund the grants so that over time it would be a self-funding arrangement.

(However, in the 2014 budget the Liberal government moved to abolish both ARENA and the CEFC. The CEFC strongly stood its ground. Unfortunately Greg Bourne, chair of ARENA, let it be known that ARENA could live without $700 million of its funding so long as the agency itself was not abolished. The Senate voted to retain both agencies but ARENA's funding was cut and the agency weakened.)

Having agreed on the architecture of the new institutions ARENA and the CEFC, and once Treasury had completed its modelling, we had to finalise the fixed price. The 450 ppm scenario would have resulted in a carbon price of $50 to $60 a tonne, so Labor rejected that outright in favour of the 550 ppm scenario price. Their proposal was for a three-year scenario of $17–$18–$19 per tonne. I argued for a higher price of around $27–$28–$29. As Bob Brown was about to meet with Prime Minister Gillard to resolve this stand-off between minister Combet and myself, we met in the corridor. Bob asked what more he could ask for if there was to be a compromise on the price. I suggested a move to protect forests, namely to amend the Renewable Energy Target regulations to prohibit native forest biomass from any longer being regarded as 'renewable' when burned to generate electricity.

The prime minister and Bob Brown met. A fixed price of $23–$24–$25 was on the table, as was the forest furnace ban. The prime minister stared at Bob for a long time and then agreed. The deal was done. The exclusion of native forest burning from the Renewable Energy Target was comprehensive and covered products, by-products and waste associated with or produced from clearing or harvesting of native forests, subject to appropriate transitional arrangements for existing accredited power stations.

A key difference between the CPRS and the Clean Energy Package was that the CPRS focused on pricing as the central response while our approach involved both pricing and substantial allocation of resources to specific actions intended to cut emissions. Many of our proposals for the overall package were rejected. Transport was an outstanding problem. We wanted mandatory fuel efficiency standards, which we thought would be an easy ask since it was consistent with what Prime Minister Gillard had promised in the 2010 election campaign. But in spite of rising emissions from our inefficient car fleet, we got no support from the government, Rob Oakeshott or Tony Windsor.

Transport was where Tony Windsor dug in. He utterly refused to have a carbon price applied to heavy vehicles, and that is why it was not included in the package. He argued that it should be decided once the period of minority government was over, following the 2013 election. Labor refused mandatory vehicle fuel efficiency standards to protect the gas guzzlers being assembled in Australia. It would have been embarrassing if new mandatory efficiency standards meant that the cars the government-subsidised multinational corporations produced in Victoria and South Australia couldn't be driven here because they didn't meet standards.

I learned long ago that the surest way to ensure a corporation leaves Australia and abandons jobs is to permit them to operate to low standards. With no capital investment to recover, industry has all the power to cut jobs and leave in its own timeframe. How different it might have been for Australia's car manufacturing industry if the Labor government had embraced a Greens plan to make subsidies contingent upon manufacturing electric vehicles in Australia. At one meeting with transport minister Anthony Albanese I had asked about integrating electric vehicles as energy storage into the management of the grid rather than just seeing them as a mode of transport. He sent for a department representative, who said no one was considering such ideas.

The issue that threatened to bring the whole carbon price effort undone was compensation to coal-fired generators and exemptions for leaky coalmines. It had become an intractable and hard-fought point of difference. In June 2011 the prime minister proposed an all-weekend meeting at Parliament House to sort it out once and for all. Parliament House at the weekend in winter is a miserable place, with no air-conditioning or heating and no cafe or coffee. Prime Minister Gillard lightened proceedings at the start by saying that if we managed to get through the day still speaking and without incident, she would have us all to the Lodge for an informal dinner.

We got under way. Ross Garnaut phoned in to the meeting. He and I agreed that it was not the obligation of government to maintain the equity value in coal-fired power stations and that they had had years to prepare for the inevitable transition away from fossil fuels. We argued our only obligation was to maintain energy security, to keep the lights on. If any coal-fired generators threatened to close down, we should provide government-guaranteed loans to maintain security of supply. The government argued for compensation to maintain profits in the face of a carbon price. All their arguments were politically motivated, all about the electoral impact on Labor constituencies in the Hunter and Latrobe valleys: Greg Combet's electorate was in the Hunter Valley. We were quite prepared to provide just transition finance to workers and communities, but not to the generators themselves, let alone exemptions to keep leaky coalmines operating. But for Greg Combet, that was a deal-breaker.

Labor brought in Matt Zema and John Pierce from the Australian Energy Market Operator (AEMO) and Australian Energy and Market Commission (AEMC). John Pierce argued that massive compensation to coal-fired generators, in addition to government-guaranteed loans, was essential. He was an advocate for the coal-fired generators, pure and simple. The government embraced his advice. Having been stymied by AEMC, I insisted John Pierce provide me with a letter saying that he advised that both compensation and the option of government-guaranteed loans to maintain energy security were necessary. I argued that people in the future would not believe that a regulatory authority had given such get-out-of-jail-free advice for the fossil fuel industry in the face of global warming and that he should bear responsibility for that advice. He provided the letter. Given we could not stop the $5.5 billion compensation to coal-fired generators, we tried to find a way to convince them to cease voluntarily, proposing a contracts-for-closure plan to close down 2000 megawatts of the dirtiest coal-fired power stations. Labor agreed to that.

We were tired and angry; it had been a long day. We knew that the coal-fired-generator operators would be gleeful and that the community was being ripped off. Admittedly this compensation for coal was less than the amount Prime Minister Rudd had offered and over a shorter period of time, but it was still a massive gift of corporate welfare to coal. In spite of all the work done in securing a carbon price, we were wondering whether we should call the whole thing off.

It was in that mood that we left for the Lodge. No one was feeling sociable. No one had partners as guests. We arrived and had pre-dinner drinks in the lounge. I had not been to the Lodge since Julia Gillard became prime minister, and I was interested to see what artwork she had chosen on loan from the National Gallery – one of the perks of office. I was disappointed when she said that she had left the choice to her partner, Tim Mathieson, who had relied on advice from the gallery. It was a conservative and safe representative collection, clearly indicating that she had no particular personal interest in the visual arts.

We moved into the dining room. No one could be bothered with conversation and no one was particularly pleased to be in a group of people with whom they so vehemently disagreed. Tim didn't bother to join us and watched TV upstairs. We noted the damage the possums had made on the ceiling and one wall and were told of the repairs that needed doing. Julia and I were the only women present, and whereas the men didn't think it was necessary to find something to talk about to satisfy the claims of civility, we did. Finally I asked the prime minister how she had enjoyed the wedding of Prince William to Kate Middleton, from which she had returned a few weeks earlier. No doubt the topic made the men even less interested in being sociable.

She told a very funny story. The timing for the royal wedding had been very precise. The political leaders of Commonwealth countries that still have the Queen as head of state are so few that they were to meet at an address in Pall Mall, where a minibus would take them for drop-off at Westminster Abbey. Prime Minister Gillard and Tim arrived at the set time and everyone else was on board. Gillard was wearing a very stylish and tall hat and miscalculated the height of the bus door, which ripped the hat from her head as she got in. There was no time for delay, as the bus was due to be at the Abbey minutes later, and they were off. Tim came to the rescue. From his coat, he immediately drew his hairdressing combs and restored the prime ministerial hairdo and hat in no time flat. The others were amazed; one wife momentarily forgot where she was and in front of everyone berated her prime ministerial husband about his uselessness compared with the Australian prime minister's partner. The bus stopped, the door opened and out our prime minister got, looking appropriately glamorous.

The minute the clock struck ten at the Lodge, the prime minister stood up. The signal to leave was met with relief.

Having had to stomach giving billions to coal, we insisted on an assessment of the timeframe for transitioning to a 100 per cent renewable-energy-powered future, negotiating a study of two future scenarios featuring a National Electricity Market (NEM) fuelled by 100 per cent renewable energy by 2030 and 2050. Gillard and Greg Combet were unenthusiastic but agreed.

AEMO deliberately undermined the report by failing to estimate a 'business as usual' cost comparison, therefore trying to make a 100 per cent renewable energy future look expensive. In spite of that, they still found that 100 per cent renewable energy was achievable and cost-effective, estimating that the cost to consumers could be as little as 6.6 cents per kilowatt-hour. The AEMO report released in April 2013 concluded, 'it is valuable to note that this operational review has uncovered no fundamental limits to 100 per cent renewables'.

We had what we needed. Interestingly, the report was leaked to the anti-renewables *Financial Review* and not launched, and was buried on the Environment Department website. Neither the government nor AEMO was looking for anything other than rejection of a 100 per cent renewable energy future.

It is now critical in 2017 that an update on that AEMO study be done as soon as possible. Not only does it need a business as usual case study but also the assumptions underpinning it need to be far less conservative than those provided by the Bureau of Resource Economics. There has been a revolution in renewable energy generation and storage technology since 2011, and prices have rushed down the cost curve, while the potential to use much less energy through efficiency measures and to reduce costs through demand management will further improve the economics of an efficient, smart, 100 per cent renewable energy system.

Australia deserves a serious annual analysis of how quickly we can achieve a 100 per cent renewable energy future and how cost-effective that will be, not to mention its enormous contribution to bringing down greenhouse gas emissions as global warming accelerates. The study must be accompanied by a radical rewrite of the rules governing the NEM. A new objective to make energy generation consistent with meeting Australia's UNFCCC greenhouse gas reduction target must be added.

Once the Clean Energy Package had passed both houses of parliament, a problem arose. We had argued long and hard for the floor price[12] but, following its passage, industry lobbied hard against it, arguing that Australian industry would have to pay a higher price than would otherwise be the case and that the price should be allowed to fall to much lower Clean Development Mechanism CERs (Certified Emission Reductions). Regulation was needed to allow the legislated floor price to take effect.

In May 2012, two months out from the whole Clean Energy Package coming into effect, Rob Oakeshott, who had signed up to it with the compromises we all had to make to secure agreement, called on the government to ditch the floor price and threatened to disallow the regulations if they came to parliament. The Coalition and business scare campaigns were having the effect they wanted. Once Oakeshott had caved in there were nervous rumblings in Labor's backbench about the feedback from industry. To their credit Prime Minister Gillard and minister Combet held firm, arguing that the Clean Energy Package had been negotiated in good faith, we had all made compromises and we should keep our word.

We could not pass the regulations without Oakeshott's support, so we compromised again by agreeing to link the Australian emissions trading scheme with the European Union scheme so that, in the absence of a floor price, the Australian price would never fall below Europe's.

The passage of the Clean Energy Package on 8 November 2011 was the highlight of my federal political career, except of course for my later honour of leading the Australian Greens. When the vote on the third reading was put, there was a sense of anticipation and gravitas in the Chamber. This was a major change in direction for Australia. The vote was 36–32 in the affirmative. Labor and the Australian Greens voted for it, and the Liberal and National parties and Nick Xenophon voted against all eighteen bills. Sadly, the Coalition and Xenophon, facilitated by the Palmer United Party, would have their way in 2014.

When the legislation passed the Senate, we were jubilant. Bob Brown and I embraced each other and our Green colleagues. Adam

Bandt and our staff were rejoicing in the galleries. For us, it was the culmination of years of work. The press gallery was full and the cameras flashed. As he often did, the Liberals' Senator Bill Heffernan immediately rushed up to disrupt the occasion. He inserted himself into the line of sight. But he was too late. The photo was taken and was splashed across the front page of every newspaper – except, predictably, that of our home state, Murdoch's Hobart *Mercury*.

History had been made. Australia had taken serious action to stand with the rest of the world in addressing global warming. We now had a legislated emissions trading scheme and a rigorous institutional architecture that would reduce emissions, create jobs and roll out new industries. There was hope at last that if fossil fuel dependent Australia could address the climate crisis, so too could the world. For the first time I felt a sense of optimism that humanity might just make it, we might actually head off the climate tipping points and avoid the point of no return. It was a great day.[13]

# 13

# Art as Activism

OBJECT: *Handwoven fabric, called* Trial, *made by Hobart artist Robyn Glade-Wright. Christine bought the material in 1992 and had it made into a suit, currently held by the Museum of Australian Democracy.*

ANYONE OPENING MY WARDROBE at Parliament House in Canberra and looking behind the suit coats would probably not have expected to see former prime minister John Howard with his lips sewn shut. If they had looked further, they would have found Howard's attorney-general Philip Ruddock in the same predicament. But people who know me would not have been surprised, just relieved that the portraits were not hanging on the wall looking down at them.

I have always been inspired by the courage and the wit of political artists, and their work has always encouraged, challenged and motivated me to keep on campaigning. Whether they use the written word, music, song, dance, theatre, film, sculpture, visual arts or fabric, I keep coming back to activist art. You are never alone as a campaigner for the natural world or for social justice; there is always an artist with you if you look for one.

I started collecting political art well before I entered politics. One of the first things I bought was a poster entitled *Rainforest,*

*Survival or Suicide* by the Austrian artist and architect Friedensreich Hundertwasser (1928–2000). I had visited Hundertwasser House in Vienna and became a fan of his work, which incorporated so many environmental themes. So I felt thoroughly at home when, elected to the Global Council of the International Union for the Conservation of Nature (IUCN) in 2000, I walked into its head office just outside Geneva and there in the foyer was a framed Hundertwasser poster *Imagine Tomorrows World* created to mark the fiftieth anniversary of the IUCN in 1998. It was great to feel part of a larger movement.

That is why I had the portraits of Howard and Ruddock in the cupboard. Having them at all was an act of solidarity. In 2005 in the Art Gallery of Wagga Wagga artist Michael Agzarian had exhibited a digital photo montage depicting Howard, former immigration minister Philip Ruddock and immigration minister Senator Amanda Vanstone with their lips sewn shut – Michael's response to the plight of refugees and their appalling treatment behind barbed wire. A visitor to the exhibition took offence and wrote to the prime minister that the work was treasonous. Howard's office referred the letter to the Department of the Arts, which then contacted the gallery to ask whether the gallery relied on public funding. The inference was clear: exhibit art that is critical of the government and your funding will be withdrawn.

I was outraged. My partner, Gary Corr, who was living in Wagga Wagga at the time, went straight to the gallery and bought the images of Howard and Ruddock for immediate transfer to Parliament House. When I resigned from the Senate, I gave them to the Museum of Australian Democracy, not just because of the human rights abuses practised by Howard and Ruddock but also as a reminder of the threat to artistic expression posed by increasingly right-wing governments. I regretted not buying the whole set at the time and am pleased to say that all three are now in the museum, providing a context of contemporary social comment to offset the usual flattering political photos, portraits and memorabilia.

The museum has gone on to collect more work by Michael Agzarian, specifically the originals of three posters that were plastered all over Australia's capital cities. Based on the iconic image by Shepard Fairey depicting President Obama over the word 'HOPE', Agzarian's work featured a drawing of then Prime Minister Tony Abbott surmounting the word 'HOPELESS', as well as Treasurer Joe Hockey branded 'CLUELESS' and Attorney-General George Brandis labelled 'HEARTLESS'. Inspired by former Prime Minister Paul Keating's takedown of Malcolm Turnbull, where he compared Turnbull to a firework – 'You light him up, there's a bit of a fizz, and then nothing … nothing' – Agzarian produced a picture of Turnbull with the word 'FIZZA' in time for the 2016 federal election. Agzarian has said, 'It's obvious that my art was resonating with the public. They saw my art as a conduit for their frustrations.'[1]

Artistic activism comes in many forms. It was the magnificent paintings of watercolourists such as Max Angus, Elspeth Vaughan and Patricia Giles, and the wilderness photographs of Olegas Truchanas and Peter Dombrovskis that introduced people who had never been there to the beauty of Lake Pedder. Bob Brown and I had the iconic Truchanas photograph of the lake and its beach hanging in our offices throughout our parliamentary careers. The Peter Dombrovskis photograph of Rock Island Bend was a major motivator for the Franklin River campaign, and no one will forget the music. When the opening chords of Shane Howard's 'Let the Franklin Flow' filled Melbourne's Rod Laver Arena during Carole King's Australian tour more than thirty years after the Franklin River campaign, the crowd still remembered and went wild.

For decades photographers, writers and artists have stood up for the forests, to the point of famously boycotting the 'Ten Days on the Island' festival in 2003 because it was sponsored by Forestry Tasmania, the destroyer of Tasmania's old-growth forests. They were joined by the writers Tim Winton, Joan London, Peter Carey and Richard Flanagan. At the time Richard Flanagan said, 'I felt [Forestry

Tasmania] were trying to use the artistic achievements of Tasmanians to veil the terrible shame of what they are doing, and I didn't want to be a party to it'.[2] In 2008 he reflected, 'I grew up surrounded by rainforest in north-western Tasmania, a place whose extraordinary beauty and wildness are unlike anywhere else in the world. When I was very young I developed a strong sense of wonder about things that are not manmade and I realised they were not just beautiful but sacred. When we destroy that land, we destroy something fundamental in our own humanity.'[3] These are powerful, effective words. It is no wonder that he was so vociferously condemned by pro-logging Labor Premier Paul Lennon, who declared, 'Richard Flanagan and his fictions are not welcome in the new Tasmania.'

~

THE ARTWORK IN PARLIAMENT HOUSE is outstanding, as anyone who has been into the Great Hall and seen the overwhelmingly beautiful tapestry of Arthur Boyd's *Untitled (Shoalhaven Landscape)* will attest. However, the collection itself is not as bold as I would have hoped an exhibition at the heart of our democracy might be, and there is a reason for that. When the new Parliament House was opened, the rules governing the acquisition of art within a set budget made clear that the work was to be from new and emerging Australian artists. This meant that more works could be collected, the flavour of the collection would always be contemporary, and new or established but uncollected artists would be acknowledged. But then John Howard and his extreme conservatives such as Ross Cameron took government in 1996. Cameron, a far-right Christian conservative, was against the contemporary art collection, which he described as engineered by the 'correct, highbrow, holier-than-thou, you-must-like-this-shit brigade'[4], and brought about a change to the acquisitions policy. Howard instigated a review of the collection, and the new rules provided for the work of established artists – including those no longer alive – to be collected. Lots of photographs and botanical drawings were added to appease the conservatives.

The committee overseeing new acquisitions consists of the Speaker of the House of Representatives, the president of the Senate and their deputies, an advisor from the National Gallery and the director of the collection. There were long periods when nothing was collected; the committee's enthusiasm was variable and subject to concern that buying art at a time of budget constraints was politically unpalatable. Budgets were not increased, and cheaper but less significant works could be collected. There is no doubt that the enthusiasm for the collection and the ideological views of the government have influenced what has been acquired; some of it has been described as 'avant-garde crap', notably by Tony Abbott. While new and interesting work is still acquired and is on public display, it's hard to see politically challenging work from contemporary Aboriginal urban artists such as those in the proppaNOW collective making the cut under conservative governments. While beautiful, decorative and interesting work enhances the lives of those who work in the parliament and those who visit, including schoolchildren, more radicalism and political comment are desperately needed.

One exception, hanging in the Senate corridor, is an acrylic painting by Richard Bell and Emory Douglas, *A White Hero for Black Australia* (2011). This depicts the defiant moment in the 1968 Mexico City Olympic Games when Australian runner Peter Norman, having won silver in the 200-metre sprint, stood on the podium wearing a human rights badge in solidarity with gold and bronze medallists African-American athletes Tommie Smith and John Carlos as they raised their fists in a Black Power salute. Norman was ostracised on his return to Australia and died never having received an apology or recognition for his athletic achievements or his courageous and important stand. Six years after his death the Australian Parliament apologised. In a 2014 interview with *The Guardian*, Richard Bell described the stand as 'a perfect example of direct visual activism', adding that, 'We should be really proud that that guy was Australian and had those attitudes at that time. We need those attitudes and that sort of courage, even now it needs to come to the fore.'[5]

I was given a valuable insight into the power of the artwork in the days leading up to my resignation as Australian Greens leader in 2015. I had been out to dinner with my Western Australian Senate colleague Rachel Siewert at a cafe in Canberra when a young Aboriginal boy, Dylan, approached our table. He said that he had seen Rachel speaking in the Senate that day. We started chatting and he explained that he was down from Daly River in the Northern Territory with two friends, Iggy and Monty, on an exchange with St Edmund's College, and was due to fly out very early the following morning. He was an interesting young man and an artist in his community, as were his friends. I was very impressed when I asked him what he wanted to do when he left school and he replied, 'I want to be chief minister.' He was eager to know about Nova Peris, the Labor senator for the Northern Territory, and was familiar with the work of the Aboriginal Affairs minister Nigel Scullion. I told him I was sorry we had not known he was in the parliament or we could have shown him around; the more I talked to him, the more I liked his curiosity and drive.

The following morning I was busy preparing for the day's sitting when my staffer took a phone call from security, saying that there was a young man at the Parliament House entrance who said that I had offered to show him around. Sure enough Dylan and his friends were there. Once we had organised a pass for them all, I asked, 'What happened to the early flight to Darwin?'

'Alarm didn't go off,' he said.

All three alarms had not gone off? Incredible!

After we sorted things out with the school, we had a wonderful day. I organised for the boys to have a guided tour of the Aboriginal works in the collection, and I joined them and their guide, the wonderful Alva Maguire. It was great to learn more about the work I passed every day. They were particularly struck by a pair of Michael Cook's works on the way to the cafeteria, images showing ninety-six per cent of the population as black and only four per cent as white, and placing black faces at the seat of power in front of Old Parliament House and at the High Court.

One of my favourite pieces in the collection is Laurie Nilsen's barbed-wire sculpture *Emu*. It is near Ozzie's coffee shop and is passed by thousands of people every day, but very few members of parliament or visitors would know the significance of the barbed wire. In an interview in *Art Collector* magazine in 2007, Nilsen spoke of witnessing the slow and agonising death of more than thirty emus caught up in barbed wire at Goolburris on the Bungil Creek in western Queensland. He pointed out that farmers use barbed wire to protect waterholes for cattle, with shocking consequences for emus when droughts force them to try to get through the fence.

'They're not like the roos or wallabies that can either jump over or crawl under,' says Nilsen. 'They seem to just pace up and down the fence and then on the second or third day they make the decision to step through and a lot of them get caught up in the top two strands, they twist over and their leg just gets caught and they lie there till they die.' Nilsen added that some of the emus he came across were still alive and he had had to put them out of their misery. The emu is the traditional totem for his people and in many respects it was like killing family members. 'I don't think I'll ever get around to making as many as I've seen perish,' he said. Barbed wire kills emus in the wild, and Nilsen uses it to restore them to life.[6]

It was good to see other pieces I didn't know we had in the collection, such as Lorraine Connelly-Northey's opossum skin cloak, also made of wire and feathers. Connelly-Northey is a Wiradjuri woman from Swan Hill in Victoria. The boys were fascinated that a possum fur cloak could be depicted in wire and feathers, and they stood for some time studying it. They were also taken with the coloured ochres in the magnificent bark paintings of John Mawurndjul; their own Daly River artwork, they said, was predominantly in black and white. Finally we got to *A White Hero for Black Australia*, and they loved it. They too found it a perfect example of direct visual activism and immediately wanted their photos taken with it, copying the Black Power salute.

Security officers opened the doors for us. The boys were visibly excited by that gesture, and I asked them why. They said how great it was to be with the 'boss lady' instead of always being stopped and searched. It was a reminder of the cultural context into which Australia places young Aboriginal people. Senator Siewert and Senator Peris made time to meet the boys, as did minister Scullion. Aboriginal and Torres Strait Islander Social Justice Commissioner Mick Gooda was in parliament that day, and he offered to have Dylan accompany him to a meeting of Aboriginal leaders taking place in Parliament House.

Before they left, Dylan announced that he was going back to Daly River to paint something suitable for the walls of Parliament House. It remains to be seen whether he ever does, and I sometimes wonder what impact that day had on Monty, Iggy and Dylan and their arts practice at Daly River.

I did try to have one work 'created' by the parliament while I was there. At that time I had visited Fireworks Gallery in Queensland and was immediately taken by the series of prints that constituted *The Ongoing Adventures of X and Ray*, a dingo and a stingray created by the late Lin Onus in collaboration with Michael Eather. I could not go past the print where X and Ray are witnessing the sinking of the last ship carrying woodchips from Australian shores.

Michael Eather told me he was looking after the last of the highly collectible Lin Onus dingo sculptures and that the Lin Onus Trust that now owns the work wanted it to go into a public collection. I thought it would be perfect for Parliament House, that we could collect the print series and combine it with a Michael Eather fibreglass stingray sculpture and a Lin Onus dingo and bring an installation of *The Adventures of X and Ray* to life in the corridors of power.

I have no doubt it would have been extremely popular. I put the idea in writing to the committee who decides such matters and it was rejected because the parliament already has one Lin Onus print.

~

IN MY EARLY YEARS IN the Tasmanian Parliament I worked with leading Tasmanian artists to develop an arts policy for the Tasmanian Greens, and I remember its first line: 'The Arts is the key to transforming Tasmania'. I believed it then and I believe it now, for both Tasmania and the nation. The arts holds up a mirror enabling us to see who we are and what we could be. Throughout my years in the Senate I held the Greens arts portfolio, as I had done previously when leader of the Tasmanian Greens. While the premier and leader of the Opposition in Tasmania took the resource-based portfolios for their parties, I took the arts and education portfolios. Despite the arts being typically regarded as a remnant or an afterthought after logging and mining and heavy industrial development, we had a vibrant and highly political arts community well ahead of its time. It is a joy to me now to see that with the cultural drawcard of the Museum of Old and New Art (MONA) to Tasmania, the arts as a sector has become 'visible', and our many artists are receiving the exposure and recognition they so rightly deserve.

In those early days in 1992 I was invited to open an exhibition of handwoven fabric by Hobart artist Robyn Glade-Wright at the Dick Bett Gallery. I was deeply impressed by her work because she was a female artist who had chosen woven fabric as her medium and incorporated strong social-justice themes into her creations at a time when the arts elites considered that women's 'crafts' were not fine art. The exhibition included pieces promoting gay rights, women's rights and justice for Aboriginal people. I bought a length of her fabric called *Trial* and had it made into a suit by a Tasmanian seamstress so I could literally wear my heart on my sleeve in the Tasmanian Parliament.

Ian Bonde described *Trial* in his introductory essay to the exhibition as arising 'from a personal view about the need to recognise Aboriginal place and justice within white Australian society'. He continued:

> The controversies surrounding black deaths in custody and the displays of questionable police morality in the media make this topic as relevant today as were the posters nailed to trees in the bush on Governor Arthur's orders in 1828. After preparing notes and assessing the potential of various images, Robyn settled on the motif of an Aboriginal facing the profile of a Hogarthian judge in full wigged regalia. She wanted to consider how Aboriginals may assess white folk within the white justice system. With a clear knowledge of the desired motif, the next stage involved its actual construction and choice of colour. This is the point where a graphed image becomes integrated within the work. In this case the Aboriginal face appears rather forceful because of its clarity and dominance, while the judge displays an almost comical, mocking European sneer. As a counterpoint dark vertical bars split the images to punctuate the field.
>
> Again the subtlety of the design belies a sinister reference. At first glance the work can be viewed as an attractive decorative fabric, but this is deceptive. The beautiful crimson colour suggests fiery warmth and passion, but it also refers to spilt blood. The rhythmic pattern has a calm and meditative effect until it is understood that the myriad staring faces refer to the 'trials' and Aboriginal deaths since the arrival of white folk to this land. Thus the piece becomes a pulsating vision with an enticing beauty and repulsive content.

I wore that suit often, including on the day the Tasmanian Parliament apologised to Tasmania's Aboriginal people for the Stolen Generations, a decade before Prime Minister Kevin Rudd made the same apology in the federal parliament. 'Bringing Them Home' is the title of the 1997 Report of the Human Rights and Equal Opportunity Commission that laid bare the cruelty of successive Australian state and federal governments in tearing Aboriginal families apart. The Howard government refused to apologise but state governments did. The apology in Tasmania occurred on 13 August 1997, during the period in which I held the balance of power in the Liberal minority government of Tony Rundle. It was one of my proudest days in politics and certainly one of the most dignified and significant. In my own speech of apology I turned to the work of Tasmanian Aboriginal poet Jim Everett to highlight the pain of a people whom government had determined, right up until the late 1960s, no longer existed.

I quoted his poem 'Yes, I Know What You Mean':

> Am I Tasmanian Aboriginal? My bloody oath I am.
> What? Not black enough? Well that don't mean a damn.
> Only part Abo is what you say. You really are a charm.
> Is it my leg, my head, my foot, or is it my right arm?
> Oh I see, I'm not full blood. Well that's a funny thing.
> Always thought I was full of blood a-pumpin' like a spring.
> But if I conform and show my wit and still claim I'm a
>     Koori,
> Whites deny my right as one and deny me my identity.
> Oh you say I'm not one of those and I know what you
>     mean.
> Then how come you distinguish those? Yes I know what
>     you mean.

The premier had intended for the Aboriginal people to stand in the meeting room near the Chamber as they were not elected members and the rules precluded them from being on the floor of the House. I strongly objected, insisting that such an arrangement only reinforced discrimination and undermined the healing process; they should join us on the floor of the parliament. It was unprecedented and against the rules but we made it happen, and it was a national first.

Annette Peardon, representing Tasmania's Aboriginal people, remarked:

> It is a welcome gesture of the government and the parliament to apologise for what must be seen as one of the most tragic events in my people's history. I believe it is the first time that any Aborigine in Tasmania has entered the Chamber of the parliament in session and I believe it is the first time anywhere in Australia an Aboriginal delegation has been invited to address the Parliament in session ... While it is true that those of us snatched from our community are a special case, there is a growing need for a plan, a policy for my people's future. We have little bits of land, we need more, when will we get it? Our people are being prosecuted in the courts for practising their culture, when will that stop?

Wearing the *Trial* never felt more powerful than on that day.

I wore that suit many times over the years, including in the Senate, but some occasions stick in my mind. One such was to an event to raise awareness of Aboriginal economic justice staged by The Body Shop in Hobart. I had been invited to speak and so had to provide a short biography for the person introducing me. All went well. Weeks after the event I received a letter informing me that I had been unsuccessful in my application for a job as a shop assistant at The Body Shop. The bio had apparently been put in the wrong tray and my skills, it seems, were not up to scratch. To this day I smile as I pass The Body Shop.

You never think of well-worn clothing as worth keeping, as having significance, except perhaps for special-occasion outfits such as a wedding dress or a twenty-first birthday outfit, and even then after a while you question the point of keeping them and rack your brain for a theatre company or similar that might use them. So what do you do with a suit that you wore when history was made, which meant a lot but has passed its prime? Wear the jacket in the garden; cut it up for cleaning cloths; send it to an op shop? Fortunately I had the option of giving my *Trial* suit to the Museum of Australian Democracy. Such collections, when viewed together, do provide some insights into the person whose apparel is on show. Kevin Rudd donated his R.M. Williams boots, Tim Fischer his ties, Dame Quentin Bryce the suit she wore when, as Australia's first woman governor-general, she swore in Julia Gillard as Australia's first woman prime minister. I donated my own statement of art as activism and solidarity with Australia's Aboriginal and Torres Strait Islander people.

# 14

# Backpacking and Beyond: Sri Lanka

OBJECT: This is not a white van, *a painting by Sri Lankan artist Chandraguptha Thenuwara. Christine bought the artwork after conversations with the artist in 2012.*

MY PASSION FOR SRI LANKA began when I was a backpacker in the early 1980s, and it has stayed with me for life. Sri Lanka is a beautiful country with a fascinating and ancient past and a brutal recent history. The painting *This is not a white van* on my wall at Parliament House epitomised social justice, courage, defiance and solidarity with the people of Sri Lanka. It shows a white van with blackened windows, and the words 'This is not a white van' written underneath in English, Sinhala and Tamil. I knew what this painting meant; it spoke truth to power in Canberra and it spoke of personal responsibility to me.

My involvement began with a personal response to one of the ethical dilemmas any backpacker faces – namely what to do as desperately poor people beg from you, day after day, in village after village. Their need is overwhelming at times, because you know that you have far more than they do but you cannot give to them all, and what you give them is so minuscule compared with their poverty. So it comes back to the value-based question: What ought one to do?

I had never really seen abject poverty up close until I travelled overseas in the late 1970s. Coming home from a year in Europe through Thailand and later backpacking through Asia, the Middle East and Africa in 1982, every day my husband Neville and I were confronted by hands held out on street corners, through the window of a tuktuk or taxi, or by children clinging on to our legs. We decided that the best way to handle all this need was to contribute when we got home in a more meaningful way than just handing out coins randomly.

Having made that decision, we were walking through a small town in the extremely poor tea-plantation district of Sri Lanka when we saw a couple of Dominican nuns walking up the street. We got talking to them about their work and went back with them to the home they ran to care for approximately forty girls. They explained that the children were mostly the daughters of poor Tamil families who could not care for them and so put them in the home, where they would be fed and educated.

I was really impressed by what the nuns were doing on next to no funding. The home was very basic but ordered, clean and organised into dormitories and attached to a school. It was a hard life for the children but at least they were being educated, housed and fed, and were no longer on the streets subject to abuse or forced into child labour. I asked what we could do to help. They explained that they wanted to buy more treadle sewing machines so the girls could be taught to sew and therefore earn money by making and selling clothes in the market. We agreed to buy a sewing machine as well as finding extra fabric.

The machine was purchased locally, and when we got home Frank's Fashions in Devonport agreed to help immediately by providing cotton fabric remnants, zips, buttons, bias binding and lace. I cannot tell you how thrilled we all were, especially the saleswomen in Frank's, when the nuns sent a photo of the children in their new dresses. But sadly all that came to an end as the civil war between the Tamil

Tigers and the Sri Lankan Army started in Sri Lanka in July 1983. In the early years of the war – which continued on and off until the Sri Lankan military defeated the Tamil Tigers in 2009 – I received a letter from one of the nuns to say they had to go to Colombo for safety and that the girls' home 'was no more'. As this was years before the internet had been invented and before telephones were accessible to the poor in Sri Lanka, their fate remained a mystery. Over the years I often wondered what had happened to them, but reports of the atrocities and human rights abuses were only occasionally given in Australia's media. In 1999 the United Nations released a report saying that Sri Lanka had one of the highest rates of disappearances in the world and that 12,000 people had disappeared after being detained by the Sri Lankan security forces.

My election to the Senate in 2005 coincided with the election of Mahinda Rajapaksa as president of Sri Lanka and a build-up of military action against the Tamil Tigers, with horrific consequences for civilians. The final onslaught by the Sri Lankan Army was a slaughter that is still the subject of international investigation: 40,000 civilians were killed in the last months of the war in 2009, with the Sri Lankan Government claiming to be the first in the world to eradicate terrorism on its own soil.[1] Thousands of mainly Tamil refugees flooded from the country as anyone suspected of being associated in any way with the Tigers was hunted down by the Rajapaksa government. Their land was taken from them and given to the military.

Many Tamils were beaten, raped and 'disappeared' in white vans without number plates, especially in Colombo and Jaffna. Being 'white vanned' was the way dissidents and critics were silenced, their dead bodies later found by the sides of the roads. The abductions were carried out with such impunity that the president's brother, Defence Secretary Gotabhaya Rajapaksa, has been accused of being the 'architect of white van abductions', and investigations continue into his role to this day.

I went back to Sri Lanka in 2012, my first opportunity after the civil war to see for myself what was going on and to try to find out what had happened to the girls' home. To my surprise I found that the home was still operating, and had been for many years. Why the nuns had told me the school and the home no longer existed became clear when I discovered that the government had taken over all church land and buildings. What had been a Catholic school was now a Tamil high school, but the girls' home had not been acquired; no doubt the government considered it an unnecessary waste of money to care for and educate poverty-stricken girls. So the girls' home existed as a separate entity in the middle of the school.

Nothing much had changed in all those years. The home was run down and basic but operating. The nun in charge told me the story of one of the girls. She had been brought up in the home and after leaving school stayed on to help look after the younger ones. She fell in love with a poor boy from the plantations, but they had no money and needed someone to sponsor their marriage. The nun in charge organised the money from her own limited resources on condition it was paid back as quickly as possible. After the wedding the young bride went to live with the nuns in Colombo while her husband went to the Middle East to work in appalling conditions as virtual slave labour to earn the necessary money. When I asked how much we were talking about, it was $250 Australian. It really brings home what suffering is being endured to repay such a small amount by our standards. I paid the bill so that at least if the young bride's husband remained in the Middle East it was for their future, not to repay a debt.

It has given me much joy to be back in contact with the home and to help them out in subsequent years. The first thing they wanted was music. A piano would have been impossible to transport there so we settled on an electric keyboard. Next came retiling the toilets and building a shower, in spite of the reluctance of the nun in charge to install one. Many of the girls, she told me, would never be able to have a shower once they left the home, so I had to consider whether it was wise to provide something beyond what life might have in store for them. However, I decided to back hope over experience and install the shower. They also wanted a vegetable garden to grow their own food, which I helped with too, and I loved hearing from them on my return about their gardening successes.

None of the children in the home high up in the centre of the island had seen the sea, even though Sri Lanka is the same size as Tasmania. I wanted to give them a present and sent them money to fund an excursion for them all to go to Trincomalee to see the ocean. I told the nun in charge that I wanted every child to have an ice-cream as a celebration when they arrived at the beach. She was reluctant; to reduce costs she had provided food for the two days they would be away, and individual ice-creams seemed way too indulgent. Having spent six years with frugal and practical nuns during my own schooldays, I was suspicious that she might use the money for something more sensible. But she kept faith with my written instructions and sent a photo showing them with ice-creams, causing everyone in my office in Hobart to be misty-eyed. We laughed too, as the nun reported that when the bus stopped at the beach, the children were so excited and so in awe of the ocean that they ran straight into the sea fully dressed.

Even though the war was over, everywhere I went when I was there in 2012 – on the roads, in the towns, outside shops, temples, in marketplaces – there were soldiers. They were often no more than children dressed in military uniform with assault rifles slung over their shoulders and leaning on walls and fences and eating ice-creams or sweets, like kids everywhere. It was quite clear that the Rajapaksa government had not stood them down after the war and continued to pay them as a ready power base.

I returned to Colombo and decided to try to understand what was really going on in Sri Lanka beneath the facade of peace. There is nowhere better to start than with artists – people courageous enough to speak truth to power. I asked about political art and was shown the work of Chandraguptha Thenuwara in a private gallery. He had become famous for *Barrelism*, which reflects on the role of the military in Sri Lanka and features barrels and camouflage. But the work whose power immediately struck me was *This is not a white van*. It is a brilliant and audacious take on *Ceci n'est pas une pipe* (*The Treachery of Images*) by René Magritte, the painting of a pipe which of course is not the pipe itself but the image.

For an artist to risk his life by drawing attention to the fact that these white death vans exist while declaring that they do not was masterful. The painting had been exhibited in the Lionel Wendt Gallery in Colombo in 2011 as part of an exhibition called The Wall and Other Works, all drawing attention to aspects of life in Sri Lanka that had remained unspoken – such as the existence of those white vans.

I decided to buy the work and bring it back to Australia to hang in my office in Parliament House. But I wanted to make sure the artist would not be 'disappeared' once the news travelled back via the diplomatic corps to Sri Lanka. I went out to the university where Chandraguptha is deputy head of the School of Fine Arts, but before I was permitted to enter the campus the security guards insisted I forfeit my passport. Handing over one's passport to the representative of an authoritarian regime is not something to be done lightly. I decided that if Chandraguptha had the courage to take on the regime with his paintings, I should be brave enough to hand over my passport.

I met him in his university office, where we talked about his art and other things. I am not able to say what specifically, just as I cannot name the girls' home; Sri Lanka is still not a safe place. He was delighted when I told him I wanted to buy his painting, and when I asked about the consequences of hanging it in Australia's national Parliament House, he assured me that, as in the case of Íngrid Betancourt, captured by the Revolutionary Armed Forces in Colombia in 2002 and released six years later, it is a form of insurance for those who speak out to have advocates abroad. The higher the profile overseas, the more difficult it is to have someone disappear with no questions asked.

Once I had bought the painting came the task of getting it home. It is quite large and was framed, so I asked the gallery if it could be sent. I was advised that since it was the most controversial painting in Sri Lanka it would disappear without trace at the border. So it came out of the frame, was rolled up, put in a canister, and – had I been asked – what I would have described as a 'Panoramic View of the Tea Plantations' was carefully carried through customs.

It hung in the foyer of my office throughout my whole period as Australian Greens leader, and over the years many visitors saw and commented on it. I was proud to have it there as a statement of commitment to the people of Sri Lanka and as a statement of the Australian Greens' support for a United Nations investigation into war crimes in that country. I wanted people to be aware that we recognised that human rights abuses were happening under the Rajapaksa regime and that, while the Australian Government was turning a blind eye, we were not.

Instead of taking a strong stand against these abuses, Australia had compromised itself. The Rudd, Gillard, Abbott and Turnbull governments wanted the Sri Lankan refugees intercepted before they left the country or, if they managed to escape by sea, turned around and sent back. Australia declared that Tamils seeking to leave Sri Lanka were not political refugees but economic migrants looking for personal advancement, in spite of the UN resolutions to the contrary.

In March 2013 the UN Human Rights Council expressed concern about 'reports of continuing violations; concern at reports of enforced disappearances, extrajudicial killings, torture, threats to the rule of law, religious discrimination and intimidation of civil society activists and journalists'. In November 2013 newly elected Prime Minister Abbott travelled to Colombo and announced that Australia would give two Bay-class patrol boats, recently retired from surveillance service in Australia, to the Sri Lankan Navy to use as interdiction vessels, capturing asylum-seeker boats before they are able to leave Sri Lankan waters. 'People smuggling is a curse. It is an evil trade ... the promises that people smugglers offer are promises of death, not life,' he said.

I condemned this $2 million gift, saying, 'The prime minister's silence on human rights abuses in Sri Lanka is inexcusable complicity, but this is nothing less than collaboration and it is abhorrent.' When it was reported that one of Rajapaksa's relatives and senior government officials were involved in the people-smuggling trade and were profiteering from dollars Australia provided to stop asylum seekers, I asked about that in the Senate and the Abbott government denied it. The Abbott government knew at the time that several senior Sri Lankan naval officers were involved in the people-smuggling trade but chose to ignore it.

The collaboration with the corrupt and cruel Rajapaksa regime is a stain on Australia's recent political history. I took up the disappearances issue with both Bob Carr and Julie Bishop as foreign ministers. Neither pursued the matter beyond raising it in diplomatic reports and noting it in resolutions of the Office of the United Nations High Commissioner for Refugees. Both were compromised by Australia's complicity with Mahinda Rajapaksa in 'stopping the boats', and both would have been well aware that the United States had decided that a hard line on human rights abuse would drive Rajapaksa further into the arms of China.

The bishop of Jaffna came to Australia to plead for his people, but when I met with him at Parliament House he expressed disappointment with the lack of empathy from Australia's leaders. I addressed rallies of people who felt sure that if they could only be heard, Australia would change its hardline position on asylum seekers. But they soon learned that the imperative in both Liberal and Labor governments was to instil fear in Australian electorates to win votes, not to win freedom from torture and abuse for people in Sri Lanka.

When Thisara Samarasinghe was appointed high commissioner to Australia in 2011 after being chief of the Sri Lankan Navy in the final years of the civil war, I called on the Gillard government and Kevin Rudd as foreign minister not to recognise his credentials. The International Commission of Jurists had already submitted evidence to the Australian Federal Police pointing out that, at the end of the war, Sri Lankan naval ships under Samarasinghe's command had fired on civilians who were fleeing the fighting in Sri Lanka's north-east. He denied it, but I refused to meet with him or attend any functions at the Sri Lankan high commission. He sent numerous invitations but I had made it clear that I did not regard him as a fit and proper person to be a high commissioner. The Australian Greens was the only party to take such a stand.

In 2014 Australia's slippery slope of appeasement of the Rajapaksa regime was complete when Julie Bishop failed to back a resolution for an independent international investigation into alleged war crimes after the release of a new report detailing 'credible' claims of civilian bombings, extrajudicial killings and other abuses. I requested that Australia, like Canada, should boycott the Commonwealth Heads of Government meeting in Colombo because of the ongoing disappearances, human rights abuses and refusal to conduct a UN investigation into war crimes; this was rejected by both Liberal and Labor. When I said to Julie Bishop in a private meeting that the Rajapaksa regime was the closest thing to a totalitarian dictatorship masquerading as a democracy in the region, her reply was, 'Christine, you need to get out more.'

Rajapaksa was defeated by Maithripala Sirisena in the Sri Lankan presidential election of 2015. The new president purged the Canberra mission and six people were recalled. I welcomed the decision, saying that Australia's decision to accept Samarasinghe's credentials in the first place had been flawed and that 'we have to now have a full and proper review into Australia's engagement with the completely discredited, anti-democratic, shocking regime that was the Rajapaksa government'.

Julie Bishop gleefully tweeted me that Rajapaksa had been ousted in a 'democratic' election, that the people had rejected him. She should have known as foreign minister that it was not as simple as that. Rajapaksa was defeated because he had upset the geopolitics of the region. He had courted the Chinese, who had invested heavily in the southern Sri Lankan port of Hambantota, giving the Chinese access to the Indian Ocean as part of China's maritime 'string of pearls' link of ports to guard its sea routes.

When the Rajapaksas permitted a nuclear-powered Chinese submarine to dock in the newly constructed port, India protested and warned that Sri Lanka must not do that again or at the very least had to inform India. The warning was ignored. Within months of a scheduled election health minister Maithripala Sirisena emerged as a presidential candidate and won. Rajapaksa was toppled as president and didn't make it back as prime minister either. It was clear that Washington's and New Delhi's strategic interests in the region had prevailed.

Afterwards, Sri Lankan Prime Minister Ranil Wickremesinghe made clear what we all knew, namely that the Australian Government's silence on alleged human rights abuses was the price it paid to secure cooperation from the former Rajapaksa government on stopping asylum-seeker boats. Australian prime ministers Kevin Rudd, Julia Gillard and Tony Abbott and their foreign and immigration ministers have this and the suffering of thousands of refugees and asylum seekers as their legacy.

As for the artist Chandraguptha Thenuwara, he continues to inspire people to stand up for human rights and freedom everywhere. His more recent exhibition featured works called *These are not white flags*. He was invited to speak at the 7th World Conference on Arts and Culture in Malta in 2016, addressing the question, 'How do we support advocacy for freedom of expression and cultural rights?' Director of Regional Arts Victoria Esther Anatolitis, who was in the audience, told me that Chandraguptha had said in his answer that his signature White Van piece was in the 'Christine Milne Collection' in Australia. Our collaboration had provided something of an answer to the question.

# 15

# Seeking Asylum

OBJECTS: *'Not Drowning', political cartoon by Cathy Wilcox, 2016;*
*'Drowning', political cartoon by Andrew Marlton,*
*First Dog on the Moon, 2012*

WHEN VIETNAMESE BOAT PEOPLE CAME to Australia between 1976 and 1981, they were subjected to ridicule and racism. As a teacher in north-west Tasmania I was horrified by the attitudes being expressed in my classroom; students proclaimed that 'we should shoot them out of the water'. I realised that in a predominantly white community like Devonport, it was unrealistic to think that the students would ever have met anyone of a different culture, and so were repeating what they had heard at home.

So in 1981 I decided to introduce a multicultural education program in the school. I approached the local migrant support worker and invited the few Filipino, Vietnamese and Chinese people living in the community to come in and talk with the students. The staff were very supportive and soon we had cooking, music, history and literature curriculum units under way. In the course of this work I heard about a Vietnamese refugee family who had arrived in Devonport sponsored by one of the churches. I decided to meet them to see how they might become involved.

That is how I met the wonderful Diep and Liem Tran and their daughters, Hang, Ha and Vi. They had left Vietnam from a beach in the countryside about 450 kilometres from Saigon, in the dark of a new-moon night in mid-1980. They were first on a small boat, and then transferred to a larger one, and were at sea for four days before landing in north-west Malaysia. I remember Diep describing her overwhelming terror that Hang, nearly three at the time, or Ha, then a baby, would cry and expose their hiding place in the nights leading up to their departure. It is almost impossible to imagine how frightened you would be as a pregnant woman with a one- and a three-year-old setting out in the dark of night on a boat, not knowing if any one of you would survive.

Vi was born in the Malaysian refugee camp where they were taken and where they stayed for five months. When Diep's family was offered resettlement in the USA, she and Liem couldn't go with them because Diep was too close to giving birth. The next country to offer asylum was Australia, and so they came here. They were sponsored by a church group and arrived in Devonport in 1981, becoming Australian citizens in 1982. Liem remembers my first meeting with them after I had volunteered to help teach them English. He laughs when he recalls how he was reluctant even to answer yes/no questions because he thought too much would be lost in translation.

Liem worked at Baker's Milk processing plant and Diep at Richie's fish factory. They worked hard but their language difficulties meant they were socially isolated and incredibly lonely. They came to visit me at my home in Ulverstone and were very excited when my sons were born. Language remained a huge barrier and so I was sad but not surprised when they decided in 1987 to go to Melbourne, where there was a large Vietnamese community with whom they could communicate fluently and in which there were many more social and economic opportunities.

Before they left, we talked about education. They were extremely grateful to the teachers at the primary school in Devonport who had been so welcoming and where the children were doing very well. They thought that if they stayed, the children might receive a better education in Tasmania than in a large multicultural Victorian school, but what was the point if the parents were not happy? I had to agree.

I lost touch with them when they went to Melbourne. We couldn't write or ring each other and so we all got on with our lives. And then out of the blue in 2008 we caught up again. They had seen me on television and so asked Hang, by then a teacher, to write a letter to the Greens to try to reconnect. We had a great day together at their home in Melbourne, where Diep and Liem and the family welcomed me with the most amazing feast, featuring every Vietnamese delicacy you could imagine. The table groaned under the weight of so much fabulous food. I met their son Duong, born after they left Tasmania, and caught up with their daughters Ha and Vi as Hang had to work that day. The children are all great young Australians, all tertiary educated and all working in education, planning, environment, accounting and business. I was pleased to learn that Liem returned to Vietnam to see his family in 1989 and that Diep had made it to the USA in 1992 to see her family again after a twelve-year separation. They are proud Australian citizens and talk often of giving back to this country. We stay in touch and I am very moved that Liem now calls me his Australian sister.

There are thousands of similar heartwarming stories in communities around Australia, not just about Vietnamese boat people but about people in every wave of refugees to this country. Most people who opposed bringing Vietnamese boat people to Australia in the 1970s and 1980s would now have changed their minds about Vietnamese refugees and would never admit to having been vehemently opposed at the time. But that story is deliberately suppressed when Australian politicians and a complicit Murdoch media decide to incite fear of refugees as a way of winning elections.

Racism is powerful in Australia. It always has been. The White Australia policy was not dismantled until the 1960s and 1970s, and its cultural legacy remains. Australians have had a long history of discriminating against Chinese and Pacific Islanders because of the fear that they would take Australian workers' jobs. One of the first pieces of legislation passed after Federation was the *Immigration Restriction Act 1901*. With a history like ours it is not difficult to stir up fear that too many new arrivals will undermine national security.

In 1988, when he was leader of the Opposition, John Howard said that Australian social cohesion might be better supported if Asian migration was slowed down. He apologised for that, but then pandered to Pauline Hanson and One Nation. When down in the polls in 2001, he fell back on the tried and true issue of border security, saying 'we will decide who comes to this country and the circumstances in which they come' to help him win the election. It did.

The refugee and asylum-seeker debate in Australia is never taken in a global context unless it suits the hate and fear agenda. It is as if the issue is peculiar to Australia and can be dealt with by adopting the 'pull up the ladder, Jack, we're okay' mentality. Wars by their very nature generate refugees. Some periods of history see more displaced people than others. At the moment there are sixty million people worldwide seeking asylum because they have been displaced, mostly by war in the Middle East, a war in which Australia was and remains involved.

It is a complete abrogation of responsibility to invade another country and then wash your hands of the results. When Prime Minister John Howard followed the United States into a war in Iraq in 2003, what did he expect would happen to the hundreds of thousands of people who would be left homeless as their villages were destroyed? Where did he think those who suffered persecution because of the unleashed sectarian violence would end up? Why is it acceptable to dump refugees out of sight and out of mind on Manus Island and Nauru rather than conduct an inquiry into Howard's role in going to war on a lie and displacing millions of people who now seek refuge? And at the same time as Prime Minister Abbott, with the support of the Shorten Labor Opposition, was begging the Iraqis to permit Australia to join the most recent 2014 disastrous intervention in the Middle East, Abbott was determined to stop the boats filled with people fleeing John Howard's previous race to follow the Americans into war. Rupert Murdoch and his newspapers cheered him on every step of the way, supporting the war and condemning the refugees.

At least in Europe there is a recognition of cause and effect. In response to Donald Trump's condemnation of Germany's action in 'letting all these illegals into the country' German Deputy Chancellor Sigmar Gabriel pointed out, 'There is a link between America's flawed interventionist policy, especially the Iraq war, and the refugee crisis.'[1] It has never suited the Liberals, the Nationals, the Labor Party or the Australian media to link asylum seekers arriving in Australia in boats to John Howard's rush into the Iraq War in 2003 and re-entry to Afghanistan thereafter. To do so would be to expose the foolhardiness of those responsible and the unjustified and inexcusable nature of their inhumane treatment of asylum seekers.

What has been equally dispiriting is that some of the strongest supporters of draconian measures against refugee boat arrivals are people who came to Australia as refugees in the previous wave. I struggled with the question of why they would not extend the same generosity to others as they had received. The answer is the rules surrounding family reunion. The Liberal–National Coalition has not only reduced the humanitarian intake but has taken a leaf out of Julia Gillard's book and manipulated family reunion rules by making them more restrictive. It is a perfect divide and rule strategy. The most recent refugees are those who are trying hardest to be reunited with their loved ones still in refugee camps somewhere in the world. They see every new refugee as a threat or delay to them ever being reunited with the people they love. No wonder they support policies taking away family reunion from anyone who arrives after them.

It is a classic case of fighting over an ever-diminishing pie, instead of making the pie bigger.

I was working in Bob Brown's office in the lead-up to the 2001 federal election. Bob was up for re-election to the Senate and the polls were showing that it was touch and go whether he would be successful. On 26 August an Indonesian fishing boat with 433 Afghan asylum seekers on board was sighted in difficulty by an Australian Coastwatch surveillance flight and a call was broadcast to ships in the vicinity to render it assistance. A Norwegian container ship, the MV *Tampa*, with a crew of twenty-seven and licensed to carry no more than fifty people, responded to the call.

The *Tampa*'s captain, Arne Rinnan, sought entry to Australia to take the asylum seekers to Christmas Island after they became very agitated about being taken back to Indonesia. He tried for two days to get permission from Australia and, receiving no reply, he proceeded into Australian waters. Prime Minister Howard then insisted that the ship go to Indonesia, saying that the asylum seekers could not be landed in Australia. After a stand-off, Howard ordered the navy and the SAS to board and take charge of the vessel, to prevent it from berthing in any Australian port.

Within hours Bob came into the office and called all his staff together, as Howard's unprecedented breach of international law required an immediate response. Bob laid it out in no uncertain terms. If the Australian Greens came out defending a humanitarian and safe response and insisting that the asylum seekers be taken to Christmas Island and that the international law of the sea and refugee convention be upheld, we would be alone in doing so. We risked the national media condemning the Greens from every quarter. I remember Bob saying specifically that the price we might have to pay for taking a stand was the loss of his Senate seat. But I was never so proud of him or the Australian Greens as when it was unanimously agreed that we had to take that risk. It was a watershed moment, and it is moments like those that define what a person or party really stands for.

Which way do you go? Become a celebrated populist and darling of the right, a flip-flopper in the middle who tries to be all things to all people, or be framed and ridiculed as a moralistic, inflexible, hardline Green by the self-declared Christians in the parliament and the media?

That is the fate of the Greens and of a Greens leader in a political process swinging to the hard right. It was exactly where I found myself when I took on the leadership eleven years later. My first three months as leader were dominated by the asylum-seeker issue, as six boat tragedies occurred. By 2012 Australians' attitudes had hardened after a decade of relentless negative scaremongering about asylum seekers, terrorism and border security. People wanted a simple 'solution' to a complex problem, a deal to put asylum seekers out of sight, out of mind, and they were annoyed with me and with the Greens when I would not go along with it. But I am proud of the team I led during this bruising time. Every Green senator, MP and party member had the courage to stand up for social justice, a key pillar of Green philosophy, human rights and international law, regardless of the abuse we received.

And all around the country organisations and individuals have held the line, including the Human Rights Law Centre, Asylum Seeker Resource Centre, the Refugee Council, Amnesty International, the Knitting Nannas and the Australian Human Rights Commission headed by the fearless Gillian Triggs, as well as community leaders such as Pamela Curr, Julian Burnside, David Manne and Eleni Poulis of the Uniting Church, and Father Rod Bower of the Anglican parish of Gosford, among many others.

Leadership can be lonely. Ultimately the buck stops with you and the consequences are laid at your door. There are not too many people to whom you can turn in order to discuss the dilemmas, or from whom you can get moral support when the criticism is heaped on you. I had wonderful parliamentary colleagues and staff with whom I could discuss these issues, but I often went back to a tried and true piece of advice from Martin Luther King against which any dilemma could be put to the test:

> Cowardice asks the question, 'Is it safe?'
> Expediency asks the question, 'Is it politic?'
> Vanity asks the question, 'Is it popular?'
> But, conscience asks the question, 'Is it right?'
> And there comes a time when we must take a position
>     that is neither safe, nor politic, nor popular, but one
>     must take it because it is right.[2]

Less than twenty-four hours after Howard's decision in 2001, the Australian Greens were out in the media condemning the SAS boarding of the *Tampa* and the Australian Government's breach of international law. The phones in Bob's office went off. At first all the calls were abusive, but then came a steady trickle that turned into a flood of supportive calls, from people who had voted Liberal or Labor all their lives saying the *Tampa* incident was the last straw. They would now back the Australian Greens. Bob Brown went on to be re-elected with a quota in his own right, without needing to rely on preferences. It was the first time that an Australian Green had been elected with a full quota, and many attributed this to his stand on the *Tampa*.

On 29 August 2001, while the asylum seekers were still being forcibly held on the *Tampa* without knowing where they would be taken, the Howard government introduced its Border Protection Bill into the federal parliament. The aim of this was to cover Howard's back, removing the right of any person using any court to prevent the forcible removal of a ship from Australian waters. It excised Christmas Island as part of Australia's migration zone to evade international obligations under the United Nations High Commission for Refugees, which states that refugees who arrive on a territory within the signatory's migration zone must be processed there. Labor initially voted against the bill but, after it became clear that Howard's actions were supported by the majority of Australians, the Opposition changed its mind. On 26 September the party supported legislation to validate Howard's actions and massively expand the government's powers in relation to asylum seekers.

The asylum seekers were sent to Nauru, and so began the cruel and inhumane so-called Pacific Solution, which has come to dominate Australian politics ever since. 'Stop the boats' was the mantra for parliamentarians. Senior public servants got the message. An interdepartmental committee known as the People Smuggling Taskforce was established to coordinate the activities of different agencies and to provide whole-of-government advice to ministers. On later examination it became evident that the taskforce established a culture of only telling the prime minister or ministers what they wanted to hear. Plausible deniability was paramount.

Hardly had the asylum seekers held on the *Tampa* been sent to Nauru than the Islamic extremist group al-Qaeda hijacked four airliners and carried out suicide attacks against US targets including the World Trade Center and the Pentagon. On 11 September 2001 Prime Minister Howard was in Washington; he immediately pledged support for the Americans in whatever response they chose.

As with the announcement of President Kennedy's assassination, everyone can remember where they were when they first heard the news. I had flown up to Canberra from Tasmania for a meeting at the Department of the Environment. I remember walking into the department to see everyone crowding around the television sets, staring in shocked and silent disbelief at footage that showed the second plane ploughing into the Twin Towers.

Three weeks after the 11 September attack, as Australians were still reeling from the horror of what had happened in the United States, Prime Minister John Howard called the Australian federal election for 10 November. The election campaign in which he declared 'We will decide who comes to this country and the circumstances in which they come' had begun. The following day the bombing of Afghanistan began and the fourth suspected illegal entry vessel (SIEV), a leaky wooden boat carrying 223 asylum seekers, was intercepted by HMAS *Adelaide* one hundred nautical miles north of Christmas Island. It then sank.

Immigration Minister Philip Ruddock told Australians that 'a number of children had been thrown overboard'. Defence Minister Peter Reith and Prime Minister John Howard repeated the claim throughout the election campaign. It had the desired effect. People around Australia were horrified that anyone would throw their own children into the sea. Except we now know they didn't. The government knew they didn't but deliberately chose not to correct the record before polling day. The Certain Maritime Incident Senate Inquiry held after the election reported:

> No children were thrown overboard from SIEV 4.
>
> Photographs released to the media on 10 October as evidence of children thrown overboard on 7 October were actually pictures taken the following day, 8 October, while SIEV 4 was sinking.

Years later I was on a domestic flight when an ex-navy airline staff member told me he had been on board HMAS *Adelaide* that day. He said he and his colleagues all saw what had happened, and they knew that the story of the children overboard was a lie. They waited for the navy to correct the record before the election, but it didn't. He lost respect for the navy and resigned. As it happened, the navy did try to correct the record, but this was ignored by the chief of the defence forces.

Three months after the election Admiral Barrie finally conceded that children had not been thrown overboard from SIEV 4. Government ministers just blamed poor advice from their advisors but, as the Senate inquiry noted, they took no action to reprimand or discipline those advisors. In fact the report said, 'It is reasonable to infer, therefore, that they had acted with ministerial approval and that the government was not displeased with their conduct.' In 2002 Jane Halton, the convenor of the People Smuggling Task Force, was awarded the Public Service Medal.

On 18 October 2001, two weeks into the election campaign, SIEV X, with 421 people on board, sailed from Indonesia en route to Australia. It was a dilapidated boat, so badly overcrowded that some passengers asked to be put ashore before it left Indonesia. The following day the boat sank in international waters, inside the Australian aerial border protection surveillance zone. In all, 353 people drowned: 146 children, 142 women and 65 men.

Survivors said that, to board that boat, some of the passengers had been transported long distances in buses with blacked-out windows. There were accounts of the Indonesian police forcing people at gunpoint to board an obviously unseaworthy boat. They said that, during the twenty hours they were in the sea after the boat sank, two boats came and shone their lights onto the water. People started to swim towards them but they switched off the lights and left, leaving them to drown. Survivors were eventually rescued by Indonesian fishermen.

On 23 October, Prime Minister Howard said that the disaster had nothing to do with Australia 'because the boat sank in Indonesian waters'. It didn't. It sank in the international waters Australia was closely monitoring. As journalist Margo Kingston has argued, this was the big lie of the 2001 campaign, greater than 'children overboard'. A cable from the Department of Foreign Affairs and Trade received by Prime Minister Howard among others on 23 October stated clearly that the SIEV X sank in international waters. More than fifteen years later there has never been a judicial inquiry into Australia's possible complicity in the sinking of the SIEV X.

When I was elected to the Senate in 2004, I pursued the SIEV X issue. I met with survivors and attended memorial services. Faris Khadem, who watched his family drown, was broken by grief.

He told me that the only thing that kept him alive was the need for the truth to be told. Author Steve Biddulph and community activist Beth Gibbons had a suitable memorial for the SIEV X created and, after a long battle, permanently displayed on Lake Burley Griffin in 2005, in line of sight to Parliament House. I was there when 1000 Canberrans raised 353 poles, each naming a person who died, all handpainted in a nationwide collaborative art project by schools, community organisations and concerned people, laid out in the shape of the boat. This memorial expressed the empathy people feel towards the families of those who drowned, as well as defiance and determination that the SIEV X will never be forgotten.

When they took government in 2007, I pressed Labor to have an independent judicial inquiry; they voted against it and have done so ever since. By then Labor had joined the Liberals in pursuing an inhumane policy towards asylum seekers. They decided to use a lame excuse that after 2004 they adopted a new platform and an inquiry into the SIEV X was no longer policy.[3] They clearly thought it was no longer in the national interest for Australians ever to know the extent of the Australian Government's involvement in the disruption activities before the SIEV X left Indonesia, its subsequent sinking and the failure to rescue survivors.

On the tenth anniversary of the sinking of the SIEV X, I made a plea:

> It's my great hope that people will come forward and say exactly what did happen. After ten years, I would hope that people who were working at the Shoal Bay tracking station, who were crew or command on the *Arunta* [the Australian naval vessel in the vicinity], people who worked in the Prime Minister's Department, there must be people who can answer these questions. And they must ask why every inquiry has deliberately precluded any investigation of the circumstances leading up to

the departure of the ship, including those disruption activities.

But rather than the soul-searching that these incidents should have provoked, 'stop the boats' remains the mantra of the Liberal, National, Labor and One Nation parties, regardless of our international responsibilities to take refugees and treat them with dignity. Not only has the 'stop the boats' policy failed, it has undermined Australia's standing in the international community. As if that is not bad enough, Liberal, Labor, National and One Nation have dressed up their inhumane and illegal treatment of asylum seekers in offshore detention centres as being motivated by the desire to save lives by stopping people from drowning at sea. This is the ultimate cynical spin doctoring of public policy. Stopping the boats was a mantra long before any of its advocates started worrying about people drowning at sea: witness SIEV X.

Public concern was growing about asylum-seeker boats, especially after December 2010 when horrified TV viewers saw people drown as a boat smashed against the rocks at Christmas Island. And so Labor and Liberal governments hit upon a new message of deterrence, ostensibly as a way of saving lives at sea. To dissuade other refugees from making the dangerous journey, those arrivals who had not drowned needed to be made an example of, punished and never permitted to come to Australia. They needed to be held indefinitely in detention and sent to Manus Island and Nauru or be swapped for other asylum seekers already in Malaysia. That would stop the boats.

Deterrence – the policy embraced not just by Labor, Liberals and Nationals but also by large swathes of the media – was inconveniently rejected by the High Court. In a judgment of six to one, the High Court said that the proposal to send 800 asylum seekers from Australia to Malaysia over a four-year period in a swap for 4000 asylum seekers already there did not uphold the human rights of the asylum seekers. It was no 'solution' to anything.

The High Court not only found the Malaysia Solution to be illegal but also cast doubt as to the legality of all existing offshore processing. Prime Minister Gillard was not in the least apologetic about abandoning international law, and introduced a bill to circumvent international law and the Human Rights Convention and to enable her Malaysia swap to proceed. All that would be required to facilitate offshore processing would be for a minister to decide it was in the national interest to designate a country as an offshore processing country. The only chance of the bill being passed was with the Coalition, but it wanted its own Pacific Solution reinstated. The bill did not proceed.

The pressure was on the government to make onshore processing work in conjunction with a regional solution, as the Australian Greens had been arguing. Australia could have embarked on a serious debate about developing a regional plan similar to the Fraser government's at the height of the Vietnamese refugee crisis. I had proposed a multi-party committee with experts, similar to the committee on climate change, as a way of responding to the new policy environment. Tony Windsor MP had begun talking to colleagues across the House of Representatives to seek support for a new way forward.

But a human tragedy intervened. As the parliament was sitting on 27 June 2012, a boat carrying at least 130 asylum seekers sank and a rescue mission was under way. In a tactical move Prime Minister Gillard announced the incident at 1.30 pm and suspended Question Time to bring on a debate on a private member's bill previously introduced by the independent Rob Oakeshott. His bill would have allowed an immigration minister to designate any nation, regardless of whether or not it was a signatory to the Refugee Convention, as an 'offshore assessment country' as long as it was party to the Bali Process. Co-chaired by Indonesia and Australia, the Bali Process was a regional forum allegedly to strengthen practical cooperation to protect refugees and to cooperate in dealing with people smuggling. Members included forty-four countries – many the very countries from which asylum seekers were fleeing, including Malaysia, Syria,

Iran, Iraq, Afghanistan, China, Malaysia, Burma and Indonesia.

Embracing the Oakeshott bill as a 'breakthrough' was a cynically timed last-ditch effort by a government determined to make legal what the High Court had determined was illegal, a final throw of the dice to secure offshore processing while people were drowning and the authorities were under pressure to sort something out.

The Labor Party was happy to permit offshore processing in any of the forty-four countries because it was so desperate to secure a political win. The Coalition wanted to reject and defeat the Malaysia Solution and return to the Pacific Solution of offshore processing on Nauru. We opposed offshore detention consistent with the High Court ruling and wanted an increase in the humanitarian intake to Australia, an increase in funds to Indonesia to assist it to process more asylum seekers faster, and a multi-party committee to develop a proposal for a regional approach consistent with international law and the Refugee Convention.

There was no way to bridge the divide. Prime Minister Gillard heaped on the pressure. 'We are on the verge of getting the laws we need … It would be a tremendous act of destruction and tremendous denial of the national interest … to conduct yourself in a way which means there are no laws,' she said.

The pressure to sort something out, to get an agreement, to seal the deal, is regularly manufactured and timed by governments, vested business interests and the media to secure the outcome they want. Like the circle in the playground chanting 'fight', parliament is full of hype, exclusive interviews are given, leaks abound, sources 'close to' say this and that, breaking news heightens expectations for a deal. Minor party politicians or independents are praised as kingmakers for securing the deal. They are players, whereas those who refuse to give ground are condemned for it. Once the dust settles, no one goes back to analyse what exactly the deal was, whether it had merit, who benefited and who lost. By the time people begin to realise the deal was a dud, 'the caravan has moved on'.

Rob Oakeshott's bill to abandon the human rights of asylum seekers, to ditch international law and to enable the dumping of people in any of forty-four countries was such a dud. It was about to pass the House of Representatives when I was invited to go on the ABC's *7.30 Report*. Just as the live interview started, a technical problem occurred that caused the debate from the House of Representatives to be fed through my earpiece. Labor minister Anthony Albanese was shouting in my ear all the time I was trying to hear Leigh Sales's questions and to respond. Normally I would have said so, but in this instance I didn't feel I could, because viewers would have thought it was an attempt to avoid her attack.

She said to me, 'The de facto asylum-seeker policy in Australia at the moment is onshore processing, which is the Greens policy. We're seeing the results of that policy: dozens of boats coming to Australia, boats sinking at sea, people dying. How many boats will have to sink before the Greens reconsider their position on this [Malaysia]?' It was a highly offensive question, ignoring the High Court ruling and implying that I was happy to see people drown so long as I got my way, and further suggesting that my concerns about upholding international law and human rights for asylum seekers if dumped in Malaysia were irrelevant, selfish considerations. I explained that 'it would be a very good thing to increase our humanitarian intake, provide safer pathways, actually approach a regional solution' and that the Greens had 'proposed a multi-party committee to work with the Prime Minister and the Leader of the Opposition, providing it's in the context of international law, and that really ought to be the basis.' Our policy of onshore processing was the 'de facto' government policy because it was deemed to be the only lawful policy, not just by the Australian Greens but by the High Court. That didn't bother Ms Sales. If ever there was a pitch to vote for offshore processing regardless of the detail, to vote for ditching human rights and international law, to nail a deal for the government, Leigh Sales's interview was it.

The day after Prime Minister Gillard's effort to reinstate offshore processing failed, she announced a panel consisting of Air Vice-Marshal Angus Houston, refugee advocate Paris Aristotle and Michael L'Estrange, former Howard government bureaucrat, to consult the community on a way of dealing with the asylum-seeker issue. Senator Hanson-Young and I met with the panel as part of its consultation. We reiterated our opposition to offshore processing and our support for an increase in the humanitarian intake, an increase in assistance to Indonesia and our commitment to a regional process for managing the flow of asylum seekers in our international neighbourhood. We emphasised that whatever they recommended needed to be consistent with international law and the Refugee Convention. I pointed out that the panel was being used to deliver offshore processing. Both Sarah and I made it plain that there was no way the government would accept any package without it. I also spelled out that there was no way the government could be compelled to implement the panel's recommendations and that it would cherry pick.

That is exactly what happened. Six weeks later, in August 2012, the panel delivered its report, recommending offshore processing in Nauru and Papua New Guinea with the caveat 'as part of a comprehensive regional network'. It recommended an increase in the refugee intake from 13,000 to 20,000, rising to 27,000 within five years, but said that those who arrived by boat should not be eligible to sponsor family members to join them. It gave the nod to boat turn-backs and increased cooperation with Indonesia on joint surveillance, law enforcement, and search and rescue. Finally it gave the prime minister a personal face-saver by suggesting that talks with Malaysia should be built on, not discarded, but more assurances should be sought about the treatment of people who might be sent there.

The prime minister gave in principle support to all the recommendations and raced back to the parliament with amendments to immediately implement the most draconian parts of the package, namely reintroduction of offshore processing on Manus Island and

Nauru and removal of family reunion concessions for people arriving by boat. Within twenty-four hours the government had legislation ready to reintroduce offshore processing and had already ditched the comprehensive regional network within which it was supposed to operate. A month later, in September, the government tabled its designation of Nauru as an offshore processing country. None of the recommendations of the independent panel had been included in the designation, including no arbitrary detention. But Angus Houston, Paris Aristotle and Michael L'Estrange had served their purpose.

Once offshore processing was reinstated, the boats didn't stop. They kept leaving Indonesia and Sri Lanka, and the detention centres on Christmas Island and Nauru were full to overflowing. When Kevin Rudd toppled Julia Gillard in June 2013, he introduced even more cruel measures, announcing a new deal with Papua New Guinea, declaring that all asylum seekers who arrived by boat would be sent for offshore processing and resettlement, and that even those found to be refugees would *never* be resettled in Australia. He went further, saying that he would return anyone not found to be a refugee to their home country. He also announced that the Australian Federal Police would pay rewards of up to $200,000 for information leading to the arrest and conviction of people organising people-smuggling ventures to Australia.

In 2016 the Papua New Guinean court declared the Rudd deal illegal, but nobody in the Turnbull government, Shorten Labor Opposition or the media cared enough to call for accountability. The Papua New Guinean Government said that Manus Island must be shut down. As for Kevin Rudd, he had moved on and was busy campaigning to be secretary-general of the United Nations.

To this day no one knows how many boats have been towed back or how many people were on board. We don't know how many sank or how many lives were lost. But we do know that the Abbott government actually paid people smugglers to turn the boats around and take the asylum seekers back. Amnesty International says that any Australian official who pays a people smuggler is engaged in transnational crime, but that hasn't stopped Australian Border Force officials from handing envelopes stuffed with thousands of dollars to people smugglers. No doubt the Australian Government would indemnify them from prosecution.

Furthermore, we know that people who were forcibly returned to the countries from which they fled have been tortured. Under the 1951 Refugee Convention, to which Australia is a party, countries cannot 'refoul' a person – that is, send them back to a place where they will face harm. But Australia thumbs its nose and sends people back to Sri Lanka, even though the British Government stopped doing it because of evidence of arbitrary arrest, police brutality and torture on their return.

Breaking people's spirits, torturing them and destroying lives is not only morally reprehensible but also costly. It does not stop the boats; nor does it stop people drowning.

Cartoonists capture the hypocrisy of 'not drowning' better than anything that I can write. I cheered when Andrew Marlton, otherwise known as First Dog on the Moon, won a Walkley Award for journalistic excellence with his cartoon 'Drowning' in 2012. Cathy Wilcox with her cartoon 'Not Drowning' in 2016 put an end to any shred of credibility that the whole shameful lie that stopping the boats to stop people from drowning has become. Both are powerful statements that sum up exactly how I feel about this disgraceful episode in Australia's history. Both remain in my archive.

The policy of deterrence continues to be an utter failure. With cruelty and abuse in the Manus Island and Nauru detention centres, riots during which Reza Barati was murdered, the death of Hamid Khazaei from septicaemia after cutting his foot, and the death of Faysal Ahmed on Christmas Eve from untreated heart and other health problems, as well as ongoing incidents of self-harm and self-immolation, you would think if deterrence was going to work, the boats would have stopped coming. But people seeking asylum are not deterred.

To hide its failure the Abbott government declared 'on water' issues to be secret. It cracked down on any leaks of information from the detention centres, refused to allow the media to film there and even wrongly accused Save the Children of leaking documents to the media. But the wheels are falling off. The United Nations Special Rapporteur on Human Rights Francois Crepeau reported in 2016, 'Some of Australia's migration policies have increasingly eroded the human rights of migrants in contravention of its international human rights and humanitarian obligations.'[4] He called on Australia to stop intercepting and pushing back asylum-seeker boats, saying the practice does not meet human rights obligations. At the same time the Australian National Audit Office has revealed a chaotic wasteful culture, with the government paying private contractors more than $2 billion without any oversight; it also failed to update its assets register so that when the $75 million facility on Nauru burned down, it was not insured.

Scott Morrison sipped champagne with alleged war criminal and leader of Cambodia Hun Sen to celebrate sending desperate asylum seekers to the poverty-stricken South East Asian country: $55 million has been paid to resettle fewer than five refugees, and once again it is the price Australia is prepared to pay to look the other way on human rights abuses, corruption and the sabotaging of democracy in that country.

There will come a day when the Australian Parliament apologises for its treatment of refugees and asylum seekers. But when it does, let us not have any hypocrisy from those who have supported and voted for offshore detention, gross cruelty and torture. Let's have no tearful mea culpas that if only they had known the full extent of it, if only they had been given better advice, they would never have allowed it. Let's not sympathise with those in the Liberal, Labor and National parties who declare that they were always opposed to it but had to respect party policy. No. They had a choice. They could have risked their ministries or shadow cabinet positions and crossed the floor, if they had been prepared to put the treatment of refugees above their personal or electoral self-interest.

As for the many cheerleading, uncritical journalists – initially in the Murdoch media but spreading throughout the rest – they, more than anyone, know exactly what is happening and have promoted and defended it and been promoted themselves. But there have been some outstanding exceptions such as Michael Gordon. Others have tried to do their job and submitted factual, often critical stories with limited success in getting them to air or into print at all or without major edits. To name them would be a career death sentence given the concentrated ownership and control of Australian media. But they are there and they are a credit to their profession.

~

THE PONTVILLE DETENTION CENTRE north of Hobart operated at various periods between 2011 and 2013 to take single men and underage boys. I visited it in August 2013 with fellow senator Peter Whish-Wilson. It is hard to visit a place set up as a prison for children who have committed no crime other than to run from persecution. High wire fences surrounded the complex, and the first thing I noticed was how cold the boys all looked, shivering in the hoodies and jumpers they had been given, having just been flown in from Darwin.

I organised for a big group of boys to be brought together so I could speak to them. I explained that not all people in power in Australia supported mandatory detention of asylum seekers and that they should hold on to the hope that they would be free. I told them that they must never, ever give up hope and asked them to repeat it after me. 'Never, ever give up.' They did so and soon we had a chant going. I asked them what they needed and they asked for more computer equipment as that was the only way they could communicate with their families and let them know they had survived.

Afterwards I noticed a small group of Vietnamese boys and went over to talk to them. I told them how I had first met Diep and Liem Tran and how they had come to Australia as boat people and had made a successful life for themselves and their children. I told them that they must hold on to stories like that, as they could and would be free.

Once back in Hobart, I rang Nick McKim, a Greens minister for education in the Tasmanian Labor Cabinet, and suggested we work together to get the boys out of detention by sending them every day to Tasmanian high schools. The federal Education Department objected, saying that they wanted to second Tasmanian teachers to go to the detention centre rather than have the boys attend local schools. But Nick insisted, arguing that the law in Tasmania made school attendance compulsory and he was going to uphold it by arranging for them to attend school. The federal government backed down.

After retiring from the Senate, I was invited to deliver the keynote address at the combined independent schools annual Justice Day seminar. Just before I spoke, a very impressive young man took the microphone to tell his story. He told of being a Vietnamese refugee who had been in the Pontville Detention Centre. While there, he had attended Claremont College every day, where a teacher had befriended and encouraged him. But he was then sent to another detention centre in Western Australia, and when he turned eighteen he was immediately sent to Darwin and put in adult detention.

One day he was told that he was to be given a bridging visa and had to leave. He had nowhere to go, so he contacted the Tasmanian teacher. This teacher invited him back to Tasmania to live with his wife and family. That young man went on to become a school captain of Guilford Young College. When he resumed his seat, he leaned over to me and said, 'I remember, you are that lady I met at the Pontville Detention Centre who told me about the Vietnamese family. I didn't forget it.'

I was deeply moved and immediately rang both Nick McKim and Peter Whish-Wilson to share the news with them. It was a classic example of taking a village to raise a child, of everyone doing what they could to help a young man dehumanised by the system and labelled an 'unaccompanied male minor'. This young man would not have left the Pontville Detention Centre to go to high school had it not been for a Greens minister and Greens senators who reached out and gave him hope and the opportunity. He would not be where he is today if a teacher at a Tasmanian state school had not befriended him, and if a private school, Guilford Young College, had not made an exception to the rules and enrolled a student who was over eighteen. He would not have made such a mark if he had not had it within himself to hold on to hope, regardless of the circumstances in which he found himself.

The story reminded me of lines from 'Yussouf' by American poet James Russell Lowell, which I used to teach at Devonport High School:

> As one lamp lights another, nor grows less,
> So nobleness enkindleth nobleness.

My hope is that the 'nobleness' in the community is ultimately enough to defeat the ignoble in the parliament. That the generosity of spirit and the fair go for which we were once known is unleashed again. That people who, up until now, have thought they could do nothing to combat what they know is wrong are inspired enough by the stories of the Tran family and this young man to do something and to vote accordingly.

# 16

# Leadership and the Importance of Timing

OBJECT: *Brenda the Civil Disobedience Penguin, created by cartoonist First Dog on the Moon. Christine uses the soft toy version of Brenda to encourage parents of newborns to take action to achieve positive change for future generations.*

TIMING IS EVERYTHING IN POLITICS. You can be elected or become leader of your party when the electoral tide is flowing in your direction, or as the tide is going out. But there is nothing you can do to avoid the inevitable ebb and flow. Governments are elected, people give them a go and then vote them out. How long that cycle takes and how far in or out the tide goes depends on political strategy and on wildcards.

The 9/11 terrorist attack and the *Tampa* incident were Howard's wildcards in the 2001 election. He exploited them politically to the fullest extent, recasting himself from being the tired, out-of-touch proponent of the GST to the self-appointed Father of the Nation, keeping out the terrorists and making us all safe. He recaptured the One Nation vote, and he won.

As to political strategy, winning power for its own sake has become the sole objective of the Liberal and Labor tribes. It is no longer about a vision for the nation. It no longer matters if you lie or cheat to get there. It no longer matters if you leak and undermine and overthrow the leader: 'whatever it takes' is the justification.

Abbott overthrew Turnbull. Gillard overthrew Rudd, who undermined her until on the third attempt he overthrew her. She spent her entire prime ministership looking over her shoulder. The internal and external speculation about her leadership got to the point where the media became players themselves. Instead of reporting the news, they worked to create it with their 'unnamed sources' for stories. A week before Rudd's success in 2013 *The Age* ran an editorial calling on Gillard to step aside 'for the sake of the nation'. Engaging in reasoned debate was exhausting, and getting media attention for policy matters was almost impossible. Conflict sells.

Abbott's three-word slogans amounted to 'Only the stuttering rifles' rapid rattle', in the words of war poet Wilfred Owen.[1] Every day when I was leader of the Australian Greens I woke up to and went to bed with 'Great Big Lie', 'Axe the Tax', 'Stop the Boats', 'Debt and Deficit'. (There were also 'Lifters not Leaners' and 'Jobs and Growth', but they came later.) Journalist Laura Tingle wrote of Tony Abbott in *The Australian Financial Review Magazine* on 24 February 2017 that 'he unleashed a feral and deadly negativism on Australian politics from which we have never really recovered … what an utter destructive force, an utter waste of space this man has been on the Australian political landscape'.[2]

Shock jock Alan Jones was Abbott's cheerleader and echo chamber from day one. His words '[Julia Gillard's] off her tree and quite frankly they should shove her and Bob Brown in a chaff bag and take them as far out to sea as they can' morphed into the failed Convoy of No Confidence, with its fewer than 200 trucks rolling into Canberra. But the infamous photos of Abbott in front of 'Ditch the Witch' and 'Bob Brown's Bitch' signs became signature Coalition politics thereafter, reaching a climax with Alan Jones saying at a Liberal Party dinner, 'The old man recently died a few weeks ago of shame. To think that he had a daughter who told lies every time she stood for parliament.' Abbott repeated the 'died of shame' line in the parliament a few weeks later, reinforcing the message but saying he was oblivious to Jones's remarks and claiming a different context.

Five years later, in February 2017, Abbott's former chief of staff Peta Credlin admitted on Sky's *Sunday Agenda* TV show the Coalition's lie about the so-called carbon tax: 'It wasn't a carbon tax, as you know ... we made it a carbon tax. We made it a fight about the hip pocket and not about the environment. That was brutal retail politics and it took Abbott about six months to cut through and when we cut through, Gillard was gone.'[3]

Abbott's immediate legacy is a generation that suffers from ongoing and deepening anxiety about what the future will bring. In the long term, the children crawling around the floor while the television in the background brought Tony Abbott into their lounge rooms are the ones who will not see the Great Barrier Reef as we have seen it. They are the ones who will inherit climate wars, who will only see photographs of animals and birds driven to extinction. They will live with the consequences of sea-level rise, food-chain collapse and a depleted planet. They will have no choice but to protest and protest hard to stop the situation getting worse. They are the victims of the global climate culture wars and Abbott's lie. The Abbott lie is a crime against humanity, not the admired killer blow of 'brutal retail politics'.

It is a hard thing for a grandmother to know. Generation Y is not alone in suffering anxiety about the future; it is shared by their parents, and I am one of them. We grew up with the anxiety generated by the threat of nuclear war and we face old age with anxiety about what global warming will do to our home the Earth and our families and grandchildren.

That's why I gave my beautiful granddaughter Eleanor the soft toy Brenda the Civil Disobedience Penguin, a creation of cartoonist First Dog on the Moon. Having fought for something so critical to life on Earth as action on climate change and to see it denigrated and the critical decade for action lost is gut-wrenching. But it is not a reason to give up. Global emissions have to peak and start to come down by 2020 if we are to have any hope of staying below two degrees of warming: that's it for a liveable planet. We are already at one degree. We have to stand up now. That's what activists do and it is a damn sight better and more effective than hand-wringing or burying our heads in the sand. In Brenda's words, 'Stick it to the man' and 'Lawyer up'.

I give Brenda to parents of newborns. She is a reminder that we do not inherit the Earth from our ancestors, we borrow it from our children. She is a gift that disarmingly says: *Get off your 'apolitical' or 'disillusioned with politics', 'disempowered' or 'self-indulgent' backsides and start doing something about it.*

~

I ASSUMED THE LEADERSHIP of the Australian Greens in April 2012, only weeks after Kevin Rudd's resignation as foreign minister and his first attempt to overthrow Julia Gillard. Labor's destructive infighting had never gone away, but now it resumed in earnest. Prime Minister Gillard was under siege internally and externally. She gave in to the hysteria generated by Tony Abbott over asylum-seeker policy and reopened the offshore detention camps, describing her motivation as concern for people dying at sea.

She responded to Abbott's hip pocket attack by fighting on the same ground, making the defence of the Clean Energy Package all about compensation for low-income households instead of the climate emergency.

I tried very hard to move the debate back on to environmental grounds. Newspaper editors and television producers were not interested, deliberately antagonistic or humouring the Abbott regime, and they refused to publish stories about global warming, extreme weather events or threats to wildlife. The fossil fuel vested interests cheered as Labor and Coalition politicians and the media condemned the Greens. When I said that global warming was so serious that choosing coal over climate action was choosing death, the *Daily Telegraph* editorial screamed that it was 'ridiculous' and 'offensive' to frame 'the coal debate in such extreme and bitterly negative terms'. But apparently it was neither ridiculous nor offensive to frame the global warming debate in the extreme and bitterly negative terms chosen by Tony Abbott.

Prime Minister Gillard tried to shift the politics of 2012 onto ground where Labor traditionally had an advantage, and that was education. The Gonski Review, released in February 2012, galvanised community support to bring an end to the debilitating political brawl over school funding. Gonski found there is an unacceptable link between low levels of achievement and educational disadvantage, particularly among students from low socio-economic and Indigenous backgrounds, and recommended an immediate boost of $5 billion a year for schools funding and a needs-based funding model that was transparent, equitable, financially sustainable and sector-blind. The unions, parents and education community welcomed it. The private schools generally didn't. But Gillard compromised the review's integrity from day one by saying that no school would lose a dollar under the plan. The vested interests of Catholic and independent schools were rewarded.

Despite my disappointment I urged the government to put the bill to parliament before Christmas 2012, knowing that if it rolled into election year 2013 it would be even further watered down. But it soon became obvious that Labor preferred to use schools funding as a key point of differentiation from the Coalition in an election campaign than to use the Labor–Greens majority vote to secure the full recommendations of the Gonski Review. And indeed Gonski and education became intense issues in the lead-up to the election.

The Gonski saga confirmed to me that for Gillard power trumped everything. Nothing she believed in couldn't be compromised or ditched if it stood between her and power. I liked Gillard and respected her decency and consultative approach to working in balance of power. I admired her dignity in handling the horrible, sexist, demeaning personal attacks she had to endure from the old white men in politics and the media. She was right when she said her gender didn't explain everything about her prime ministership but it didn't explain nothing either. However, there was no escaping it: for her, Labor being in government was an end in itself, to be secured with whatever it took.

After the shock revelations of the *News of the World* phone hacking in the United Kingdom and the recommendations of the Finkelstein Review, Stephen Conroy was determined to see media reform legislation passed before Christmas 2012. We all knew that the prime minister would not take on media regulation and Rupert Murdoch in an election year. I put to the prime minister that we sit an additional week in parliament to deal with the issue. She said she would not sit a minute longer than necessary; it was clear that she feared Kevin Rudd would force a leadership challenge before Christmas. The Rudd–Gillard war cost Australia serious media reform.

The 2013 election year started with the announcement of a Royal Commission into institutional responses to child sexual abuse. I had asked the prime minister the previous year to set up such a Royal Commission but she had refused, saying she considered that the states had the matter in hand. But the *7.30 Report* appearance of former New South Wales detective Peter Fox was explosive in its exposé of child sexual abuse. Public opinion made the prime minister change her mind. As I now see the harrowing reports, the extent of the abuse and the response of the victims believed at last, I regard this Royal Commission as one of the great achievements of the Gillard minority government.

I had met with Gillard every week that the parliament sat, as was set down in our agreement of 2010. But after the first meeting in 2013 it was clear that the agreement was over. Gillard was courteous as always, but it was patently obvious that she had no intention of moving to deliver the unfinished business in the agreement. Furthermore she backed Tony Burke's decision to support the mining of the Tarkine and reject the Australian Heritage Council's advice to protect it; she and he had decided that giving mining the big tick was their best hope of retaining the seat of Braddon for Labor. Even with written agreements between the Greens and the minority government, if the government reneged the Greens' only recourse was to live with it, bring the government down or refuse to cooperate.

But living with it invited an abusive power relationship in which mutual respect was evaporating. With an election looming and Labor tearing itself apart, with no prospect of new policy outcomes, I decided the best course of action was to tell the public what I had experienced in private.

I was not going to do this without informing Prime Minister Gillard first. Minutes before I went on stage at the National Press Club, I called to tell her of my announcement that the Labor–Greens agreement was dead. Interestingly, her only response was to ask whether I intended to attack her trustworthiness at a personal level. I reassured her that my speech was not personal, but policy- and issues-based. She was fine with that. Clearly the Abbott and Rudd personal attacks were weighing heavily on her mind.

Within weeks Simon Crean called for a Labor leadership ballot; Gillard survived. Crean had made his call on a day when 800 people were gathered in the Great Hall to hear the prime minister's apology to those who had endured a lifetime's suffering as a result of forced adoptions; his insensitive and disrespectful action showed just how consumed Labor was by its internal war. The ritual of apology was an incredibly moving and dignified ceremony. I was particularly proud of my colleague Rachel Siewert, who had initiated and chaired the Senate inquiry into forced adoptions. It was a great community and Greens initiative that has made a permanent contribution to the nation.

Every year in June, before the parliament rises for the winter break, the Press Club ball is held. This is not a social event; it is the most politically charged gathering you can imagine. Who talks with whom, the body language, the loosened tongues and the leaks are what it is about. In 2013 I was invited to sit at the prime minister's table and I invited our newest Greens senator, Peter Whish-Wilson, to join me. Not one of Julia Gillard's colleagues came over to talk to her and nor did any of the big business or media owners, who were all in the room. Peter and I chatted with Julia and her partner Tim, and to their credit they kept up appearances, but I suspect the ball was the last place they wanted to be.

As we left, I said to Peter, 'Gillard is gone.' He was taken aback. But six days later Kevin Rudd defeated her in a leadership ballot she called to try to head off a petition for a caucus vote. Ministers Peter Garrett and Craig Emerson announced their retirement from politics at the forthcoming election, and ministers Swan, Conroy, Ludwig and Combet all went to the backbench. Such a loss of experience in key portfolio areas ten weeks out from an election was disastrous for Labor.

Having never seen fit to meet with the Greens when he was prime minister before, Rudd now needed us: we were balance-of-power holders in both Houses, and Greens support was crucial. The meeting was icy and courteous, and it would be an understatement to say that there was no love in the room on either side. Rudd asked for our support until the election. I wrote to the governor-general, undertaking to provide that support until 30 September 2013, ensuring an election would be held before that date. Rudd called the election on 5 August for 7 September 2013.

Few people realise what a tragedy it was for progressive politics and the Greens in particular that Rudd took back the prime ministership weeks out from an election; he did not campaign on any of the Labor–Green achievements of the Gillard years, or any of his predecessor's achievements. There was no attempt to sell the Clean

Energy Package, the Australian Renewable Energy Agency, the Clean Energy Finance Corporation, Climate Change Authority, Denticare, the National Disability Scheme, the Royal Commission into Child Sexual Abuse, the Apology for Forced Adoptions or the Parliamentary Budget Office. It was as if they had never happened. Instead Rudd rushed out with his fear-and-border-security megaphone, doing deals with Papua New Guinea and Nauru to rev up offshore detention of asylum seekers. He announced his own carbon trading scheme, fuelling criticism of and undermining the Gillard–Green Clean Energy Package, but could not explain what his new scheme would do to reduce greenhouse gases. Meanwhile, Tony Abbott was ready with his amplifier: 'We will scrap the carbon tax, we will get the Budget back under control, we will build the infrastructure of the future and we will stop the boats.'

Given Abbott's attacks and Rudd's selective amnesia it was left to the Greens, with our small microphone, to campaign on the global warming emergency and to talk about inequality, corporate power, housing affordability, renewable energy and Australia's legal responsibility to welcome refugees. It was left to us to sell the Clean Energy Package and the achievements of the Gillard minority government with Greens in balance of power. It had been the most progressive, reformist period of government for decades – something few people knew. The electorate was exhausted from the internal Labor brawling and had been reduced to anticipating their promised $550 in savings from Tony Abbott when he 'axed the tax'.

We Australian Greens were always vulnerable to criticism about costing our promises because, unlike the government and the Opposition, Treasury was precluded from assessing them. We were always being accused of making unfunded promises. That is why we had been so proud of securing the Parliamentary Budget Office (PBO) as part of our agreement with Labor.

We went into the 2013 election with a detailed and, for the first time, fully costed policy platform – a source of enormous pride for me, for which I owe a debt of gratitude to my colleagues and my staff, especially Clare Ozich who oversaw the whole process for my Leader's office. But after all his debt-and-deficit and return-to-surplus rhetoric, Abbott refused to have his 'stop the boats', 'direct action' and 'broadband' policies costed by the PBO, saying instead they were bulletproof. Big business wanted him to win and so he got away with it. In doing so, he tore down the idea that any party has to take costing of election promises seriously any more: another blow to our democracy and to our national accounts.

It is ironic that the Liberal Party, which has always claimed to be the best money manager and is lauded as being so by big business and the financial press, is actually the biggest cheat and squanderer of public money. They have frittered away the income from the mining boom and have paid $55 million to resettle four asylum seekers in Cambodia; Direct Action has cost taxpayers $2.5 billion as greenhouse gases continue to rise; coal is subsidised; native forest logging and land clearing are encouraged; and the rollout of broadband has been an expensive debacle.

The election campaign was brutal. My job was to hold all our seats and try to win more as the Abbott tide surged. I campaigned hard around the country, and when we did hold all our seats and won one more with Senator Janet Rice's election in Victoria – notwithstanding the saga of the Western Australian recount and new Senate election – I was gratified. We would return to the parliament with ten senators and one member of the House of Representatives, the largest team the Australian Greens had ever had.

Even though Abbott had won a majority in the House of Representatives, the Australian Greens still held balance of power in the Senate. I wrote to the prime minister and asked for a meeting to discuss his alarming election promise to excise 74,000 hectares of forest from the Tasmanian Wilderness World Heritage Area. We met in his office and in small talk he said that he had considered getting Menzies' desk brought in to use – it showed how much he thought himself Menzies' heir. It was an important 'reading the person' meeting. It was also the first engagement between balance-of-power players.

The most critical element in a balance-of-power relationship is always trust. The parties don't have to agree, but both have to know that whatever is agreed will be delivered; otherwise there is no point. I had that relationship with Liberal Premier Tony Rundle until his final betrayal when he went to the media to announce not only a reduction in the numbers in the Tasmanian Parliament, but done in a way designed to wipe out the Greens – a breach of an undertaking to me – and I had it with Julia Gillard.

But never with Tony Abbott. I was shocked when he said that he had not campaigned to take the forests out of the World Heritage Area so they could be logged. He said he would not do it. The fact that it was a fundamental plank in the Liberal Party campaign in Tasmania had been deleted from his memory. He said that as far as he was concerned, what was 'locked up was locked up'. Peta Credlin was at the meeting, as was my chief of staff Emma Bull. I asked for Abbott's undertaking not to excise anything from the Tasmanian Wilderness World Heritage Area in writing, and he agreed to provide it. He never did.

Meanwhile Abbott was keen to demonstrate his 'axe the tax' credentials by personally introducing the legislation to abolish the carbon price on the first sitting day of his government, 13 November 2013. Labor and many of the environmental groups were keen to send the issue off to committees and delay the vote until the New Year. Labor feared giving Abbott a double dissolution trigger and the groups wanted it held over so they could use the summer to campaign for the Clean Energy Package's retention.

I was keen to have the vote and defeat the bill before Christmas, because we still had the numbers. Postponing it over the summer break was too risky; I was afraid that those Labor MPs who had always opposed the carbon price would use the election defeat to change Labor's position. Abbott started the 'Electricity Bill' attack, suggesting that new Labor leader Bill Shorten wanted to retain carbon pricing in order to keep electricity prices high, and no one knew for how long Shorten would hold the line. In the end the Senate talked it out. The bills were debated and not voted on, and the groups that had wanted the summer to campaign were given the opportunity to do so and didn't.

At the same time Treasurer Hockey moved to increase Australia's debt ceiling. Labor had introduced the political weapon of a legislated debt ceiling in 2008 as a gesture of insurance that their stimulus package, introduced to combat the Global Financial Crisis, would not lead to massive overspending and recklessness. They then increased it three times under sustained Liberal attack. I had no time for the Abbott government but neither did I consider it good practice to create mayhem in the economy every time the limit was approached, just for the sake of cheap politics. Ultimately, the electorate would judge the economic management credentials of the government at the next election.

Like Premier Rundle so many years before, Treasurer Hockey refused to be seen with us, insisting on negotiating by phone and via staffers. We reached an agreement under which the Coalition would have to table a statement in parliament every time the nation's debt increased by $50 billion, explaining the factors behind the increase. Also it had to enhance the ten-year, medium-term projections in the Budget and Mid-Year Economic and Fiscal Outlook Report, with a focus on infrastructure funding. Hockey also agreed that a debt statement with details regarding government spending on climate change would be included in future Budgets and key economic reports. All future Intergenerational Reports would include a section on the environment and global warming, and the effect of these government policies on the nation and the Budget. He undertook to consult with the Australian Greens on the scope of what could be included. The deal was concluded and in writing.

Prime Minister Abbott reneged on his undertaking regarding the forests and wrote to UNESCO in February 2014 to try to excise 74,000 hectares for logging. And Hockey reneged on his agreements too, ultimately turning the Intergenerational Report into Liberal party-political junk. That was the beginning and the end of any constructive relationship in balance of power with the Abbott government. It is impossible to work with people who don't keep their word.

Hockey and his colleague Mathias Cormann were very pleased with themselves about their Budget. They smoked cigars together and Hockey even danced in his office to the tune of 'Best Day of My Life' as he was about to deliver a Budget that slashed support for pensioners, the elderly, the sick and the disabled, while the wealthy were rewarded with tax cuts. The government's strategy was to ingratiate itself with the new Palmer United Party senators so they could bypass the Greens and the Labor Party, abolish the carbon price and the mining tax and get the Budget passed. We made a decision to oppose Abbott's Budget with everything we had. Rallies were held around Australia.

I was roundly criticised for refusing to negotiate with Abbott, with those same critics refusing to acknowledge that he had already shown he couldn't be trusted to negotiate in good faith. Those critics and commentators failed to understand that not negotiating in balance of power is just as strong and valid a position as negotiating, especially if you reject the proposals on the table outright when there is no room to compromise. In the end it was not the crossbench deal makers on the 2014 Budget who brought Abbott and his budget undone: it was those, like we Greens, who stood up to him.

The most bizarre event of 2014 was the Clive Palmer press conference in the week leading up to the new Senate. I knew nothing about it until a flurry of activity occurred in Parliament House and breathless journalists reported that Clive Palmer and Al Gore were about to do a joint press conference in the Great Hall. I couldn't believe that Al Gore, the champion of environmental responsibility, would give credibility and political cover to a coal baron who had stood for election to destroy carbon pricing. I later asked the US ambassador to Australia informally why he had given the go-ahead for the former vice-president to do it. He graciously replied that had Al Gore asked for advice from the American embassy, he would have been given it, but as he had not, only Al Gore himself could explain his decision.

Since then it has been revealed that, in the 2013–14 financial year, Clive Palmer's company Queensland Nickel donated $15 million to set up the Palmer United Party. Palmer said that it was to abolish the carbon 'tax' and that it had been money well spent, as it saved his refinery $24 million a year. Clive Palmer voting down the carbon price saved just one of his companies $24 million. For those who set up the spectacle – Don Henry, Ben Oquist, Andrew Crook and John Clements – it was a tactical manoeuvre, but for Al Gore it was in another league. His credibility in Australia was all but destroyed in a single day.

The carbon pricing scheme was abolished on 17 July 2014. In the House of Representatives Greg Hunt, Kelly O'Dwyer and Christopher Pyne all hugged each other and danced, and so did Clive Palmer's senators Jacqui Lambie, Glenn Lazarus and Dio Wang up the back of the Senate as they all condemned future generations to living in a climate emergency. I am glad that the dancing photos are recorded; for everyone who voted to abolish the carbon pricing bills, whatever else they do in their careers that vote will stand as their political legacy. Future generations will hold them responsible for Australia's utter failure to pull its weight in the crucial decade when action on climate change could have made a huge difference.

After the vote I went straight from the Senate to my office and had a good cry. Peter Whish-Wilson came straight around, declaring that because Bob Brown had given me a hug when we celebrated the passage of the bill, he would give me a hug when there was cause for grief. It was such a thoughtful gesture.

During the following winter break in 2014 I thought long and hard about how to advance climate policy within the Australian Parliament. It was obvious that even if Abbott were rolled, his successor Turnbull wouldn't act on climate change: the conservatives who gave him the leadership would not allow it. Labor, on the other hand, would never stand up against coal because of the unions and because of corporate donations.

My fears were confirmed when the politically motivated Warburton Review of the Renewable Energy Target was released in August. Dick Warburton is a former Caltex chair, climate denier and nuclear advocate. He went way beyond his brief to recommend the Renewable Energy Target be scrapped altogether. I dumped the report in a bin. It was not worth the paper it was written on, but it signalled where the next attack on renewable energy would be focused. Sure enough, Labor voted with Abbott for a reduction in the Renewable Energy Target and announced its support for the Adani coalmine.

At the same time I moved for a Senate inquiry into tax avoidance in Australia. The cosy relationship between big business, especially the resource-based industries, and the Liberal and Labor parties needed to be exposed. Both the Coalition and Labor had already refused to introduce a national commission against corruption, despite the revelations coming out of New South Wales's Independent Commission Against Corruption (ICAC) about the corruption of Australia's resource-based industries, and the Abbott government continued to support tax cuts for big business while attacking the poor. Just as I had expected, the big business entities that screamed about the mining tax and carbon pricing and constantly called for the abolition of penalty rates didn't pay tax in Australia. Nor did Apple or Google or Facebook. The greatest and ongoing legacy of the Inquiry was to change the national debate around corruption, political donations and budget repair. The Inquiry destroyed the idea of trickle-down economics. People saw big business running overseas with tax-free profits and expecting more tax cuts and corporate welfare to be provided to them by government by cutting pensions, school and health funding. The Inquiry brought home the extent of the gap between the rich and the poor in Australia and brought inequality and redistributive justice to the Budget and federal election conversations. It brought a national ICAC, political donations and tax reform to the top of the political agenda.

Meanwhile, the war in Afghanistan remained as a constant backdrop with the prime minister and the leader of the Opposition attending every funeral of every dead soldier until there were too many and they stopped. I kept calling for the troops to be brought home and was even more determined after reading Major General John Cantwell's book, *Exit Wounds*. He asked:

> What measure of success in the campaign to fight the
> Taliban and build Afghanistan's army could possibly
> warrant the grim procession of dead men that I
> supervised? [. . .] Is what we have achieved in Afghanistan
> worth the lives lost and damaged? [. . .] It is not worth
> it. I cannot justify any one of the Australian lives lost in
> Afghanistan.[4]

Just as the Greens under Bob Brown's leadership had opposed Howard's invasion of Iraq in 2003, and had introduced legislation for the Parliament rather than the Executive to decide when Australia goes to war, under my leadership, Scott Ludlam did the same. I opposed Abbott's later desperate efforts, supported by Bill Shorten, to beg the Americans and Iraqis for Australia to be included in the ongoing war in the Middle East. As I predicted, it became and remains a quagmire.

But the Australian Parliament can rise to occasions too; parliamentarians from all parties can come together to mourn, commemorate or honour individuals. On 5 March 2015 I attended a dawn vigil at Parliament House to plead for the lives of Andrew Chan and Myuran Sukumaran, two Australians on death row in Indonesia for smuggling drugs. It was inspiring to see the outpouring of support from all around the country and another reminder why it is so important to oppose the death penalty as a matter of principle.

Foreign minister Julie Bishop invited Tanya Plibersek and me to join her in her office very early that day to rehearse how the event would proceed. This was clearly her event. When we turned up, she was furious as Tony Abbott had decided to crash the occasion, inviting leader of the Opposition Bill Shorten to join him. We went down to the Great Hall; it was nearly time for us to go out to the forecourt, and Abbott hadn't turned up. I suggested we proceed as agreed and when the prime minister and Bill Shorten turned up they could join us. She was more than pleased. We were well into the ceremony by the time they arrived. It was my first personal insight into the deterioration of the Liberal leadership.

~

GIVEN WHAT I KNEW ABOUT the global warming emergency, the need for global emissions to peak by 2020 and the extent to which both sides of politics in Australia were now owned by the banks, the fossil fuel and mining industries, the gambling, communications and property industries, I had to ask myself some hard questions. In the few years I had left to work at a high level, would I be more effective as a Green activist inside the Australian parliament or working beyond it globally? It was clear nothing was going to change in Australian politics within five years to seriously address global warming, so perhaps I needed to rejoin the global activist community. I was sixty-two. The next federal election was in 2016, and I was up for re-election for a six-year term. I knew that there was no way I wanted to still be in the Senate travelling backwards and forwards to Canberra at the age of sixty-nine. Nature and I didn't have time to wait. Besides, I had a grandchild soon to be born and an aged mother to cherish.

I sought inspiration in the words of my favourite philosopher, Henry David Thoreau: 'I left the woods for as good a reason as I went there. Perhaps it seemed to me that I had several more lives to live, and could not spare any more time for that one.'[5] I could have followed others and stood, been elected and then retired, handing my replacement a five-year term. But I didn't want to stand in press conferences and community meetings and lie to the very people who had supported me for more than twenty years.

I discussed the pros and cons of staying or going often and at great length with my partner, Gary, and my sons, Tom and James. They were all great sounding boards, and they said unanimously that I was the only person who knew in my gut what I really wanted, and that they would support me whatever I decided.

So I made up my mind to go. I knew I needed to resign from the Greens leadership and the Senate early enough for the next leader to become established before the 2016 election. A carefully executed strategy was needed. I took my chief of staff, Emma Bull, and my office manager, Wendy McLeod, into my confidence; they had to help make it happen, and together we needed to make sure that no word of my plan leaked. Timing was everything, and every detail had to be considered.

I didn't want to make a valedictory speech in the parliament; I simply couldn't bear hearing those who had done everything they could to destroy the Greens mouthing platitudes about how they respected my contribution though we didn't agree. So I organised a National Press Club pre-Budget speech and timed my resignation for the day before so I could make that speech my valedictory.

My final sitting days as leader were quite surreal. I knew when the parliament resumed for the Budget session that I would not be leader, but no other MP did. Asking my last question as leader, making my last speech: all those things were quite emotional. I was trying to close the circle on as many outstanding issues as I could. One of the most beautiful things about that last week was the visit to Parliament House by journalist Peter Greste, recently freed from an Egyptian jail. I had advocated for him in the media and through the parliament, as had Julie Bishop and so many others, and he came with his whole family to thank us all. As we sat in my office, I saw the joy in his mother's face and the relief of his father and all his family. I could not have imagined a more heartening note on which to leave the leadership.

On the morning of my resignation I woke up early. I checked all the media: so far so good; there was nothing about me. I checked in with Emma and finalised the tweet and the social media statement that would break the news. To calm myself I walked up to Parliament House alone, along the Democracy Walk linking Parliament House with the city, the walk that Bob Brown had made happen. I remembered the day the walk was opened and we had stood together along that pathway.

It was a beautiful May morning in Canberra, quite clear, with lots of birds in the trees and ants in the gravel; I reflected that I need not have organised for Gary and the boys to fly in the night before to avoid the Canberra fog. I had made sure they didn't fly together: seeing them all would have caused speculation as they rarely came to Canberra, and never all at the same time. They would stay in the hotel until after the announcement before coming up to the parliament for the press conference. Nothing was left to chance.

I was happy that my family would be there. We had lived my political life together, and it was important to me that we ended it together. I remembered what the boys had been through growing up: the 'you know whose son that is' whispers behind their backs, being taken home from school by the police because of death threats. They would be relieved that whatever they did from then on would attract no comment from the media. But I knew they were proud of what we had achieved together, and I wanted them to know how proud I was of them in return. I thought about what a rock Gary had been for fifteen years and rejoiced that at last we might actually be able to spend our lives living under the same roof in the same city.

I thought about my colleagues who I would be meeting in a short while and thought how much I would miss them. I was anxious for my staff, who owned all that we had achieved together and who would now be faced with redundancy. They didn't deserve that, but the life of political staffers is inherently unfair. They are paid well because at any moment they can lose their jobs: as leaders change, so do they. I tried to anticipate the media's questions. I knew that, for them, the substance of my career over decades meant nothing. All they would want to know was 'Why?', 'Who knew?', before moving on to the new leader. I was approaching my rooster-to-feather-duster moment.

It is amazing how much ground the mind can cover as you walk even a relatively short distance. I arrived at the doors; I was ready. My work was done.

Richard Di Natale, Larissa Waters and Scott Ludlam were elected as a great leadership team to succeed me. In my last speech I said, 'I'm not leaving politics, I'm not leaving the Greens, I'm leaving political representation, but, for the Greens, activism is everything in and out of the parliament.

'And I will be there as an activist, in purple stockings and more dangerous than ever.'

Then, as a representative of the Global Greens, I flew to the meeting of the United Nations Framework Convention on Climate Change in Paris, at which the groundbreaking Paris Agreement was negotiated and agreed. Although it was a good start, it is nowhere near good enough. If all the pledges made in Paris were to be delivered, it would still leave the world on track for at least three additional degrees of warming – far from the 1.5 degrees everyone agreed needed to be pursued.

There was still a great deal more to do. That is when I started buying Brendas.

# 17

# The Tasmanian Activism App

OBJECT: *Freezer owned by Christine since the 1980s.*
*Covered in paint and campaign stickers. It is a snapshot*
*of the political, environmental and community campaigns*
*of a twenty-year period in Australian history.*

FROM THE VERY BEGINNING, I was captivated by information technology's enormous and disruptive power to revolutionise everything. It excited me to think about how IT might enable Tasmania to overcome the disadvantages of geographical isolation and become a beacon, a small wild island in the southern hemisphere where human potential knows no bounds. So I became an advocate for its widespread adoption. In 1996 my photograph appeared on the cover of an IT magazine as a leader in the field of information technology, believe it or not.

I established the IT portfolio for the Greens in the early 1990s. I added it to my portfolios of arts and education and started advocating for an alternative 'Clean, Green and Clever' future for the state, based on protecting our wilderness, powering industry with renewable energy, maintaining clean air, clean water and uncontaminated soils to underpin our food and wines, and linking to the rest of the world with IT.

At this point anyone who has worked with me will be laughing – especially the IT help desk at Parliament House, to whom I will always be incredibly grateful. I recognised the enormous potential of IT and could talk about its huge benefits, but I struggled to understand how it actually worked and had no intuitive feel for making it do so on my own computer.

In 1989 the Tasmanian Greens were the first party in the Tasmanian parliamentary offices to have computers. We had been persuaded by Ahmet Bektas, who had just joined our Greens team from working with Apple, to get new Macintosh Portables and, for the staff, desktop computers. All other MPs and Upper House members still used stenographers to type dictated or hand-drafted letters, press releases or draft documents. The standard equipment for newly elected MPs was a desk and a phone, not even a fax machine, so moving to computers was regarded as a radical and subversive thing to do.

Others looked at us with suspicion. Who knew what our staff were up to? When the Liberal government of Ray Groom was elected in 1992, so suspicious were they that they sent people to take our staff desktop computers away. Dr Gerry Bates, who understood the usefulness of computers best, locked the doors to stop their removal, and the government backed down. Gradually other parliamentary offices adopted the new technology; the threat posed by the Greens and their machines was over.

Over my twenty-five years in politics, information technology has exploded. Mobile phones, laptops, the internet, the iPad made life easier and harder. It meant that, apart from being in the air, there never was a place or time when you were out of contact, but on the other hand you could access the world and information of every kind at any time and broadcast whatever you wanted at the click of a button. IT has changed the way we do everything, including how we relate to each other, how we spend our recreational time and how we relate to wild places. People rarely leave home without their phones. There are now virtually no places on Earth where you can really be alone in the wild and beyond a satellite's or a signal's reach.

Online environments have become more real to some than the physical reality of the world around them. You can don 3D and play games or experience the Arctic, Antarctic, tropical jungles or extreme sporting events from your own lounge room. In every profession, from the complexities of modern medicine right down to renovating a house, the new tools have been transformative. What this has meant is that physical buildings such as museums and interpretation centres have been supplemented by apps.

I am excited by this opportunity. I have argued for decades for the establishment of a World Heritage interpretation centre in Tasmania in a prominent position on the Hobart waterfront. Thousands of people from all over Australia and around the world stood with Tasmanians during the Franklin dam campaign and during the forest campaigns over thirty years, but there is nowhere they can go to learn about the wilderness or the forests or deposit their stories and photos. Nor is there a place where they can go to see memorabilia from the 1970–2015 period and relive what was possibly the most exciting and meaningful time of their lives except for a small display at the Tasmanian Museum and Art Gallery. Sadly such a centre will not happen, because showcasing the struggle would highlight the past and current failures of Liberal and Labor governments, of Forestry Tasmania and Hydro Tasmania, who resisted every effort to protect forests and wild areas from logging and mining and hydro development, and continue to do so in the face of pressure from not only resource extraction but inappropriate tourism development.

The history of the struggle to protect Tasmania's wild places and natural beauty has been largely written out of the Tasmanian story. Many who did nothing to save these places immediately moved to cash in on the global and national awareness delivered by the campaigns. Profiting from other people's principles, I call it. As I had hoped when I produced the Greens' Business and Industry strategy for Tasmania in 1992, everything from beer and wine to cheese and fruits, beef, lamb and shellfish and tourism are all sold on the back of the cleanest air in the world and the global reputation of the Tasmanian Wilderness. But rarely do those producers or tourism operators acknowledge that their brand has been built by the passion of the protesters and their supporters in the community. It is way past time for them to realise that maintaining the authenticity of the Tasmanian brand, not just marketing and profiting from it, is their responsibility too and should not be left to the environment campaigners alone.

But now we can bypass all that and tell our own story.

All around Tasmania there are special places – individual trees, forests, conservation areas, stretches of river, coastal environments, hilltops and ridges, heritage buildings, bridges, farmland – preserved by the efforts of local people who have campaigned for their protection. But the stories and photographs of that struggle have been lost or remain in albums with no names or labels.

The best memory prompt I have is my old freezer. When I lived on Tasmania's north-west coast in the early 1980s, I had a tub freezer in my garage. My son Thomas knocked a couple of tins of paint from a shelf and the lids came off, covering the white freezer with green and pink streaks. I didn't discover it until the paint had dried. So I covered the paint with environment and Green campaign stickers until 2005, when I moved house. The stickers are a great summary of Green history of those twenty years. They are the stuff of local stories but over time these tales are lost, especially if protection attempts have been successful. When you drive through a beautiful forest, along an undeveloped coast, or marvel at a bumper crop in the richness of the red soils, how can you know that if not for the efforts of local people they would be gone?

We need an app so that these stories are not left to those who can remember or have a sticker on a wardrobe door or a freezer. Tasmanians and tourists alike should be able to enjoy a much-enriched experience of the landscapes and stories in which they live or travel. The Franklin blockade, the campaign against the Wesley Vale and Gunns pulp mill[1] and the fight for Lake Pedder are well-known stories but there are so many others. I want people to know about the fight for the forests of the Great Western Tiers, the Observer Tree, the site of Miranda Gibson's longest tree sit in Australia's history and the location in the Southern Forests where the now world-famous 'Angels' first came to national prominence.[2] I'm sure Australians would love to know how and where BHP got away with the biggest oil spill in Tasmania's history, why the Friendly Beaches weren't sand mined, why the beautiful east coast remains undeveloped and how the French came to plant a vegetable garden in Tasmania.

Laurie Goldsworthy had been one of my support candidates in three Tasmanian state elections and was passionate about the area in which he lived. He acted as our guide when my colleagues and I set up a mobile office in the forest to report on the logging proposed for Mother Cummings Peak near Deloraine in the state's north. He took us to a sphagnum moss swamp, a relic of the last ice age containing small King Billy pines that would be destroyed by the bulldozers. It was a fairyland of water, lichens, mosses and fungi deep in the forest. Glades of man ferns and myrtle and sassafras on towering ridges were certainly worth fighting for. A great many local people put themselves on the line, and on a day when many were arrested at Scotts Road in Meander, Hector the Protector made his stand. From a computer in a tree, Hector, whose real name was Neil Smith, was the first person in Tasmania to tell the world in real time what was actually going on in the forests:

Wed, 4 Mar 1998 12:02:45 +1100 (EST)
(Message sent to The Hon Tony Rundle MHA, Premier of Tasmania, and The Hon John Beswick MHA, Minister for Forests, with copies to all State members of Parliament.)
Dear Ministers,
This message comes to you from 25 metres up a tree

(*Eucalyptus delegatensis*) in proposed logging coupe
HU-307 on the Great Western Tiers.

I am sorely concerned at the devastation wreaked on
this hitherto pristine ecosystem, at the way in which this
exercise appears to have been engineered to smash totally
the conservation movement in Tasmania, and at the blatant
disregard for human safety which was part of the exercise.

Not only is this coupe (if I must use the term) of
outstanding biodiversity significance, containing forest
types inadequately reserved in the RFA [Regional Forest
Agreement], but also it is, at 850 metres elevation,
silviculturally questionable. The success of regeneration
would be anybody's guess.

For the time being I'm adopting the name Hector.
It isn't my real name, but I want to deflect as much
as possible the threats and recriminations which will
inevitably follow myself and my family given the
questionable standards of behaviour adopted by many
involved in the vile forestry industry in this state.

Today a peaceful blockade mounted by
environmentalists on Scotts Road, Meander, was broken
by a large show of strength involving workers from
Forestry Tasmania and the Tasmania Police. Chainsaws
were produced and approximately one hundred trees of
all sizes were felled along the course of a planned logging
road into this coupe. The very first tree felled was one
of the largest, only 80 metres from my site, despite the
fact that I was located some 500 metres into the coupe.
It was felled in my direction and I felt the shock wave
transmitted through the ground and up the trunk when
the tree fell.

When the saws were briefly silent, I called out to reveal
my presence on my platform ... I also suggested (very

loudly) that the workers had a duty to halt dangerous practices like tree felling when there was a possibility of people in the coupe. There were other protesters at various places in the forest and no reasonable attempt had been made to scour them out prior to commencement of work. I informed the workers of the presence of others hidden in the understorey, but they continued with what they were doing. Only after at least twenty more trees had been felled was there a desultory attempt to search the immediate surroundings of the work in hand.

Apart from the first and largest tree, several smaller ones nearby were felled directly towards me after I had engaged the workers in conversation. At least ten police officers stood by while all this occurred. Other sources may be able to state that there were even more.

When all but one of the police and forestry vehicles had left the scene just on nightfall after the two-hour display, a single shot was fired from a rifle and the last car left. I can only assume that the shot was meant to scare me. Just after dark, 'the noises' began – two or three sinister commando-like characters circling quietly in the bush around me and making fake animal sounds, possibly with small electronic trillers or maybe with voice. From this height I can hear every small twig that is broken underfoot, and track the route of the intruders fairly accurately. This activity is a repetition of last night, when such people circled menacingly all night, disappearing one by one to the northwest just before dawn. On both occasions these people have refused to identify themselves when challenged (in the case of last night, by my wife who was herself on the ground alone). We have talked about these people as 'the gooks' but their identity remains a mystery.

Tonight I have friends camped on the ground below
my tree. Through a third party I requested a police
guard, since I fear for my safety. A police vehicle arrived
and I talked to one of the officers by shouting loudly
over the intervening 500 metres. They declined to stay
overnight but said they would be around 'for a while'.
The officer also said it could be 'a possum'. I told them
of last night's goings-on including that there was a fixed
light marking a supposed camp or rendezvous spot on a
bearing of 35 degrees and about 500 to 600 metres from
me. I suggested that they might find something there
if they looked. The police then departed immediately
without fulfilling even their promise to stay 'for a while'.

Is this sort of atrocious behaviour – with equal
disregard for places of extreme conservation significance
and for people's safety – the outcome of your much-
touted RFA which was supposed to bring 'peace in the
forests'? I can't see much possibility of peace.

Yours sincerely,

Hector

Eight days later, on Thursday 12 March 1998, Hector was forcibly
removed from his platform by Tasmania Police. Logging company
North Ltd's Chris Oldfield told protesters that their action had cost
North $80,000, and that North will 'rip that forest regardless of the
costs'. And they did.

Even before the Mother Cummings protests, in an effort to
understand where each opposing force was coming from after years
of ongoing forest conflict, local farmer Ned Terry and artist Niecy
Brown began a project called Yarns, intended to record the history
of the district and the stories of families old and new in an artwork
that the community itself would make under the watchful eye of
works coordinator Lexie Young. It consisted of four panels of silk,

representing the life of the district throughout the four seasons. The result was dazzling. The appliqué, embroidery, cross-stitch, weaving and quilting skills of the established rural community joined with the artistic skills of new settlers to create a truly remarkable work, right down to the jewellery makers who created silver icicles on waterfalls.

Three hundred people were involved in the storytelling, design and making of Yarns. It was a triumph of community arts. As leader of the Tasmanian Greens I was invited to its unveiling and was thrilled to be there; having witnessed for so long the conflict and animosity towards 'greenies', this was at last something really positive, and an event at which to move beyond that conflict. The artwork still hangs in Deloraine. But how much deeper would the experience be if instead of just seeing depictions of the forest conflict, there was an app that you could consult while viewing Yarns to read Hector's messages and look at the photographs of the protests and feel the depth of emotion on both sides. Apart from that, a Tasmanian environmental interpretation app could also provide a map so that people could go to Mother Cummings Peak and to where Hector's tree had stood, and experience the loss and the joy of knowing that the World Heritage listing of the Great Western Tiers had finally been successful because of people like Hector and the hundreds of people who stood for the forests.

At the climate talks in Paris in 2015 the now-famous Angels or Climate Guardians were a huge hit as they posed in angel iconography in front of landmarks and called for climate action. But few people realise that the first to create such a presence was Allana Beltran, with her sculptural performance art piece known as the Weld Angel. As an artist and filmmaker she had joined the campaign to save the forests of the Weld Valley. Dressed as an angel, with handmade wings and in full costume and body paint, she sat atop tall wooden poles and ropes and disrupted the logging. She made world news. Yet people now driving along the forestry roads in southern Tasmania would have no idea about her or the location of her action. With an app, you could see Allana again in full costume in the forests in the very place of her groundbreaking performance art of activism.

From the forests to the coasts, another focus for the app would be Tasmania's magnificent coastal environment. Eaglehawk Neck on Tasmania's east coast was critical to the decision to site a convict prison at Port Arthur, as it was such a narrow land bridge that escape was almost impossible. Convicts had to brave a dog chain across the Neck or swim for it, risking drowning or shark attack. The Tasmanian Department of Main Roads decided in 1989 to build a four-lane highway, filling in Eaglehawk Bay to accommodate the road and destroying Eaglehawk Neck. I couldn't believe that such an assault on the landscape or the integrity of our history would be allowed. But this was a time when Tasmanians didn't particularly value our convict ancestry and it was still a matter of shame to have a convict forebear. The Coal Mines site on the Saltwater River on the Peninsula was not protected either; people from Hobart would go down at weekends to steal the sandstone slabs for their gardens.

I had done my honours thesis at the University of Tasmania on the development of Tasmanian tourism from the end of transportation to 1900, and so felt strongly about the need to protect not only the heritage of the Port Arthur site but also the convict sites on the whole peninsula.

The amazing thing about Eaglehawk Neck was that the field of view from the officers' quarters had not changed since the penal colony was established. It seemed an abomination to me that Labor minister Judy Jackson was prepared to allow a shop to be built right in front of the officers' quarters, let alone that the government was prepared to destroy the Neck.

I joined the historians including Peter MacFie in insisting that the minister Ken Wriedt visit the site, accompanied by the Port Arthur Authority experts. Wriedt agreed that the Neck should not be widened to accommodate the new road. It was a victory for common sense, for the environment and for our convict history. Now with World Heritage listing of the Port Arthur site and the restoration of the Coal Mines site, it is hard to imagine that anyone thought destroying Eaglehawk Neck was a good idea. The fact that they did, and the stand taken to protect it, should be part of the story.

As they drive down the east coast of Tasmania, overseas and interstate visitors marvel at the fact that it is largely unspoiled, unlike almost the entire eastern seaboard of Australia. They appreciate the magnificence of the wide coastal seascapes from the Bay of Fires in the far north to Swansea and Bicheno, with Freycinet Peninsula and Maria Island in the background. There is a reason for that: local people and the Tasmanian Greens fought to keep the landscape that way. For decades, while Lesley Nicklason fought to save the forests of the Blue Tier, Bill Manning, Todd Dudley and Jay Yulumara fought through the planning schemes to stop subdivisions and inappropriate development up and down the entire coast, including an area known as The Gardens. As a result of their experiences and my own – having been condemned as the Princess of Piermont for stopping a subdivision – we campaigned for a statewide coastal policy that would properly protect our coasts and incorporate genuine principles of sustainable development.[3] It was formulated in 1996 and it has remained in place ever since as the overriding legislative framework when conflicts occur between local planning schemes and the state coastal policy.

Further up the coast are the magnificent wild Friendly Beaches. People who marvel at their beauty and surfers who flock there would be shocked to learn that the Labor government gave approval for the development of a sand mine during the time of the Labor–Green Accord. We Greens were totally opposed to such a venture and approached the Liberal shadow minister John Bennett to work with us to prevent it. He was a four-wheel driver who took his vehicle onto the beach and didn't want to see a sand mine in the vicinity. Together we defeated the Labor Party proposal. We then worked with

Labor and had the area declared a national park. Not even bicycles are permitted on the beach. It was a big win for Lyons, for Tasmania and for the shorebirds.

When Graham Richardson was Labor minister for the environment, he asked me about the Bay of Fires Coastal Preservation Lobby. He said it must be a remarkable organisation as he received well-researched letters or a submission to inquiries nearly every week, highlighting environmental issues as diverse as tuna fishing in the Pacific, logging Tasmania's forests, the Wesley Vale pulp mill, the protection of Binalong Bay and the Bay of Fires, and the Ranger uranium mine in the Northern Territory. I agreed it was a remarkable, well-organised group of people not to be taken lightly. I didn't tell him that it was effectively a dedicated two-person campaign, run by Jay Yulumara and Jim Henley from a kitchen table at Binalong Bay. Jay continued the struggle to protect wild places for more than twenty-five years. She set up a cabin on her land, and when my boys were little we spent very happy and relaxing beach holidays with her there. We also enjoyed the hospitality of Jeff Weston, one of the great characters of the east coast.[4]

But the fight for the east coast and Tasmania's coastal vistas goes on, with a Property Council of Australia-driven new statewide planning scheme under consideration that would give developers a free hand. When visitors go to unspoiled Binalong Bay and see the intact heathland known as Black's Land, it would be wonderful if they were inspired by the efforts of the Bay of Fires Coastal Preservation Lobby and their dedicated team of volunteers and decided to work for the protection of their own special places, wherever they might be.

If people could see and read about the struggle, they might be less willing to facilitate a new planning scheme and coastal property boom at the expense of the environment.

On 10 July 1995 the BHP-chartered bulk carrier *Iron Baron*, transporting manganese to the TEMCO smelter at Bell Bay, ran aground on Hebe Reef as it approached the mouth of the Tamar

River and began leaking bunker fuel oil. It leaked approximately 550 tonnes of oil over twenty days before being towed to an offshore anchorage and eventually scuttled east of Flinders Island on 30 July. Twenty-five thousand penguins died, with thousands killed on Ninth Island alone. It sparked a major clean-up and wildlife rescue operation. Hundreds of oiled seabirds were rescued from affected areas and moved to Low Head for treatment and rehabilitation. Most were penguins from the Low Head colony, but cormorants, pelicans and black swans were also rescued.

I visited the clean-up site to thank and encourage the volunteers who were working long hours with the Department of Parks and Wildlife staff and veterinarians to save the birds. But my overwhelming memory of the episode is the difficulty of exposing the seriousness and long-term consequences of the spill for Bass Strait's ecosystem in the face of the public relations campaign from BHP. I don't know if they won PR awards for their efforts, but they should have done. It was masterful. Criticising the company for the spill, calling for prosecution and condemning the government for the utterly inadequate fines and penalties was seen as 'negative' and 'ungrateful' for the dollars BHP invested in the clean-up and search-and-rescue operation. Their PR people were constantly on all the media, talking up the company's response. It was considered impolite to sheet home responsibility for killing 25,000 penguins and plastering oil along the coast or pointing out the long-term damage of oil pollution on Bass Strait's marine flora and fauna. Better to highlight the workers cleaning the birds and dressing them in the knitted coats that volunteers so quickly and decently produced. It was heartening to see the community response, to see the generosity of Tasmanians everywhere doing what they could to help, but it was also an insight into the level of preparedness of big business to protect their brand from their own disasters and their profits from governments that might be tempted to actually properly regulate and fine them.

Visitors to the Tamar Valley love the wildlife, and I am sure they would be inspired to hear how a community came together to save its birds, while they would be horrified by how a company got away financially and publicly with causing an environmental disaster and the biggest oil spill in Tasmania's history.

According to the late John Mulvaney, one of Australia's most distinguished archaeologists and anthropologists, two sites in Australia have special significance for science and history: Botany Bay in New South Wales and Recherche Bay in Tasmania.[5] At both places, botanists collected many of Australia's unique plants for the first time, and they became the type specimens to which later botanists referred. But apart from the specialists, who in Australia even knows about Recherche Bay?

Most Tasmanians, let alone others, know very little about the French visits to Tasmania in the late 1700s. Recherche Bay in southern Tasmania was named after one of the French ships, the *Recherche*, on the Bruny d'Entrecasteaux expedition in search of French explorer La Pérouse, who had vanished somewhere in Oceania on a previous voyage of discovery. He had last been seen leaving Botany Bay in 1788. D'Entrecasteaux's ships the *Recherche* and *Esperance* sailed into Recherche Bay in 1792 and returned in early 1793. It was also a scientific expedition, and they established friendly contact with Tasmania's Aboriginal people. The botanist Labillardière made several voyages locally to collect botanical samples, and the gardener Félix Delahaye planted a garden in the hope that when they returned there would be fresh vegetables. Rossel set up his equipment to observe the stars and measure the Earth's magnetism. One sailor died, and no one knows where he is buried.

Over the years the area was home to whalers and to sawmills and was eventually bought by a family determined to log it. Local people like Wren Fraser Cameron formed the Recherche Bay Protection Group to campaign to save it. A singing group called the Recherche Baybes, with Deborah Wace's powerful voice and creative talent, wrote songs for the campaign. I was working in Bob Brown's office at the time and, together with Bob and senior staffer Margaret Blakers, began to study the area with a view to securing its protection as a natural and cultural site. I can still remember the excitement when reports came into the office that Helen Gee and Bob Graham had found a rock formation they thought matched the description of the French garden.

We accompanied archaeologist John Mulvaney to the site and were delighted when he determined that it was indeed the garden. I flew to Paris to do a search through the museums to try to find the diaries of Félix Delahaye, the artwork of the ship's artist Piron and anything else that might help us to better understand the detail of the journey. I cannot describe the wonder of being taken into the bowels of the Natural History Museum in Paris and being shown the samples of *Eucalyptus globulus* and *Diplarenna moreae* collected by Labillardière on that voyage. Right there in front of me from halfway around the world were the type specimens – the botanical term for the specimen on which the description and name of a new species is based – collected from my own home 200 years before.

I found the diary of the gardener De La Haie – that was the original spelling – but while it didn't provide much more information than we already had, again it was incredible to be turning the pages of a book written in the hand of the person who had planted the French garden at Recherche Bay. I drew a blank searching for Piron's drawings. He made so many on the voyage that are held in various collections that it does not make sense that there were so few from Tasmania. I have searched everywhere for more of his drawings over the years, but my search has been in vain. It seems that the few that are known are all that remain in existence.

I visited Malmaison, Empress Josephine's home where gardener De La Haie worked on his return from the expedition. Napoleon and Josephine had a lake there on which swam black swans from Tasmania and around which emus grazed. They built a large glasshouse in which to show off the tropical plants collected from the South Seas. I had hoped that some of the eucalypts planted on her estate had survived, but sadly the gardens had been subsumed by Paris suburbia, and the small gardens now surrounding Malmaison did not feature any Tasmanian trees.

The campaign to protect Recherche Bay from logging had gained such public interest and momentum that it was ultimately saved, thanks to a generous donation by philanthropist Dick Smith. It is currently owned and managed by the Tasmanian Land Conservancy. The opportunities for tourism and cultural engagement related to the French experience in Tasmania, their friendly engagement with Aboriginal people and retracing the local exploration voyages and fieldwork of the French scientists of the d'Entrecasteaux expedition are boundless. Such tourism experiences will be enhanced through awareness that Recherche Bay was almost lost to logging and was saved by people who cared enough to fight for it.

So the challenge is out there. We need a way of collating, digitising and showcasing the fight for Tasmania. Non-violent direct action, protest, standing up for what we believe in has become part of Tasmanian culture. We need to save and celebrate it. It cannot be the preserve of the government or Federal hotels. We need an app that belongs to the community that will give life and shape to real stories that matter and enhance our sense of place. History is made by those who show up, said Disraeli, and he was right, but it is a pity that many of those who did show up to 'save our state' have never been recognised and their photos, stories and memorabilia are being lost.

If we are to preserve our multilayered history and value the hopes and disappointments, passions and actions of people who have cared enough about Tasmania to fight for it, we need to grab the opportunities that new technology affords and get on with it.

# 18

# Green Leadership

OBJECT: *Claudio Alcorso's note, sent to Christine in 1996 for the launch of the Tasmanian Greens election campaign, framed by her staff as a sixtieth birthday present in 2013.*

AT THE LAUNCH OF OUR 1996 Tasmanian election campaign I read out the handwritten note sent to me by the great Claudio Alcorso, industrialist, winemaker, cultural warrior and futurist. He wrote:

The Greens will be the dominant political and social influence of the next century.

The Greens are the only Party understanding the interrelationship between Humanity and Nature based on the principle of 'being part of it' rather than of unlimited exploitation.

The Greens are the only party with a social programme based on human values. The other traditional parties have espoused the gods of 'Money and Markets'.

Our grandchildren will look in wonder and disbelief at the blindness of Australia's traditional Parties at the end of the 20th Century.

For my sixtieth birthday seventeen years after that launch, my staff had Claudio Alcorso's note framed for me. It felt as prescient as it had in 1996.

As I walked onto the stage in Liverpool, England, to address the opening plenary of the fourth Global Greens Conference in March 2017, I thought of these things, and especially of Claudio. The Global Greens has been a fledgling organisation, operating on a shoestring budget since its 2001 establishment in Canberra. Its existence constitutes a new threshold for the Greens; after forty-five years we are finally a global political movement. Admittedly this had happened more slowly than I had hoped when elected to the Tasmanian Parliament as an independent in 1989, and more slowly than the Earth needs. However, we had completed stage one of the challenge expressed by philosopher Henry David Thoreau: 'If you have built castles in the air, your work need not be lost; that is where they should be. Now put the foundations under them.'[1]

Looking out at an audience representing Green parties from more than ninety countries in the world, I thought about how far we had come from the idea of giving the Earth political expression, first articulated in 1972 in our United Tasmania Group (UTG) manifesto, 'The New Ethic'.[2] It seemed almost unbelievable that an idea conceived in Tasmania had now been built into an organised, futuristic, global, political force from the bottom up, but so it is. Green parties are well established, with representation in many parliaments of the world. They often hold balance of power and sometimes ministries – the deputy prime ministership of Sweden and the Austrian presidency, for example. Regional structures such as the European Greens are strong, and others such as the Asia Pacific Greens, the African Greens Federation and the Green parties of the Americas are evolving.

It excites me that all the Greens parties are based on the same principles, whether in Rwanda, Colombia, Germany or Australia. Because of this, we have the capacity to work together. Those principles that define being Green are clearly set out in the Global Greens Charter and are the four pillars of the New Ethic: ecology, social justice, peace and non-violence, and participatory democracy. The charter was largely drafted by Dr Louise Crossley, a giant of the environmental movement. Together with Margaret Blakers OAM, she guided it to ratification at the first Global Greens Conference in Canberra in 2001.

Getting the charter through the conference had not been entirely easy. Jeanette Fitzsimmons, a co-leader of the Greens in New Zealand and chair of the final conference session, had been charged with ratification, but she had to leave, so I was roped in to do the job. This was a matter of some urgency: the time was right, people of all cultures were thinking of new ideas for a new millennium, and if the charter wasn't ratified by the end of the conference, it might never be. Besides, we had brought together people from all over the world – not something we could easily do again, considering our shoestring budget.

Having been to the European Greens meeting in Paris two years before, I knew the problems I would have to face: a dogged adherence to process and a tendency to parochial Eurocentrism. There had been some resistance to the next meeting being held in Australia on global warming grounds that delegates had not wanted to fly. How much more difficult would it be to get final sign-off on the wording of a charter that had been years in the drafting?

It soon became obvious that I had to make a choice: either stick to strict Green meeting procedure and lose the charter as we ran out of time, or force the issue. The point of contention was a paragraph rejecting discrimination on the basis of race, religion, gender or sexuality. Our African delegates from the Kenyan Greens, including the much-loved and highly respected Wangari Maathai, sought to remove sexuality from the list, and stated their view strongly.

From the chair I decided to run a very hard line, refusing to reopen the matter for debate. I chose not to recognise further intervention and ignored a European Greens delegate who protested that I was not following Greens meeting procedure. (Normally, procedure would have required everyone to listen carefully as the Kenyan Greens reiterated their reasons, even though their objection had already been heard and rejected.) Then I put to the vote all the remaining paragraphs. When they were passed, I put the charter as a whole for ratification. It was agreed by acclamation; people clapped and cheered and hugged each other.

Did the end justify the means? Extending the Kenyans the courtesy of reply would have cost us a great deal. So many people had put everything into making that day happen, writing policies and letters and submissions, keeping notes and writing minutes, working through interpreters, spending hours on phone link-ups with constant technological challenges, raising funds to pay airfares and organising the whole event. I wasn't going to see our commitment to end discrimination compromised or the moment lost.

Fast-forward to 2017. In spite of many African countries making homosexuality illegal – subject to a life sentence in Uganda and Sierra Leone; punishable by death in Sudan, northern Nigeria and southern Somalia – the African Greens supported an amendment to the charter to end discrimination against all LGBTIQ people. Sixteen years after that Canberra plenary, far from wanting 'sexuality' removed, our African delegates had put their lives on the line for social justice. It is true that, as Victor Hugo said, 'No army can stop an idea whose time has come.'[3]

'Moved by the need for a new ethic which unites man with Nature to prevent the collapse of the life support systems of the Earth' was the New Ethic of the UTG, and it was the profound new global idea of 1972. Reuniting humanity with nature instead of assuming humanity is separate from and superior to it was a radical idea. Christianity has done a very good job of persuading people that humanity is separate from the Earth and from all other creatures, that it is the duty of humans to go out and conquer the Earth and, having done so, leave it behind for an afterlife in another realm. According to this view the Earth exists as a convenience to be used, abused and abandoned. The idea that we exist as part of nature was regarded as subversive and pagan.

Thinking about the environment on a planetary scale began in the late 1960s and early 1970s. The Club of Rome produced its report 'Limits to Growth' in 1972, and later that year the United Nations Conference on the Human Environment was convened in Stockholm. The image of the Blue Marble, the most famous image of the Earth from space and taken by the crew of *Apollo 17*, was released, searing the appearance and physical reality of the Earth as a self-contained ball in space with interrelated ecosystems into people's consciousness.

But it had not entered the consciousness of politics or economics. Every political party around the world until 1972 started from the assumption that the resources of the natural world were free, unlimited and there for the taking. They also assumed that the Earth could absorb all the wastes generated from the transformation and use of those resources without a problem, and that dumping them was free. There was no limit to what could be taken or dumped.

The natural environment did not exist for them except as a quarry or a tip or, in rare circumstances, as an area to be protected for its beauty, not for its own sake but as a playground or a zoo for the use of humanity. People could dam or poison rivers, log forests, fish the oceans, drill oil, mine ore bodies, clear vegetation, spray chemicals, dump pollutants and garbage into rivers, oceans and landfills, and pump whatever came out of a stack or chimney into the air to their heart's content. Wildlife could be destroyed. Extinction didn't matter.

The basic faultline in politics between left and right came down to the same issue: how it would affect whoever already had wealth or made money, and how the proposal would influence how that money was shared. Conservative politics worldwide concentrated on representing the people of the developed world who owned the land and the corporations, exploiting the natural world to ensure they kept the lion's share of the profits. Labour politics worldwide concentrated on organising and representing the people who worked to transform the resources of the natural world into marketable items so that they got secure jobs, good working conditions and a wage that represented a fair share of the profits generated.

The idea that digging up, cutting down, drilling, dredging, dumping and extracting might lead to collapse did not enter their heads. Economics evolved to support that view by making the physical world, our Earth, the place where we live, an externality. In the pursuit of jobs or in the corporate accounts, clean air, clean water, uncontaminated soil, other species or natural beauty were expendable externalities without intrinsic value.

Green politics turned that thinking on its head. It didn't just add an environment policy as a negotiable extra or an offset to wealth generation and distribution; rather, it put the protection of nature and the Earth's ecosystems at the ethical centre and as the starting point of political engagement.

It recognised that to do this properly on a global scale you had to protect the global commons such as oceans, rivers, forests, mountains, deserts, grasslands, wetlands and the atmosphere so that ecosystems and Earth systems could continue to function to support life. Because limits needed to be placed on the use of non-renewable resources, the profits derived from them should be distributed justly and equitably. At the same time renewable resources needed to be developed and promoted, and waste and resource use minimised by a process of recovery, reuse and recycling. All species had the right to exist and occupied a niche in nature deserving of respect. All people needed to be treated and respected equally, and conflicts resolved peacefully and non-violently. As many people as possible had to be involved in any decision affecting them. Hence the four pillars of the Greens: ecology, social justice, peace and non-violence, and participatory democracy.

The idea that politics could be changed to give expression to these ideas was new and radical. The UTG gave political expression to these ideas in the campaign to save Lake Pedder. It didn't win any seats in the 1972 election but it was a world first in environmental politics, paving the way for the future success of Green candidates Bob Brown, Dr Gerry Bates and Jo Vallentine (who started as a senator for the Nuclear Disarmament Party in 1984 but became a Green in 1990). The five independents – of which I was one – who got elected to the Tasmanian Parliament in 1989 through to the Tasmanian and Australian Greens all ran on a platform consistent with the New Ethic and the Brundtland Commission report 'Our Common Future', which had been released in 1987.

That report put environmentalism on the global political stage. It injected an urgency and depth to the debate and reinforced the ideas that the global environment imposed limits to growth and that poverty reduction, gender equity and wealth redistribution were crucial to environmental protection. It formulated the first definition of ecologically sustainable development as 'development that meets the needs of the present without compromising the ability of future generations to meet their own needs'. It was an unwelcome message to those vested interests that continue to make their money from driving ecological collapse. It has made them fight harder to maintain control of conservative and labour parties and to destroy any challengers.

This fierce resistance continues to this day. Economics adapted. Instead of treating the environment as an externality, it turned it into a trade-off. For years I struggled with understanding how economics turned the Brundtland definition of ecologically sustainable development into business as usual via the triple bottom line and trade-offs. I got my answer in 2007 when I was invited to a meeting of globally respected environmental thinkers in Zurich. They included Muhammad Yunus, founder of the Grameen Bank, Sylvia Earle, known as Her Deepness for her love of oceans, Lester Brown of the

Earth Policy Institute and Ashok Khosla, later to become president of the International Union for the Conservation of Nature.

Ashok mentioned that he had been part of the Brundtland Commission, and so I asked him what had happened. He said that the commission had decided that there were only two real things in the world: people and nature. They recognised that economics was merely a human construct, a tool that governed the relationship between them. They recognised that the tool was making the relationship unsustainable by regarding the environment as an externality. It had to be redesigned. Economics needed a rethink.

Their report was sent to the World Bank, where its conclusions were fundamentally undermined. Far from being reconstructed, economics was promoted from being a tool governing the relationship between two real things to being an equivalent real thing itself. A diagrammatic triangle came out of the World Bank to represent the relationship. Environment, Society and Economics became equivalents in the triple bottom line.

Ever since, in cost–benefit analyses of developments from one end of the planet to the other, socio-economic factors have been constantly combined to defeat environmental considerations. Whereas previously people and capital unapologetically combined to destroy nature via the market, now destroying nature was legitimised if the benefits to people and the market were deemed greater than saving the environment. 'Jobs versus environment' was born, and it has acted as the get-out-of-jail-free card for corporations and governments ever since.

The Brundtland Commission made the initial mistake of seeing people and nature as separate, not as one integrated whole. The World Bank exacerbated this fundamental error by refusing to recognise the need to rewrite economics to drive ecological sustainability. Instead it locked in a system of ecologically unsustainable trade-offs. The World Bank has a lot to answer for.

As we pored over and exposed the shoddy science and false claims in every environmental impact study of every major mine or pulp mill, we never really realised the extent to which the triangle and the Ecologically Sustainable Development idea itself had been co-opted to make winning our battles all the more difficult. The whole thrust of the argument of the pro-Wesley Vale pulp mill, pro-Whale Point woodchip mill, pro-Jabiluka uranium, pro-Tamar Valley pulp mill, pro-Adani, pro-James Price Point or Liverpool Plains Gas supporters was socio-economic: jobs and economic activity outweighed the coasts, rivers, groundwater, forests, wetlands, farmlands, oceans, coral reefs or Aboriginal culture. Every day in parliaments around the world Greens stand up to make a claim for the environment and for the future generations ignored by the World Bank.

Every Green candidate, every Green MP and every environmental activist should commit to memory this quote from *The Prince* by sixteenth-century Florentine politician and philosopher Niccolò Machiavelli – a book that has been on my shelves during my whole career. It will be their experience:

> And it ought to be remembered that there is nothing
> more difficult to take in hand, more perilous to conduct,
> or more uncertain in its success, than to take the lead
> in the introduction of a new order of things. Because
> the innovator has for enemies all those who have done
> well under the old conditions, and lukewarm defenders
> in those who may do well under the new. This coolness
> arises partly from fear of the opponents, who have the
> laws on their side, and partly from the incredulity of
> men, who do not readily believe in new things until they
> have had a long experience of them. Thus it happens that
> whenever those who are hostile have the opportunity to
> attack they do it like partisans, while the others defend
> lukewarmly, in such wise that the prince is endangered
> along with them.[4]

As a leader in changing the political and economic order of things, the Australian Greens have built our party in spite of powerful enemies. Unlike the United Kingdom Independence Party, Berlusconi, One Nation or the Palmer United Party – which with varying combinations of money, celebrity, populism, shock value, stunts and good timing have gone off like a skyrocket at a bonfire and sped into the sky, exploded with a bang and created showers of attention-grabbing sparks before falling to the ground as a dead stick – the Greens have a unifying philosophy, a strong membership and a solid organisational foundation that challenges the status quo. It is no wonder we have attracted such powerful enemies as the Business Council of Australia, the Australian Chamber of Commerce and Industry, the Minerals Council of Australia, Rupert Murdoch and his media empire and those in the political establishment generally. We also have lukewarm defenders in the old established environment and social justice groups and in many of the renewable energy and service and information businesses of the new economy who try to keep the door open to the old order while seeking to make way in the new.

Defending lukewarmly not only endangers policies such as a strong greenhouse gas reduction target or strong renewable energy target but it also slows the transition to the zero carbon, innovative economy and endangers the Greens. To stand up for these policies in parliament the Australian Greens have to be elected, and unless those who support the policies stand strongly with us, this will not happen.

Appeasement is a lose–lose strategy. Staying silent and trying to retain access and approval from the old order of politics out of fear of retribution when an apolitical analysis reveals that the Australian Greens have the best policy on an issue is 'lukewarm'. It is not apolitical; it is being highly partisan.

This has been the Australian Greens' experience since the 1980s, when Bob Hawke lured the environment movement off the streets and into the backrooms of parliament as 'insiders' and 'players'. It is almost unheard of that a political party has more radical policies than the movement advocating for those causes. The movement should be driving the Greens, rather than seeking to water down policies so as to keep the other parties in the race.

As to the broader community, I cannot calculate the number of times over the years that people have said to me how much they appreciate what we have done to protect forests or the Reef and then add that they never vote for us but are glad we are there. They vote for the old order and the short-term gratification of tax cuts or self-interest and are grateful that someone else's vote will save them from themselves.

That was the milieu of ideas out of which Green politics evolved. In 1989 we five Green independent MPs from Tasmania held a meeting in Sydney with a number of supportive people, including academics Ian Marsh and Frank Stilwell and broadcaster Peter Thompson to discuss the pros and cons of forming a political party. Ian Marsh urged caution; research in the United Kingdom indicated that people were becoming more interested in being part of movements, often several at a time, than joining political parties with set platforms.

He put to us that as leaders of a new movement in environmental politics we should consider remaining as a movement instead of forming a party structure. At one level I agreed but at another I wanted the certainty of knowing who I represented, and having a mechanism to talk with them and work on policies together. What gives me strength in politics is representing other people. I would never make the same sacrifices or work as hard for my own benefit as I do for people who believe in that cause and in me. After being an independent for a few years with unidentified supporters in a large sprawling electorate, I had no way of keeping regular contact to give or receive feedback from a broader group than my known supporters. I wanted genuine connection with like-minded people. But I also wanted to influence the direction of the state and the nation.

I always remember how far ahead of his time Ian Marsh was in challenging us to think about how politics might evolve. Social media has now created this opportunity. With a whole new world of communication and databases that people can opt to join, there is a mechanism for a two-way conversation that does not require a political party structure. It has enabled the rise of independents, but also the rise of movements such as Brexit and Trumpism. It has become the modus operandi of organisations such as Get Up. Everyone is chasing clicks, data and dollars.

But, as the Labor–Green Accord had shown, a team of like-minded independents working together can achieve far more than unaligned independents. If we had grown larger without a structure, how would we have developed an agreed shared vision, divided up responsibilities and leadership, and held together? Social media could have helped us remain in touch with our supporters on the ground and to run election campaigns. But no one has been able to demonstrate how to stay together over a reasonable length of time without a shared vision, shared responsibilities and accountability, and a party structure for delivering them. Unaligned independents can serve an electorate, but they cannot deliver and implement a vision for a country.

Harnessing the power of a popular movement or idea such as the New Ethic, working to nurture its growth and hold on to its meaning over time while underpinning its rollout with resilient structures, is hard work. It requires passion and toughness from the entire membership, parliamentary team and the leader. Putting the foundations under the idea and building the Green party has been a large part of my life's work.

A key issue for me in deciding whether to go from being a Green independent to being part of forming the Tasmanian and Australian Greens Party was the conscience vote. I had never been able to understand how people could stand in a parliament and vote against what they believed was right because the party said so. I would not then, nor would I now, join a political party that did not allow its elected members a conscience vote on every issue, because every issue has at its heart a values dimension.

If you don't extend that respect to candidates, how do you expect people of integrity to stand for parliament? How can you maintain your self-respect and personal integrity if you sell out your own values? I have watched people in the Liberal, National and Labor parties vote for offshore detention and torture of refugees, or abstain from the vote and then proclaim in the electorate that they strongly oppose it. If they genuinely oppose it but don't vote against it, then obviously being a member of parliament, keeping preselection or a position in that party is more important to them than the people who suffer.

Values in politics have now conveniently been restricted by the Coalition and Labor to matters of personal morality, such as the reproductive rights of women, the rights of the LGBTIQ community and euthanasia. Those who purport to be Christian loudly proclaim their religious faith and engage in parliamentary debates on personal moral issues while deliberately refusing to acknowledge the social morality of decisions on pensions, going to war, global warming or sending refugees to offshore detention and torture on Nauru or Manus Island. It is so politically convenient to declare some issues as matters of conscience and others not as a way of keeping the numbers in line. How much better would decision-making be if a conscience vote was extended to everyone on everything?

If a party's platform was aligned with its values, its numbers on a vote in parliament would rarely be thwarted by internal dissenting opinions, as the Greens' experience demonstrates. If not, you have to wonder why people joined parties whose policies are out of line with their platform and their values.

This issue of the conscience vote is fundamental to understanding the difference between the New South Wales Greens and the rest of the Australian Greens. Except in New South Wales, Green members of parliament are trustees of the Green philosophy on behalf of our members. If a Green MP votes differently from colleagues, the party may ask him or her to explain the rationale for the decision. If the party is not satisfied, the member may lose preselection. But the New South Wales Greens refused to join the Australian Greens if a conscience vote was allowed on everything. They held the view that members of parliament are not the trustees of the party philosophy: they are delegates of the party members, empowered to vote only as directed by party policy or by the party's advisory committee, thus handing extraordinary power to that committee. They are not permitted to vote against the party line, even if a real-time parliamentary compromise is on the table. No other state Greens party agreed with this. To enable the Australian Greens Party to be formed, New South Wales was granted an exemption from the conscience vote provisions. That difference remains to this day.

The media understand very little about the Greens. It always surprises them when we don't collapse with a change of leader, but they never analyse why. They never stop to notice that whereas Bob Brown was the first Greens leader and was loved and respected over decades as the embodiment of Greens in politics, he had a dedicated team who shared his philosophical view and backed him up in his work, as well as assisting him to become the highly skilled parliamentarian he was. Green politics was never just about Petra Kelly, Caroline Lucas, Elizabeth May, Jo Vallentine, Bob Brown, Christine Milne, Richard Di Natale, Peg Putt, Nick McKim or Greg Barber, Giz Watson, Mark Parnell or Shane Rattenbury – it was always about what we stood for.

Of course a small number of Greens MPs don't need the same structure and formalised procedures as a larger group; as an individual MP you don't have to consult and stick to a plan, and you can act immediately, responding to every opportunity in the best way possible. But when there is a larger team of Green MPs, as you move from the founding stage of a political party to the consolidation stage, new structures need to be put in place. Consultation and inclusiveness mean more democracy but less flexibility. In Tasmania and nationally my leadership coincided with the consolidation phase of the Greens.

Changing the Westminster parliamentary structures to permanently accommodate third parties doesn't sound like the work of an activist but believe me it is. No one gives up power easily. Proportional representation should be introduced in all democracies in the houses of government and multi-party governments should be commonplace.

When I became leader in Tasmania in 1993, the Greens were not recognised as a party in the parliament. Over several years I worked on the Parliamentary Reform Committee to change that, and as a result the Greens secured party status: the third question in Question Time, the third call on any bill being debated, for example. It meant that the Greens view was heard on all parliamentary business as a recognised, legitimate third force. It is just as important as a Greens leader to make structural change as it is to secure policy outcomes. After all, we ultimately want to form government. We are not just there to 'keep the bastards honest'; we want to replace them in a transformed system to implement the policies that will set the nation on an ecologically sustainable and socially just path for the future.

When Bob resumed activism outside parliament in Tasmania in 1993, and federally in 2012, I was unanimously elected as leader, but the 'honeymoon' that the first woman to lead the Greens in both Tasmania and nationally might have expected did not occur, as the male-dominated media were in overdrive talking up 'not Bob Brown' and collapse.

It was not easy, even though the second time I knew something about what to expect. As leader and deputy leader Bob and I developed a close friendship over decades, working well together and thoroughly understanding each other and the system we worked in. We learned to anticipate where the next move would come from and how to deflect or stymie it with the parliamentary procedures at our disposal. We could anticipate who would lead an attack and why, and be in the chamber beforehand. If an attack was mounted against one of us or one of our team out of the blue, the other would be in the chamber in minutes to launch a counterattack. We had a shared corporate knowledge of the Australian Greens and of Australian politics and its players. We knew the history of our political opponents: when an individual appeared in the chamber unexpectedly at a critical time in a debate, we would immediately go into problem-solving mode to work out what was going on.

Bob knew the standing orders of both the Tasmanian Parliament and the Senate inside out, and so did I. If you are in a parliamentary minority, it is essential to know the procedures and how to utilise them to best effect. Parliament is a theatre as well as a debating chamber. An intervention or interjection or suspension of standing orders at the right time can win or derail an argument. The timing of a debate or a question or a speech is often determined by the media cycle. You need to understand it and to anticipate what forthcoming events might enable a Greens angle to be covered in the media. You need to be in a state of constant alert and readiness to prevent being ambushed.

Bob and I had four years together in the Tasmanian Parliament and seven years in the Senate. We worked as a tag team, and when he left and I took over, no one really picked up on the experience gap I had to cover. Thank goodness for Rachel Siewert, who carried the baton on procedures. Six of our ten elected members had been elected in 2010, and five of those new senators took their seats in July 2011. They had had only twelve weeks' experience of sitting in the Senate when I was elected leader in 2012.

Leadership for me has always been about inclusion, lifting the team, increasing the confidence and experience of my colleagues and bringing them on to achieve their full potential. Perhaps this is the teacher in me. It has been about sharing the ideas and the reasoning behind decision-making. It means encouraging and sharing the media opportunities and appearances, sharing information so that proper decisions can be made and experience passed on. It is leadership based on the trust of those in the team. Such leadership builds resilience and collaboration; it is all about the team.

But it is also the antithesis of what is now regarded as 'strong' leadership. I found the descent of politics from being a contest of policies to becoming a presidential, superficial popularity contest between leaders incredibly frustrating, distracting and stressful. How can you be an authentic inclusive leader when a hierarchical, top-down leadership style, with the leader making the party about him/her, is the praised norm and the standard by which you are judged? In that style personified by Kevin Rudd, Tony Abbott, Malcolm Turnbull, Bill Shorten, Clive Palmer or Pauline Hanson, for example, other MPs are disempowered and follow because they think the leader will do the right thing by the party and its elected members and will remain popular enough to get them re-elected, regardless of what policies are actually implemented.

The leader makes the good news announcements, holds on to information and makes decisions that others then have no choice but to own or reject. Ultimately that battle produces a new leader. Insider knowledge as power is a recipe for competition, cronyism, undermining, factionalism and distrust. It deals the disaffected backbenchers and the press gallery in as players, and they love the game. They forget that outside the Canberra bubble people actually want the news reported, not just the 'who is stabbing who' exclusive of the gossip columns.

If you haven't got both a shared and a consistent philosophy, you are dependent for votes and electoral success on the public face of the leader, which has more in common with reality TV than with something of substance. This is fundamentally what has gone wrong in Australian politics. The contest of ideas between Labor and the Liberal–National Coalition has largely disappeared as both major parties have embraced neoliberalism and attracted corporate donations to varying degrees. Elections have become questions about which political party can create, embed and promote the image of the leader as a marketable product to win a short-term popularity contest, with the capture of power being an end in itself. Refreshing the image is more important than developing good policy.

This has been made worse by the transition from television and print as the major media for communication to an integrated platform of social and mainstream media. Electoral popularity now comes down to clicks and instant stories: designer clothes, botox, expensive cars, hard hats, high-visibility vests or Akubras, parading of families, jackets, budgie-smugglers and cycling lycra, hair, jewellery, front-page fashion shoots, fruit bowls with or without fruit, personal relationship and celebrity dramas. It is what you look like and how you sound, not what you have to say, that matters. It doesn't matter what you say as long as it's shocking or you look and sound like some acceptable 'role model', from a tradie to a Kardashian. It is 'authenticity' in the most fake way possible.

For many people on all sides of politics who are genuinely intelligent, committed, passionate and dedicated to driving change, whether you agree with them or not, their authenticity is increasingly seen as outdated, mainstream, boring and staid. The community is seeing less and less of the people who are actually most like them, and more and more of the people who pretend to be. And the ultimate example of fake authenticity is of a privileged, white, narcissistic, sexist, super-rich septuagenarian businessman pretending to know what it is like to be poor and marginalised in the United States of America. A popular TV show and extreme wealth delivered him the presidency.

Politicians pay consultants to refine their image and even that of their partner to become a brand. People no longer know who is the real Julia or the real Kevin, Tony, Bill or Malcolm. As they say, if you can fake sincerity you've got it made. 'Saying the unsayable' generates outrage: hate speech becomes show business. 'Balance' is the excuse for deliberately generated conflict and publicity generated by false equivalence.

But they need enablers. Referring to United Kingdom far-right fallen hero Yiannopoulos, author Dorian Lynskey asked, 'How was this smirking void ever taken seriously?'[5] The answer is Twitter, Facebook, shock jocks, morning television and programs such as ABC TV's *Q&A*. Choosing guests or paying them to deliver 'shocking' one-liners deliberately designed to create sensationalism and lift the program's ratings via clicks is the new media norm, consistent with reality TV.

Inviting climate denier Senator Malcolm Roberts on the program with renowned English physicist Brian Cox is a case in point. Inviting a notorious 'void' onto the program to make it look as if there is serious debate about the reality of global warming is a classic case of the use of the clickbait-driven media technique of false equivalence. It is demoralising as a lifelong viewer of the ABC to see it fall so low.

The Rudd/Gillard/Rudd followed by the Turnbull/Abbott/ Turnbull revolving doors was all about the polls, winning and 'saving the furniture'; namely, how many backbenchers would hold their seats at an election. It wasn't about policy. Turnbull adopted all of Abbott's policies but remains vulnerable to the 'refresh' button that is likely to be pressed when the party wants a lift in the polls and a quick run to an election.

The Greens avoid this style of leadership because of our philosophy, the breadth and activism of our membership, and our structural foundations. The grassroots members of the party are directly involved in policy development, and feedback loops give us our strength and durability. Giving visibility to the elected members of parliament is a far cry from the cult of the leader. But someone has to be ultimately responsible for implementing the vision, strategic direction and policies of the party. Someone has to have the final say and take responsibility for decisions made. I am not a subscriber to the 'no leader' view. It is no way to deliver a long-term vision and ultimately disempowers the elected Greens members of parliament: if the MPs do not choose a leader, whoever best courts the media will become the de facto leader.

But no leader can succeed without the work of dedicated teams of people. Over twenty-five years I had people as parliamentary colleagues and as staff members who brought different ideas and perspectives to the table, who worked long hours doing everything from research, pitching and posting stories, negotiating, finessing policy, writing speeches and media releases, answering phones, talking to constituents, booking airline tickets and hotels, and reminding me where I had to be and with whom. They organised as they made the tea. They indulged me by listening to me think out loud or tell stories. I never want to be surrounded by 'yes' people, so I looked forward to being told whether something was a good idea or not. I was often under huge pressure, and I took great comfort in the support and confidence of people I could trust with my deepest hopes and fears.

I have always been inspired by the stories of Antarctic explorer Ernest Shackleton's endurance and leadership, and from my time as leader I can say that this resonated time and time again:

> Loneliness is the penalty of leadership, but the man who
> has to make the decisions is assisted greatly if he feels that
> there is no uncertainty in the minds of those who follow
> him, and that his orders will be carried out confidently
> and in expectation of success.[6]

The words of Frank Worsley, with Shackleton on the *James Caird*, also struck a chord with me: 'While I steered, his arm thrown over my shoulder, we discussed plans and yarned in low tones ... I often recall with proud affection memories of those hours with a great soul.'[7]

During my time as leader I spent hours 'with a great soul' in intense conversation with my parliamentary colleagues, my friend Margaret Blakers, whose home I shared in Canberra, my chief of staff Emma Bull, my friend and ex-staffer Tim Hollo, and my office manager Wendy McLeod. My partner, family and friends also provided support and counsel.

However, there is a long road and a political minefield between being in parliament and growing to the point of being in government, and it is a road on which a wrong move results in disaster. After the Labor–Green Accord I became acutely aware that there is an inverse relationship between electoral success and securing Green outcomes. As a lightning rod for the community, the less power you have and the fewer outcomes you achieve, the higher your vote becomes, because you have the maximum opportunity to criticise the government of the day.

Maximum publicity for 'sticking it to the bastards' results in maximum community support. But the more influence you have in balance of power and the more outcomes you achieve, the lower your vote. This is because you have less opportunity to criticise the government and a limited capacity to own the policy wins that you achieve without the government pocketing them. The result is reduced community support for 'cosying up to the bastards' and almost nil credit for what has been achieved.

Balance of power means spending political capital and losing votes but securing policy. It is the trade-off that gives Green MPs the opportunity to deliver Green policy, such as almost doubling the size of the Tasmanian Wilderness World Heritage Area or implementing the carbon price, securing the Climate Change Authority, Australian Renewable Energy Agency and the Clean Energy Finance Corporation, or Denticare, establishing the Parliamentary Budget Office, achieving gay law reform, gun law reform and an apology to the Stolen Generations in Tasmania, or a vote on Australia becoming a republic. Holding seats in the face of a reduced primary vote coming out of a period of balance of power is the challenge at the subsequent election. It was my challenge in 2013. Using those seats to rebuild political capital from Opposition shapes the next political cycle and was the task inherited by my successor, Richard Di Natale.

The more successful the Greens become, the harder the partisans of the old order fight to lock us out of power by changing electoral systems and resisting reforms to political donations, transparency and anti-corruption measures. As democracies have become the plutocracies of the old vested interests, the struggle gets harder while the evidence of environmental collapse gets stronger. The gods of markets and money identified by Claudio Alcorso so many years ago do not give up their power easily.

How do you maximise the primary vote for the Greens and increase your representation at the same time as you engage in power sharing to advance your aims? This is the major question facing Green parties around the world in 2017. We have now had enough experience of power sharing in Australia and Europe to begin to draw some conclusions and act upon them. If nature is to continue to sustain humanity in this century, the Anthropocene needs to be short-lived. We have virtually no time left to find the political way and be in government to deliver it so that humanity can once again be part of nature and the planet on which we live, instead of being a visiting freeloader.

I am proud to say that following the end of the Gillard minority government, in spite of the shift in the national mood that saw Tony Abbott elected in 2013 with a Liberal majority government, when I retired as Australian Greens leader in 2015 I led the largest elected team that the Australian Greens had ever had in federal politics, with ten senators and one member of the House of Representatives and the primary vote trending up again. I had also facilitated a culture of equality and inclusiveness throughout the parliamentary offices, working to break down barriers and see the establishment of an Australian Greens National Council ready to strengthen and build national cohesion and better communication between all levels of Green politics.

The Asia Pacific Greens had also been formalised as a regional member of the Global Greens. Bob had the vision of a Global Green movement in 2001; Margaret Blakers and Louise Crossley and a team of volunteers made it happen. The same volunteers pulled together the second meeting in São Paulo, Brazil, and Dakar in Senegal. Being on the stage in Liverpool after my retirement and speaking as the first Global Greens ambassador in the opening plenary of the fourth meeting in 2017, seeing the ongoing strengthening of the Global Greens, and being honoured by a standing ovation, was life-affirming.[8]

# Afterword

The surface of the earth is soft and impressible by the feet
of men; and so with the paths which the mind travels.
How worn and dusty, then, must be the highways of the
world, how deep the ruts of tradition and conformity!
I did not wish to take a cabin passage, but rather to go
before the mast and on the deck of the world, for there I
could best see the moonlight amid the mountains. I do
not wish to go below now.[1]

MURUJUGA (BURRUP PENINSULA) in Western Australia is the
home of the world's largest and oldest rock art gallery. Aboriginal
petroglyphs etched into the rock surface from at least 40,000 years
ago tell the story of continuous human habitation, dating from
before the last ice age. They record species such as the thylacine, which
once roamed the area, to the coming of marine species after the ice
melted and the sea level rose. It is a unique expression of Aboriginal
culture and life on Earth over millennia. It is of outstanding universal
value and should be on UNESCO's World Heritage List.

But the Western Australian government, with the support of the
federal government, decided to make the area a heavy industrial
site for bringing gas onshore. Petroglyphs were bulldozed to make

way for Woodside's, BHP's, BP's, Japan Australia LNG's, Shell's and Chevron's North West Shelf Project; the Pluto gas liquefaction facility and YARA International's fertiliser plant. A new YARA technical ammonium nitrate plant is about to be licensed to operate. The industrial emissions from all these plants are acidic and are already progressively destroying the petroglyphs. The new YARA plant will accelerate the process so that the petroglyphs will be gone in a generation.

Whereas France built replicas to protect its famous Lascaux caves from the damage caused by its visitors, the Australian Government continues to facilitate the industrial-scale destruction of the petroglyphs and with them Aboriginal culture.

It is aided and abetted by the CSIRO. I never thought I would ever be able to write, let alone think, such a thing of Australia's premier scientific organisation, which throughout my life has been regarded as an almost infallible icon. But sadly, government failure to fund public interest or pure research has turned the CSIRO into a servant of industry.

The two CSIRO reports on which the governments of Western Australia and the Commonwealth rely to argue that the industrial emissions from the already constructed $800 million YARA International's ammonium nitrate plant will not destroy the petroglyphs are fundamentally flawed. The governments know it, but won't act unless CSIRO retracts and it refuses to do so, no doubt fearing YARA compensation claims.

Rather than retire, I left activism in the parliament to resume activism in the community – here and around the world, working to strengthen the climate ambition of the Paris Agreement, for 100 per cent renewable energy, for the rollout of solar energy and for fossil fuel-sector climate accountability. I am also supporting the Green parties of the world as their ambassador.

I am determined to see the Aboriginal petroglyphs of Murujuga join the Tasmanian forests and the coral reefs of New Caledonia on the World Heritage List. Returning scientific independence to the CSIRO would be a bonus.

The protection of the Tarkine, ending native forest logging nationwide, stopping Adani and coal mining in the Galilee Basin, restoring respect for and adherence to environmental and international human rights law, ending the offshore detention of asylum seekers, ending discrimination against LGBTIQ people, securing marriage equality and a ban on automatic and semi-automatic hand guns also remain on my list of unfinished business and campaigns I support.

Taking a cabin passage is not an option.

At this stage of my life, I am loving being a grandmother, having the time to read the texts that inspire me, being able to be still, to think, to enjoy Nature, to fight for justice and for our beautiful, awe-inspiring, interconnected planet.

For their very survival, my granddaughter, her generation and all our fellow species are relying on us to once again reconnect with and live within the limits of the Earth's natural systems. We cannot let them down.

From my bookshelves – hewn from salvaged Tasmanian oak scarred from the 1967 bushfires – Tennyson gives me the nod:

> I am part of all that I have met;
> Yet all experience is an arch wherethro'
> Gleams that untravell'd world, whose margin fades
> For ever and for ever when I move.[2]

# Acknowledgements

IN *MIDDLEMARCH* GEORGE ELIOT WROTE that there are no heroes, only heroic acts. In that spirit, I thank the activists who have shared my activist life. These are the people who have put themselves on the line and made heroic choices for the Earth, for a more just and peaceful society and to restore democracy and integrity to politics. All these people will continue to inspire me and future generations.

These are the people derided as dirty ferals, greenies and hardliners at protest meetings and in the parliaments as Green MPs or staffers because they refuse to accept an easier life of 'reasonable' compromise or 'the politically possible and acceptable'. They are the men and women who kept on organising, marching, handing out 'how to votes', blockading, advocating and singing from computers, microphones and loud hailers, tractors and paddy wagons and from the pages of their books, the lenses of their cameras and their colour palettes, regardless of the personal consequences.

To the people who organised meetings, rallies, court cases – people like Margaret Blakers and Jill McCulloch – who have been part of the nitty gritty of organising for thirty years, I say we could not have done it without you.

I say thank you to the Tasmanian Wilderness photographers and artists who have been champions of the wild. First Olegas Truchanas and Peter Dombrovskis, then photographers like Tasmania's Rob Blakers, Chris Bell, Geoffrey Lea, Wolfgang Glowacki, Grant Dixon, Matthew Newton and Ted Mead, and so many others who have donated their brilliant images, bringing the beauty of the forests and wilderness to people in Australia and around the world.

I pay tribute to the men and women who founded the Tasmanian, Australian and Global Greens, who worked behind the scenes and who stood for election successfully and unsuccessfully. I thank those who supported the Australian Greens in whatever professional, staff or personal capacity, including those who read and fact-checked parts of this book. My fellow elected members and staff became my friends and were a key part of all that I have achieved. I especially thank Bob Brown for his inspiration and friendship for more than a quarter of a century.

Nor could I have continued to take a stand over decades without the love and support of my partner Gary Corr, my parents, my former husband Neville, my sons Thomas and James, my late sister Gaylene, my extended family and my friends. Thank you.

To Julie Payne, a big thank you for your beautiful pencil drawings that illustrate this book and to Karen Brown for supporting me and the Greens with your photographic images for decades.

To the staff at the Tasmanian Parliamentary Library, thank you for your generous assistance in tracking down the details.

Finally, I want to thank all those who brought this book to fruition, in particular all at University of Queensland Press. Non-fiction publisher Alexandra Payne and project editor Vanessa Pellatt were terrific. I am very grateful for their encouragement and support. To my editors Jacquie Kent and Kevin O'Brien – thank you for your guidance, patience and expertise.

# About the illustrator

Julie Payne has exhibited nationally in the fields of sculpture and drawing, and has lectured in sculpture, architecture and furniture design. She has been shortlisted for many prestigious art prizes nationally and has won awards at the Museum of South Australia for her natural history drawings and at the Queensland Art Gallery for her political based sculpture. In her arts practice, Julie utilises a diversity of materials and techniques to devise rich visual stories on a wide range of interests.

# Notes

## Preface

1   It came as no surprise then that when Premier Rundle decided to reduce the numbers in the parliament while promising that the design of the new system would not disadvantage the Greens, Jim Bacon and Labor pushed for a model that would remove the Greens from the parliament. Bacon secured the support of Liberal members Bob Cheek and Michael Hodgman who threatened to cross the floor to support Labor's plan unless Tony Rundle changed his mind and supported it too. Rather than lose a parliamentary vote on his key policy, Premier Rundle caved in and betrayed his commitment to me by backing a plan that was designed to get rid of the Greens from the parliament and by not having the decency to inform me first before going to the media.

## Chapter 1 My Blood's Country

1   Judith Wright, 'South of My Days', *Collected Poems: 1942 to 1985*, HarperCollins Publishers, Sydney, 2016, p. 19.

## Chapter 2 The Power of Lake Pedder: Awakening

1   Peter A. Tyler, John Sherwood, Colin Magilton, Dominic Hodgson, 'A Geophysical Survey of Lake Pedder and Region: A Report to the Lake Pedder Study Group', Deakin University, School of Aquatic Science and Natural Resource Management, 1993.

2   Dr Tom Grant, a recognised Australian expert in the biology and ecology of the platypus and author of a report to the Australian National Parks and Wildlife Service, *Distribution of the platypus in Australia with guidelines for management*, made a submission to the House of Representatives committee in which he gave examples of Professor Forteath's lack of knowledge of the biology of the species. Excerpts from the inquiry report state:

> [3.49] Dr Grant pointed out that even in mark-release-recapture studies there are great difficulties in estimating platypus populations. He suggested that the numbers estimated by Professor Forteath on the basis of incidental observation could not possibly be substantiated. In addition, because platypuses can forage

over considerable distances, it is impossible to distinguish between unmarked individuals, so that such an estimate would almost certainly have involved the double counting of many individuals.

[3.50] He emphasised the need for a full environmental impact assessment before the lake was drained.

(*See* 'Inquiry into the Proposal to Drain and Restore Lake Pedder', House of Representatives Standing Committee on Environmental Recreation and the Arts, June 1995.)

3   Ibid.

## Chapter 3 Saving the Franklin: Empowerment

1   Peter Dwyer, *The Advocate*, 10 February 1983.

## Chapter 4 Wesley Vale: First Steps in Activism

1   Early on I met John Morgan, one of the North Broken Hill executives, who told me his company would win because every man has his price. North Broken Hill offered the farmers and the Latrobe Council an all-expenses-paid trip to Canada and Finland to see their mills. It was clear to me that this was a divide-and-rule tactic, which proved to be correct. When the farmers refused to participate, the trip was cancelled.

## Chapter 5 The Case of Port Arthur: Gun Law Reform

1   'The degreening of Tasmania', *Times on Sunday*, 22 March 1987.

2   Labor's decision not to negotiate with the Greens to form government in 1996 was a consequence of its massive electoral defeat at the end of the Labor–Green Accord in 1992. It was also a consequence of the misplaced acrimony that Labor directed at the Greens because of the way the Accord ended.

The final crisis for the Labor–Green Accord was over forestry. Following the World Heritage Area expansion, Labor decided to throw in its lot with the forest industry to try to win back blue-collar votes. The industry worked with Labor, which brought forward Resource Security legislation to lock in logging in many high-conservation forests that the Greens had identified for protection. We announced that if Labor proceeded, it would be a matter of No Confidence in the government. The Liberals were excited. This was their moment to bring down the government. But we had made it clear, as we did in all Balance of Power arrangements, that we would not support a No Confidence motion from any other party but reserved the right to move our own.

The legislation was introduced. Michael Field and Bob Brown met to discuss the inevitable consequence, which was the fall of the government. But Bob put it to Premier Field that we would move a No Confidence motion that would say that we had no confidence in the government because of Resource Security legislation. The Liberals would think the government had fallen. Premier Field would announce to the House that Resource Security legislation was dead and would not be reintroduced in the life of the government. He would then say that he would use the next vote as a test of Confidence in the government and immediately move that the House do now adjourn. We Greens would vote for it because our No Confidence motion was conditional on Resource Security legislation. The government would be saved and Resource Security would be defeated.

Clearly Premier Field had not told some of his front bench of the plan because when the No Confidence motion was successfully moved, they clearly thought the government had just fallen. The Minister for Forests David Llewellyn walked straight out of the parliament and into talks with the forest industry to get Resource Security back on track.

Premier Field had thought the government would be credited with a clever victory over the Liberals but instead the media ridiculed Labor, and the logging industry went into meltdown calling for the legislation to be reintroduced. Within days, Premier Field began to backtrack. He lost his nerve and clearly did not have the energy to give the Labor–Green Accord a new start. Liberal leader Robin Gray offered to protect Labor from Greens' No Confidence motions until Christmas to enable the Resource Security legislation to pass both Houses. Labor accepted.

It was an ignoble end to the Labor–Green Accord, watching Labor being protected by the Liberals to deliver the forests to the chainsaws. Importantly, the fallout poisoned the relationship between Labor and the Tasmanian Greens for more than fifteen years.

3    In my speech welcoming gun law reform I also credited balance of power politics with playing a major role. I said, '… one has to speculate, if there had been a majority government in Tasmania, whether we would have reached a point where that majority government would have consulted to the same extent with the other parties in the House, whether there would have been a negotiated and agreed set of agreements, and whether there could have been avoided the normality of Australian politics of finding fault with whatever position was arrived at by the majority party and others going further than that for the purposes of fulfilling an ideological position or simply for playing politics.'

## Chapter 6 Pride

1    Liberal federal member Chris Miles co-founded the Lyons Forum in the 1990s. It was a group of deeply conservative Christian MPs that included Eric Abetz and Kevin Andrews.

When Turnbull took on the leadership in 2015 and dumped Abetz and Andrews, Chris Miles re-emerged as an anti-gay spokesperson. He reappeared in 2016 as the authoriser of a grossly misleading and offensive pamphlet claiming children of same-sex couples may be more likely to be victims of sexual abuse, abuse drugs or suffer depression. It claimed that adult children raised by gay and lesbian parents are more likely to be drug users, unemployed, carriers of sexually transmitted diseases and sexually abused. It has never been revealed who was paying for and printing these pamphlets.

What we do know is John Howard developed the Liberal Party relationship with the Exclusive Brethren when he was prime minister and Damien Mantach worked in his office. When he legislated in 2004 to define marriage for the first time as between a man and a woman, Michael Bachelard wrote that Exclusive Brethren members were present in parliament every day of the debate and thanked Howard for giving 'the true definition of marriage'.

In the Senate Eric Abetz denied Liberal involvement with the Exclusive Brethren and the hate pamphlets. The now-jailed former director of Victoria and Tasmania's Liberal Party, Damien Mantach, denied it too. As the result of a very brave stand by Martine Delaney, it was revealed that the newspaper ads for the Exclusive Brethren had been billed to the Liberal Party advertising agency accounts. It was revealed in the course of the 2016 federal election that in 2010 the Exclusive Brethren gave $67,000 to the

Liberal Party in one day and that they donate through the Liberal Party's Free Enterprise Foundation. Prime Minister Turnbull said, 'I've got no criticisms or complaints about that organisation … As you know, everybody is free to make political contributions.' (*See* Susannah Guthrie, 'Turnbull unfazed by Brethren donations', *The New Daily*, 18 June 2016.)

2　The HIV AIDS Preventative Measures Bill was drafted. Its appalling preamble demonstrates where the Labor Party stood at the time:

> Whereas the Parliament believes that HIV/AIDS prevention is best served by support for marriage and stable family, community and personal relationships, and is least served by heterosexual and homosexual promiscuity;
>
> And whereas, while the Parliament believes that criminal penalties should not apply for sexual intercourse between persons of the same sex, it does not endorse such behaviour, or condone attempts to promote the conduct of such behaviour.

3　Navi Pillay 28/7/2011 www.youtube.com/watch?v=NT5aBa-1bXs
4　Oodgeroo Noonuccal, 'Song of Hope', *My People*, John Wiley and Sons, Brisbane, 1990, p. 40.
5　Ibid.

## Chapter 7 Demolishing Democracy: Dirty Tricks

1　The government set up the Carter Royal Commission to determine if others were involved in the bribery attempt. It is a fantastic read and should be compulsory for anyone involved in Tasmanian politics because the individual players and the tactics remained the same for a generation.

　　It revealed that Paul Lennon, later to become a Labor premier, would have preferred a Liberal government to the Labor–Green Accord. The Royal Commission questioned Paul Lennon's credibility as a witness overall.

　　It exposed donations in brown paper bags handed over on the steps of the Launceston post office and kept in Robin Gray's freezer, a Gunns petty cash box containing thousands of dollars in unmarked notes accessed by David McQuestin for Edmund Rouse. Rouse went to jail and McQuestin was found guilty of corporate crime with a conviction recorded that should have seen him barred from board positions for five years. But he appealed. His guilty verdict was upheld but his conviction was overturned as it was a first offence. He returned to the board of Gunns where he remained until his death in 2008. John Gay had been Gunns Managing Director at the time of the Rouse bribery affair but, as there was no evidence of his involvement, he was appointed to the board where he was joined by Robin Gray and later Paul Lennon.

　　Nobody believed that Rouse had acted alone but the Royal Commission failed to secure the necessary evidence against any other people.

2　Nick O'Malley, 'There Is Nothing Illegal about Stephen Conroy's New Job – But it Smells Bad', *The Sydney Morning Herald*, 8 December 2016.
3　Adele Ferguson, 'Anna Bligh Will Win Where Bankers Failed', *The Sydney Morning Herald*, 17 February 2017.
4　Bob Burton, *Inside Spin: The dark underbelly of the PR industry*, Allen & Unwin, Sydney, 2007, pp. 151–2.
5　The Forest Industry Association of Tasmania and the Forest Protection Society held meetings that very week in Smithton because they were 'deeply concerned that the

present federal government, in an effort to gain the Green vote, could announce World Heritage Listing for the area'. They were not interviewed. (*The Advocate*, 8 March 1993.)

6   This tactic of creating a 'citizen activist group' as a front for industry or politics has been used with dire consequences in Tasmania. Concerned Citizens of Tasmania sprang out of nowhere supporting a second election when the Gray government lost its majority in 1989. The Royal Commission revealed that it was set up by the Liberals and run out of Liberal John Barker's office. Tasmanians for a Better Future materialised in the lead-up to the 2006 election when polling suggested that Paul Lennon's Labor government might lose its majority and a hung parliament might result. It was cashed up, advertised heavily but had no spokesperson except the public relations firm headed by a former staffer of Robin Gray, Tony Harrison. Its members and donors were never disclosed, except for Michael Kent, who outed himself. With no donations disclosure and no effective ICAC, Tasmanians still don't know who bought the 2006 election. But the campaign won a PR award, and on the Public Relations Institute of Australia website they boast 'the campaign was instrumental in raising stable, majority government as a key issue and is credited by political and media observers as playing a major role in the return of a Labor Government', which coincidentally campaigned 'For a Better Tasmania'.

7   Rosemary Bolger, 'Forest war: Premier backs down', *The Examiner*, 20 February 2012.

8   In 2002 novelist Richard Flanagan wrote, 'The only sight sadder in Tasmania than the stuffed thylacine in the Hobart Museum is that of a desperate politician reworking the oldest trick in the island's politics. It goes like this: when your fortunes are low, denounce Greenies as troublemakers who lose us jobs and who will do anything to win their arguments. The hoary old favourite was most recently trotted out by Deputy Premier Paul Lennon who, faced both with an imminent election and the recent destruction of heavy forestry machinery, felt the need to associate conservationists with this lamentable vandalism, and in so doing attempted to take us all back to brawling in the clearfells.' (See more at http://tasmaniantimes.com/index.php/article/what-lara-said.-the-true-history-of-forest-violence#sthash.9QjphRnM.dpuf.)

9   Anne Davies, 'Australia's flawed political donations laws', *The Sydney Morning Herald*, 27 July 2015.

10  E. F. Schumacher, *Good Work*, Jonathan Cape, London, 1979, p. 100.

## Chapter 8 Being a Woman in Politics

1   Andrew Darby, 'Mrs Milne's no joke', Letters to the Editor, *The Examiner*, 12 December 1993, p. 8.

2   Andrea Mayes, 'It's Julie vs Julia', *Daily Telegraph*, 12 August 2007.

## Chapter 9 In Praise of Knitted Berets

1   Bill Ryan, 'At 92, I was arrested for protesting against mining. I'm glad I took a stand', in Mining/Opinion, *The Guardian*, 1 April 2014.

2   A recent audit of the Environment Assessment and Compliance Division of the Department of the Environment and Energy found that in 2016 more than 20 per cent of the projects covered by the *Environment Protection and Biodiversity Conservation Act 1999* (EPBC) were in breach of their conditions. Of the 462 EPBC Act projects that were monitored, 96 were found to be non-compliant with some of the Commonwealth's requirements.

3   The critical factor for protecting carbon in the landscape is that it needs to protect the carbon store for the long term. Carbon needs to be secured for one hundred years and not just for a short term, to be released twenty-five years later. That doesn't make a serious contribution to saving the climate; it is just playing with numbers using too tricky by half accounting methods to meet a target at a particular time.

Although the Carbon Farming Initiative would have permitted offsetting fossil fuel emissions with stored green carbon, in 2017 there is no longer any capacity to do so. The remaining carbon budget for 2–1.5 degrees does not allow for it. Allowing the sale of carbon credits from the land sector to offset fossil fuel emissions will delay the phase-out of fossil fuels and prolong the use of coal and gas to the detriment of the climate.

4   The Emission Reduction Fund kept some good projects funded under the Carbon Farming Initiative, like Savanna Burning and capture of methane from tips but beyond that, it will be shown to be a complete waste of public funds. Almost all the money, approximately a billion dollars, has gone to prevent the short-term clearing of mulga. By reducing the time that vegetation has to stay in the landscape from one hundred to twenty-five years, the Turnbull government has destroyed any notion of permanence and by allowing New South Wales and Queensland to resume land clearing, any reduction in emissions has been offset by increased emissions elsewhere. It has been a flawed policy, done nothing for the climate and is a pork barrel for Liberal and National Party farmers in New South Wales and Queensland. Just as Managed Investment Schemes, particularly for plantations forests, enriched the middle man and did nothing for the long-term sustainability of forestry, so too will the Emission Reduction Fund be a monumental and expensive failure: the legacy of Abbott, Turnbull and Hunt.

5   Michael Coulter, 'The long-running war on drugs has failed: we need to legalise now', *The Sydney Morning Herald*, 23 May 2015.

## Chapter 10 Climate in a Bottle

1   William Laurance, 'The World's Tropical Forests Are Already Feeling the Heat', *Yale Environment 360*, 2 May 2011.

2   Ibid.

3   Philip Walker, 'Australian Miners in South Africa', *The Saturday Paper*, 9 April 2016.

## Chapter 11 Global Citizenship and World Heritage

1   I wished I had bigger hands because my hand couldn't cover all of the area identified as the Lower Gordon River catchment that had identified World Heritage Values and that had been specifically listed in the Labor–Green Accord to be immediately considered for listing.

The World Heritage Planning team in the Lands, Parks and Wildlife Department were instructed to prepare a report on the appropriate boundaries of a Western Tasmania World Heritage Area and 'any National Estate forests within the Greater Western Tasmania National Estate Area that a Labor Government agrees to protect will also be nominated for World Heritage.' This stipulation looks straightforward enough but therein lies the heart of the long and acrimonious three-way battle for the forests between the Australian Greens and the Tasmanian and federal Labor parties that lasted a quarter of a century.

The Tasmanian Labor government was far from enthusiastic and brought in its experts from the Forestry Commission and the Mines Department, who were vociferous in arguing high-mineral-prospectivity as a reason to exclude whole mountain ranges from the proposed World Heritage Area. The arguments went on, day after day.

The Greens and our advisors were on one side of the table, the government and its advisors were on the other, and the maps were in the middle. When a compromise became impossible, it was determined that Graham Richardson needed to become involved. He became increasingly exasperated by the intransigence of the miners and loggers and their Labor ministers, Michael Weldon and David Llewellyn in particular. On the day in question, we were arguing the merits of protecting a large swathe of land south of Macquarie Harbour. It was specifically identified for protection in the Accord as part of the Gordon River catchment and also because it was important habitat for the critically endangered orange-bellied parrot, which breeds in south-west Tasmania.

Andrew Reeves, Secretary of the Mines Department, was once again putting the case for the mineral prospectivity of the area. I had my hand over part of the area the conservation community had determined was critical and which was named in the Accord. Graham Richardson had had enough and that is when he declared the new boundary south of Macquarie Harbour to be the outline of my hand. It was good but way short of the entire Lower Gordon catchment.

2   If you don't think about planetary systems of air and water and carbon or ever stop to think that the oxygen you breathe comes from forests and plankton across the planet, you just deal with where you live as if it is separate from the rest of the world. But if you do, then you can't help but see the Earth's ecosystems as a whole and recognise that what is done locally across the planet could cumulatively bring about collapse. There is no option but to act locally and globally at the same time. We are part of one beautiful, complex and awe-inspiring Earth.

## Chapter 12 What Price Carbon?

1   Kevin Rudd, Australian Labor Party Climate Change Summit, Parliament House, Canberra, 31 March 2007.

2   Professor Barry Brook, Director of Climate Science at the University of Adelaide's Environment Institute, and other experts were cited in 'Rapid Roundup: Carbon Pollution Reduction Scheme – White Paper – experts respond', published by the *Australian Science Media Centre*, 15 December 2008. Professor Brook stated that 'the 14% cut in our total emissions by 2020 announced today is such a pitifully inadequate attempt to stop dangerous climate change that we may as well wave the white flag now.'

3   In his article 'Boosting smoke and mirrors rather than cutting emissions', published in *The Age* the next day, Adam Morton wrote:

But we know the Government also thinks this almost certainly won't happen. Why? Because Penny Wong told us so in December. Ignore yesterday's spin about recent progress in international climate talks. The Government believes that a new deal won't meet the strict conditions it has put in place for Australia to sign up for a 25 per cent cut. If it is right – and there are plenty familiar with the climate talks who believe it is – Australia's ultimate target will be in the range it was before yesterday: between 5 and 15 per cent. No change, then.

4   Pressure for stronger global action was building strongly in the lead-up to the UNFCCC meeting in Copenhagen. Expectations were high that at last the world would agree to the serious, legally binding cuts in emissions that the Intergovernmental Panel on

Climate Change recommended to give the world a fifty per cent chance of keeping global warming to less than two degrees. Campaigners everywhere, especially the local Climate Action groups, the Australian Youth Climate Coalition, Greenpeace, and Friends of the Earth, were making the case for higher targets including in Australia. All rejected the CPRS as grossly inadequate and joined the Australian Greens in opposing it.

But the Australian Conservation Foundation, the Climate Institute, WWF and the Australian Council of Trade Unions (ACTU), having formed a Southern Cross Climate Coalition, instead of pressing for a higher level of ambition supported the ineffectual browned down scheme arguing it was better than nothing. Chilling climate ambition ahead of Copenhagen had more to do with the Labor-aligned ACTU'S involvement in the Southern Cross Climate Coalition than with good climate policy.

5   The Grattan Institute described these handouts as '$20 billion waste at the expense of the rest of the Australian community' and estimated that the free permits would cost about $65,000 per employee on average, and $161,100 in the aluminium industry and $103,300 in liquefied natural gas. John Daley, 'Facing up to economic reality in a climate of fear', published in *The Australian Financial Review*, Thursday 22 April 2010; and John Daley and Tristan Edis, *Restructuring the Australian Economy to Emit Less Carbon: Main Report*, The Grattan Institute, April 2010.

6   The Australian Greens refused to support the disgraceful Liberal–Labor deal and called on Labor to work with us to develop an effective serious policy response to reducing emissions. They refused and the legislation was defeated. We Greens were prepared to fight an election on what was necessary to address the climate challenge and the utter failure of the Rudd government to deliver on what the science demanded. I was relieved that we still had the opportunity to get it right in 2010, post what we all thought would be a successful Copenhagen Conference. No one watching Prime Minister Rudd rub shoulders with world leaders in Copenhagen could have guessed that he would abandon carbon pricing within two months. Rudd gave no indication either in Copenhagen or on his return that he intended to dump climate policy. He was still making strong statements of intent. We Greens worked on the assumption that the prime minister would now work with us to secure the numbers to pass a better scheme. We assumed he would enter discussions in the new year so we spent the summer working on a compromise to replace the CPRS with an effective cap-and-trade scheme.

7   In hindsight, I think the reason Rudd Labor loyalists see the CPRS as the be-all and end-all is that it is Rudd's and not Gillard's policy. It is a reflection of the Rudd–Gillard internal Labor leadership quagmire. When he overthrew Prime Minister Gillard in 2013, he ignored all she had achieved especially the Clean Energy Package. Secondly, Labor refuses to ever talk about its successes in minority government with the Australian Greens in balance of power. That would give credit to the Australian Greens and normalise minority or multi-party government when Labor wants to go to elections reinforcing the two party system with messaging that says 'majority government is good', minority government is bad'. Thirdly, Labor had not been on the global journey to address climate change over a long period of time. They were completely out of touch with global developments. Without a global context or a long-term passion for addressing global warming, Labor dipped in and out of climate commitment depending on its appeal to voters and its impact on political donations from fossil fuel corporations

or mining unions. The inherent contradiction of espousing strong interest in action on climate change but adopting globally insulting targets went uncontested within the party.

8    Bernard Keane and Paul Barry, 'Rudd's downfall: his own handiwork, and years in the making', Crikey.com, 23 June 2011, https://www.crikey.com.au/2011/06/23/rudds-downfall-his-own-handiwork-and-years-in-the-making/

9    Post Copenhagen, climate policy had outlived its political usefulness for Rudd. When he refused to either go to a double dissolution or work with the Greens to secure a better scheme, and abandoned carbon pricing in 2010, he was ridiculed for abandoning the greatest moral challenge of our time and lost huge credibility. His refusal to heed ministerial advice or to delegate caused ructions in the Labor Party. This was compounded by scandals in two other climate programs. Four people died because the speed of the rollout was prioritised over safety and probity in the Home Insulation Program. The Green Loans program was also scandal ridden. After Gillard became prime minister both programs were abandoned, but the debacle undermined community confidence in energy efficiency and home insulation and set the industry back decades.

10   Heather Ewart, 'Gillard explains carbon scheme', *The 7.30 Report*, ABC, 24 February 2011.

11   A fixed price ETS moving to a floating price was the only option to start the process of bringing down domestic emissions while we worked out how to bridge the gap between Labor's weak 5 per cent below the 2000 target and the Greens' strong UNFCCC 25–40 per cent below the 1999 target. A fully functioning cap-and-trade scheme needs a legislated cap.

12   The floor price was a mechanism to prevent price collapse and industry disruption when the scheme transitioned to a floating price. When independent MP Rob Oakeshott reneged on his agreement to a floor price, a new solution had to be found. We Greens reluctantly agreed to linking the Australian scheme with the EU Emissions Trading Scheme as an alternative. In hindsight, the advice regarding the European price from the EU Commission was wrong.

13   I was heartened by how well the scheme had worked in bringing down greenhouse gas emissions, but it is now clear – with the dissenting reports of Clive Hamilton and David Karoly – that the days of the Climate Change Authority providing science-based reports are over. The advice on targets is no longer independent and fearless, and the Authority has now caved in to what they think the government might accept, not what is needed to give us all a fighting chance of avoiding the impending climate tipping points. The fact that chief scientist Alan Finkel argues for what is politically possible rather than strictly according to the objectives of the Act feels like a total betrayal. As Green parliamentarians we stood our ground for science and for a safe climate, only to have the chief scientist fail to stand his ground and undermine the urgency of addressing global warming. The CEFC also stood its ground and remains inspiring in what it and ARENA have achieved in driving down emissions and creating jobs and new businesses in rural and regional Australia.

## Chapter 13 Art as Activism

1    Yu Ye Wu, 'Q&A with Michael Agzarian', National Association for the Visual Arts, 21 September 2016, https://visualarts.net.au/news-opinion/2016/q-michael-agzarian/

2   Paul Pritchard, 'Tasmania's ancient forest in danger', *The Guardian*, 7 April 2003.
3   'A Letter from Richard Flanagan', *Australian Story*, ABC, 3 November 2008.
4   Jane Cadzow, 'The right thing', *The Sydney Morning Herald – Good Weekend*, 14 August 2004.
5   Van Badham and Richard Bell, 'Asylum-Seeker Policy Is a Manifestation of Australian Racism', *The Guardian*, 21 February 2014.
6   Ashley Crawford, 'Laurie Nilsen: Birds on a Wire', *Art Collector*, Issue 42, October – December 2007.

## Chapter 14 Backpacking and Beyond: Sri Lanka

1   Ministry of Defence, Sri Lanka, defence.lk, 22 May 2010.

## Chapter 15 Seeking Asylum

1   Philip Oltermann, *The Guardian*, 17 January 2017.
2   Dr Martin Luther King Jr., 'A Proper Sense of Priorities: Conscience Asks the Question', *The Trumpet of Conscience*, 1968.
3   When Labor refused to conduct a judicial inquiry, I was disgusted. I could not imagine the pain of the survivors who had waited so long for a change of government and the inquiry they had been promised. After the vote was taken in which John Faulkner abstained, I asked him why Labor had changed its position and now rejected the judicial inquiry that he had so long pursued. Remembering that he had said, 'I intend to keep pressing for an independent judicial inquiry into these very serious matters' I asked him why Kevin Rudd as the incoming prime minister had retained Jane Halton, who had been Howard's Chair of the People Smuggling Taskforce in the Children Overboard and SIEV X affairs. He looked at me with a steely expression and said, 'Don't ask me.'
4   *SBS News*, 18 November 2016.

## Chapter 16 Leadership and the Importance of Timing

1   Jon Stallworthy (ed.), *Wilfred Owen: The War Poems*, Chatto & Windus, London, 1994.
2   Laura Tingle, 'Tony Abbott: Even his friends now say he is a liar and a clunkhead', *Australian Financial Review Magazine*, 24 February 2017.
3   Peta Credlin, *Sunday Agenda*, Sky News, 12 February 2017.
4   Major General John Cantwell, *Exit Wounds*, Melbourne University Press, Melbourne, 2012, pp. 358–9.
5   Henry David Thoreau, *Walden, Or, Life in the Woods*, Charles E. Merrill Publishing Company, Columbus, 1969, p. 345.

## Chapter 17 The Tasmanian Activism App

1   The very day I announced my candidacy for the Senate in 2004, Gunns announced it intended to build a pulp mill in the Tamar Valley. After the harrowing experience of Wesley Vale I felt stalked by pulp mills. The headlines ran, 'Pulp Mill Warrior Back.'
    The first thing I remember was Labor's Paul Lennon and John Gay from Gunns getting caught drawing up a pulp mill plan literally on the back of an envelope in a Hobart cafe. The next was former Forestry Tasmania's Bob Gordon making the outrageous

claim to morning radio personality Tim Cox that there would be no pollution of Bass Strait. Premier Lennon, fearful that the community would once again reject a native forest-based pulp mill, set up a Pulp Mill Task Force to persuade Tasmanians how good it was all going to be. It all came unstuck when John Gay demanded that the pulp mill be removed from the normal assessment process as it was taking too long and that it had to be fast-tracked. Nobody believed it was anything other than a deal for mates.

The saga of the Tamar Valley pulp mill deserves a book of its own. It is a set piece in Gunns' corporate lies and deception but it is also a set piece in community resistance. Peter Cundall, gardening guru and environmentalist; local wine producer Peter Whish-Wilson; Jeremy Ball, a Launceston alderman; local activists Bob McMahon, Anne Layton-Bennett and Lucy Langdon-Lane; and the Greens team in the Tasmanian Parliament: Peg Putt, Kim Booth, Nick McKim and Cassy O'Connor, all come to mind as household names in the struggle.

2    A sixty-metre old-growth eucalyptus tree in the Styx Valley, the Observor Tree was home to Miranda Gibson. She was hoisted onto her platform and vowed to stay there until the forests of the Styx Valley were protected. She lived there continuously for 451 days, which remains the longest tree sit in Australia's history.

3    In the early 1990s a German Baron arrived in Swansea and immediately applied for planning permission to develop a 200-unit estate at Piermont, a property on Great Oyster Bay overlooking Freycinet Peninsula. As an agricultural property Piermont was sold in part because it had no water. It was ridiculous to then propose a massive tourism development be established on it and even more inexcusable for local council to approve it. The water source was to be a black polythene pipe running from the town, which did not have an adequate water supply to begin with. Dr Gerry Bates and I fought the local council and the developer through the Planning Appeals Tribunal and we won. Piermont remains a beautiful place with a small number of tourist cabins. But in the very public and hard fought campaign, I acquired another title: the Princess of Piermont.

4    No Green can visit the east coast without fondly remembering Jeff Weston who put St Marys on the global map. Jeff, a long-time conservationist and one of the first group ever to go down the Franklin River in 1959, ran a backpackers' hostel on his Seaview Farm at German Town Forest Reserve in the hills behind St Marys overlooking Scamander. He was famous for his quirky sense of humour and his extraordinary generosity and was known all over the world as an essential stop on a backpacker itinerary. He had so many stories to tell.

5    John Mulvaney and Hugh Tyndale-Biscoe (eds), *Rediscovering Recherche Bay*, Academy of the Social Sciences in Australia, Canberra, 2007.

## Chapter 18 Green leadership

1    Henry David Thoreau, *Walden, Or, Life in the Woods*, Charles E. Merrill Publishing Company, Columbus, 1969, p. 346.

2    Cassandra Pybus and Richard Flanagan, 'The New Ethic: United Tasmania Group', *The Rest of the World is Watching*, Pan Macmillan Publishers, Sydney, Australia, 1990, p. 34.

3    Victor Hugo, *The History of a Crime*, 1877.

4    Niccolò Machiavelli, *The Prince*.

5    Dorian Lynskey, 'The rise and fall of Milo Yiannopoulos – how a shallow actor played

the bad guy for money', *The Guardian*, 22 February 2017.

6   Ernest Shackleton, *South: The story of Shackleton's 1914–1917 expedition*, Heinemann, London, 1927, p. 84.

7   F. A. Worsley, *Shackleton's boat journey*, Wakefield Press, Kent Town, 2007, p. 53.

8   Plenary Address by Christine Milne, Greens 2017 Congress, Liverpool, UK, 30 March 2017: https://www.globalgreens.org/news/greens2017-congress-christine-milne-keynote-speech

## Afterword

1   Henry David Thoreau, *Walden, Or, Life in the Woods*, Charles E. Merrill Publishing Company, Columbus, 1969, p. 346.

2   Alfred, Lord Tennyson, 'Ulysses', in W. M. Smyth, *A Book of Poetry*, Edward Arnold, London, 1961, p. 220.

# Index

# Index

# Credits

## Text

Judith Wright's 'South of My Days' reproduced with permission from HarperCollins Publishers.

Oodgeroo Noonuccal's 'Song of Hope' reproduced with permission from John Wiley and Sons.

'Conscience Asks the Question', Dr Martin Luther King Jr., reprinted by arrangement with The Heirs to the Estate of Martin Luther King Jr., c/o Writers House as agent for the proprietor New York, NY.

Extract from 'Anthem for Doomed Youth' reproduced with permission of the estate of Wilfred Owen.

## Images

Page 315: Christine Milne on the Loanes' farm at Wesley Vale, 1988. Photo courtesy of Bruce Montgomery.

Picture section page 2: Wesley Vale protest speech photo courtesy of Jon Paice; page 5: United Nations Climate Change Conference photo courtesy of Alex Gordon; page 6: Knitting Nannas photo featuring Jenny Leunig, Larissa Waters, Christine Milne, Jennie Dell and Daniele Voinot Sledge courtesy AAP Image/Lukas Coch; 'Not drowning' reproduced with Cathy Wilcox's permission; Brenda reproduced with the permission of First Dog on the Moon;

page 7: National Day of Climate Action photo provided by Harrison Saragossi; final day as leader of the Australian Greens photo courtesy of David Foote, Copyright AUSPIC/DPS; page 8: Christine and Eleanor photo courtesy of Karen Brown Photography.